WORKSHOP MAINTENANCE MANUAL

FOR THE

Royal Enfield
'Made like a Gun'

SPRING FRAME O.H.V.

"250 CLIPPER," "CRUSADER 250,"

"CRUSADER SPORTS," "CRUSADER SUPER 5"

"CONTINENTAL," "350 BULLET" & "250 TRIALS"

1956 - 1966

MOTOR CYCLES

including "AIRFLOW" Models where applicable

**A Floyd Clymer Publication
This edition published in 2023 by
www.VelocePress.com**

All rights reserved. This work may not be reproduced or transmitted in any form without the express written consent of the publisher.

INTRODUCTION

Welcome to the world of digital publishing ~ the book you now hold in your hand was printed using the latest state of the art digital technology. The advent of print-on-demand has forever changed the publishing process, never has information been so accessible and it is our hope that this book serves your informational needs for years to come. If this is your first exposure to digital publishing, we hope that you are pleased with the results. Many more titles of interest to the classic automobile and motorcycle enthusiast, collector and restorer are available via our website at www.VelocePress.com. We hope that you find this title as interesting as we do.

NOTE FROM THE PUBLISHER

The information presented is true and complete to the best of our knowledge. All recommendations are made without any guarantees on the part of the author or the publisher, who also disclaim all liability incurred with the use of this information.

TRADEMARKS

We recognize that some words, model names and designations, for example, mentioned herein are the property of the trademark holder. We use them for identification purposes only. This is not an official publication.

INFORMATION ON THE USE OF THIS PUBLICATION

This manual is an invaluable resource for those interested in performing their own maintenance. However, in today's information age we are constantly subject to changes in common practice, new technology, availability of improved materials and increased awareness of chemical toxicity. As such, it is advised that the user consult with an experienced professional prior to undertaking any procedure described herein. While every care has been taken to ensure correctness of information, it is obviously not possible to guarantee complete freedom from errors or omissions or to accept liability arising from such errors or omissions. Therefore, any individual that uses the information contained within, or elects to perform or participate in do-it-yourself repairs or modifications acknowledges that there is a risk factor involved and that the publisher or its associates cannot be held responsible for personal injury or property damage resulting from the use of the information or the outcome of such procedures.

WARNING!

One final word of advice, this publication is intended to be used as a reference guide, and when in doubt the reader should consult with a qualified technician.

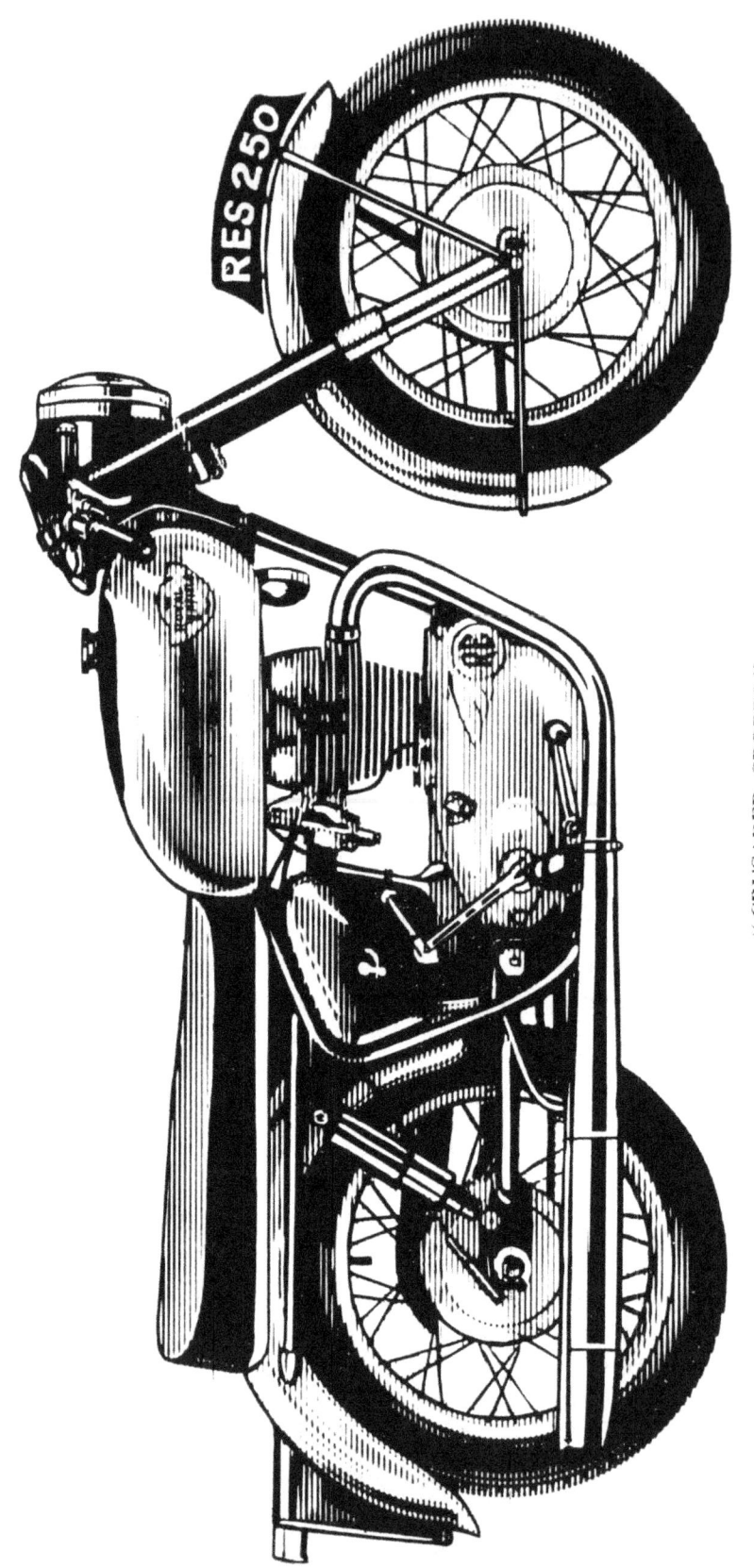

"CRUSADER SPORTS"
(*Frontispiece*)

"CONTINENTAL"
(*Frontispiece*)

ROYAL ENFIELD WORKSHOP MANUAL

Contents

1956-62 "Crusader 250", 1958-65 "250 Clipper", 1959-66 "Crusader Sports", 1961-63 "Crusader Super 5" and "250 Trials", 1963-66 "Continental" and "350 Bullet"

SECTION A16a	ENGINE DATA (250 c.c. models)
SECTION A16b	ENGINE DATA (350 c.c. models)
SECTION B16	ENGINE SPECIFICATION
SECTION C18	SERVICE OPERATIONS WITH ENGINE IN FRAME
SECTION D6a	SERVICE OPERATIONS WITH ENGINE REMOVED
SECTION E11	GEARBOX AND CLUTCH
SECTION F4	CARBURETTER
SECTION G2f	LIGHTING-IGNITION SYSTEM
SECTION G4a	BATTERY MODEL PUZ7E
SECTION G4c	BATTERY MODEL MLZ9E
SECTION G5d	HEAD AND TAIL LAMPS
SECTION H6	FRAME
SECTION J7	FRONT FORK
SECTION J8	FRONT FORK (Super-5)
SECTION K4	FRONT WHEEL (6 in. BRAKE)
SECTION K5	FRONT WHEEL (7 in. BRAKE)
SECTION L6	REAR WHEEL (QUICKLY DETACHABLE)
SECTION L10	REAR WHEEL (NON-DETACHABLE)
SECTION M7	SPECIAL TOOLS
SECTION N2	ACCESSORIES
SECTION P1	"AIRFLOW" FAIRING

SECTION A16a
Technical Data

"250 Clipper", "Crusader 250", "Crusader Sports",
"Crusader Super 5", "Continental" and "250 Trials"

Cubic Capacity	247·4 c.c. (15·094 cu. in.)
Stroke	64·5 mm. (2·5394 in.)
Bore	Nominal 70 mm.
	Actual 69·876 mm. (2·751 in.)

(Rebore to ·020 in. when wear exceeds ·0065 in. and again to ·040 in. after further ·0065 in. wear.)

Compression Ratio:
  Earlier Models:
    "250 Clipper" ... 7·5 to 1
    "Crusader 250" ... 8 to 1
    "Crusader Sports" ... 8·5 to 1
  Later Models:
    "250 Clipper", "Crusader 250", "Crusader Sports", "250 Trials" ... 8·75 to 1
    "Super 5" ... 9·75 to 1
  1963 models onwards:
    "250 Clipper," "Crusader Sports," "Super 5," "Continental" and "250 Trials" ... 9 to 1

Piston Diameter:
  Bottom of Skirt—Fore and aft ... 2·7485/2·7475 in.
  2nd and 3rd Lands ... 2·729/2·726 in.
  Top Land ... 2·725/2·722 in.

Piston Rings:
  Width—Plain Rings ... ·0635/·0625 in.
    Scraper Ring ... ·156/·155 in.
  Radial Thickness ... ·1215/·1135 in.
  Gap when in unworn Cylinder ... ·020/·015 in.
  Clearance in grooves—
    Compression Rings ... ·005/·003 in.
    Scraper Ring ... ·004/·002 in.
    (Renew Piston Rings when gap exceeds 1/16 in.)

Oversize Pistons and Rings available ... ·020 and ·040 in.
Piston Boss Internal Diameter ... ·7501/·7499 in.
Gudgeon Pin Diameter ... ·7501/·7499 in.
Con. Rod Small End Internal Diameter ·7507/·7505 in.
Big End Internal Diameter ... 1·8540/1·8535 in.
Bearing Shell Internal Diameter ... 1·7515/1·7505 in.
Crank Pin Diameter ... 1·7500/1·7495 in.

Driving Side Main Ball Bearing:
  Type ... S.K.F. 6207
    Hoffman—135 or
    R. and M.—LJ35
  Outside Diameter ... 72 mm. (2·8347 in.)
  Inside Diameter ... 35 mm. (1·3780 in.)
  Width ... 17 mm. (·6693 in.)

Generator Side Main Roller Bearing:
  Type ... S.K.F. N.207
    Hoffman—R.135 or
    R. and M.—LRJ35
  Outside Diameter ... 72 mm. (2·8347 in.)
  Inside Diameter ... 35 mm. (1·3780 in.)
  Width ... 17 mm. (·6693 in.)

Rocker Bearing Inside Diameter (old)	·026/·625 in.
Rocker Spindle Diameter (old)	·6240/·6235 in.
Rocker Bearing Inside Diameter (new)	·6880/·6875 in.
Rocker Spindle Diameter (new)	·6871/·6862 in.
Inlet Valve Stem Diameter	·3430/·3425 in.
Exhaust Valve Stem Diameter	·3410/·3405 in.
Valve Guide Internal Diameter	·3447/·3437 in.

Cast Iron Cylinder Head:
  Valve Guide External Diameter ... ·624/·623 in.
  Valve Guide Hole in Cylinder Head, Diameter ... ·623/·622 in.

Aluminium Cylinder Head:
  Valve Guide External Diameter ... ·6275/·6270 in.
  Valve Guide Hole in Cylinder Head Diameter ... ·626/·625 in.

Cam Follower Spindle Diameter ... ·5005/·4995 in.
Cam Follower Internal Diameter ... ·5020/·5010 in.
Idler Pinion Spindle Diameter ... ·5005/·4995 in.
Idler Pinion Internal Diameter ... ·5025/·5015 in.
Contact Breaker and Pump Spindle Diameter ... ·4370/·4365 in.
Contact Breaker and Pump Spindle Bearing Internal Diameter ... ·4377/·4375 in.
(After assembly with Mandrel.)

Valve Clearance with Cold Engine:

	Cast Iron Head	Alloy Head
Inlet	·004 in.	Zero
Exhaust	·006 in.	·002 in.

Valve Spring Free Length:

	"250 Clipper" and "Crusader 250"	"Crusader Sports," "Super 5," "Continental" and "250 Trials"
Inner	2 1/32 in.	1 1/2 in.
Outer	2 3/32 in.	1 11/16 in.

Renew when reduced by 1/8 in.

Valve Timing with ·015 in. Clearance:
  "250 Clipper" and "Crusader 250":
    Exhaust opens ... 80° before B.D.C.
    Exhaust closes ... 30° after T.D.C.
    Inlet opens ... 50° before T.D.C.
    Inlet closes ... 60° after B.D.C.

Valve Timing with ·015 in. Clearance:
  "Crusader Sports," "Super 5," "250 Trials" and "250 Continental":
    Exhaust opens ... 57° before B.D.C.
    Exhaust closes ... 31° after T.D.C.
    Inlet opens ... 27° before T.D.C.
    Inlet closes ... 55° after B.D.C.

Camshaft Bearing External Diameter	·562/·561 in.
Camshaft Bearing Internal Diameter	·5627/·5625 in.
(After assembly with Mandrel.)	
Timing Sprocket	14 Teeth
Camshaft Sprocket	28 Teeth

(Continued overleaf)

Technical Data (continued)

Timing Chain:
    Type... 114500
    Length ... ...38 Pitches (Endless)
    Width ... ... ·340 in. (Duplex)
    Pitch ... ... 8 mm. (·315 in.)
    Roller Diameter ... ... 5 mm. (·197 in.)

Contact Breaker and Oil Pump Drive:
    Camshaft Pinion ... ... 24 Teeth
    Idler Pinion ... ... 23 Teeth
    Contact Breaker and Pump Pinion 24 Teeth

Contact Breaker:
    Points ... ... ·015 in.
    Timing—Advanced ... $\tfrac{3}{16}-\tfrac{7}{32}$ in. before T.D.C.

Engine Sprocket... ... ... 23 Teeth

Clutch Sprocket ... ... 49 Teeth

Final Drive Sprocket ... ... 17 Teeth

Primary Chain:
    Type... 110038
    Length ... ...70 Pitches (Endless)
    Width ... ... ·225 in. (Simple)
    Pitch ... ... ·375 in.
    Roller Diameter ... ... ·25 in.

Feed Oil Pump:
    Speed ... ... $\tfrac{1}{2}$ Engine Speed
    Piston Diameter ... ... ·12475/·12450 in.
    Stroke ... ... ·375 in.

Return Oil Pump:
    Speed ... ... $\tfrac{1}{2}$ Engine Speed
    Piston Diameter ... ... ·31225/·31200 in.
    Stroke ... ... ·375 in.

Sparking Plug ("250 Clipper," "Crusader 250," "250 Trials")
    Type... ... Lodge 2.H.N. Champion L7
        K.L.G. F.80 or L10.S.
    ("Crusader Sports," "Super 5" and "Continental")
    Type... ... Lodge 3.H.N. Champion L5
        K.L.G. F.100 or L11.S.

SECTION A16b

Technical Data

"350 Bullet"

Cubic capacity	346 c.c.
Stroke	90 mm.
Bore ... Nominal	70 mm.
Actual	69·876 mm. (2·751 in.)

(Rebore to ·020 in. when wear exceeds ·0065 in. and again to ·040 in. after further ·0065 in. wear.)

Compression Ratio	7·5 to 1
Piston Diameter:	
Bottom of Skirt—Fore and aft	2·7485/2·7475 in.
Top land	2·728/2·726 in.
Piston Rings:	
Width—Plain Rings	·0635/·0625 in.
Scraper Ring	·156/·155 in.
Radial Thickness	·1215/·1135 in.
Gap when in unworn Cylinder	·011/·015 in.
Clearance in grooves—	
Compression Rings	·005/·003 in.
Scraper Ring	·004/·002 in.

(Renew Piston Rings when gap exceeds $\frac{1}{16}$ in.)

Oversize Pistons and Rings available	·020 and ·040 in.
Piston Boss Internal Diameter	·7501/·7499 in.
Gudgeon Pin Diameter	·7500/·7498 in.
Con. Rod Small End Internal Diameter	·7507/·7505 in.
Big End Internal Bore (of Bush)	1·62625/1·62575 in.
Big End Floating Bush	O/D 1·6235/1·6230 in.
	I/D 1·2502/1·2498 in.
Crank Pin	1·24900/1·24875 in.
Outrigger Bearing:	
Bearing Journal	1·8105/1·8100 in.
Plain Bearing Bush	1·8132/1·8125 in.
Driving Side Main Ball Bearing:	
Type	S.K.F. 6207
	Hoffman—135 or
	R. and M.—LJ35
Outside Diameter	72 mm. (2·8347 in.)
Inside Diameter	35 mm. (1·3780 in.)
Width	17 mm. (·6693 in.)
Generator Side Main Roller Bearing:	
Type	S.K.F. N.207
	Hoffman—R.135 or
	R. and M.—LRJ35
Outside Diameter	72 mm. (2·8347 in.)
Inside Diameter	35 mm. (1·3780 in.)
Width	17 mm. (·6693 in.)
Rocker Bearing Inside Diameter	·6880/·6875 in.
Rocker Spindle Diameter	·6871/·6868 in.
Inlet Valve Stem Diameter	·3430/·3425 in.
Exhaust Valve Stem Diameter	·3410/·3405 in.
Valve Guide Internal Diameter	·3447/·3437 in.
Aluminium Cylinder Head:	
Valve Guide External Diameter	·6275/·6270 in.
Valve Guide Hole in Cylinder Head Diameter	·626/·625 in.
Cam Follower Spindle Diameter	·5005/·4995 in.
Cam Follower Internal Diameter	·5020/·5010 in.
Idler Pinion Spindle Diameter	·5005/·4995 in.
Idler Pinion Internal Diameter	·5025/·5015 in.
Contact Breaker and Pump Spindle Diameter	·4370/·4365 in.
Contact Breaker and Pump Spindle Bearing Internal Diameter	·4377/·4375 in.

(After assembly with Mandrel.)

Valve Clearance with cold engine:	
Inlet	Zero
Exhaust	·002 in.
Valve Spring Free Length:	
Inner	1½ in.
Outer	1 $\frac{11}{16}$ in.

(Renew when reduced by ⅛ in.)

Valve Timing with ·015 in. clearance:	
Exhaust opens	57° before B.D.C.
Exhaust closes	31° after T.D.C.
Inlet opens	27° before T.D.C.
Inlet closes	55° after B.D.C.
Camshaft Bearing External Diameter	·562/·561 in.
Camshaft Bearing Internal Diameter	·5627/·5625 in.

(After assembly with Mandrel.)

Timing Sprocket	14 Teeth
Camshaft Sprocket	28 Teeth
Timing Chain:	
Type	114500
Length	38 Pitches (Endless)
Width	·340 in. (Duplex)
Pitch	8 mm. (·315 in.)
Roller Diameter	5 mm. (·197 in.)
Contact Breaker and Oil Pump Drive:	
Camshaft Pinion	24 Teeth
Idler Pinion	23 Teeth
Contact Breaker and Pump Pinion	24 Teeth
Contact Breaker:	
Points	·015 in.
Timing—Advanced	$\frac{5}{16}$–$\frac{3}{8}$ in. before T.D.C.
Engine Sprocket	23 Teeth
Clutch Sprocket	49 Teeth
Final Drive Sprocket	19 Teeth
Primary Chain:	
Type	110038
Length	70 Pitches (Endless)
Width	·225 in. (Simple)
Pitch	·375 in.
Roller Diameter	·25 in.
Feed Oil Pump:	
Speed	½ Engine Speed
Piston Diameter	·12475/·12450 in.
Stroke	·375 in.
Return Oil Pump:	
Speed	½ Engine Speed
Piston Diameter	·31225/·31200 in.
Stroke	·375 in.
Sparking Plug:	
Type	Lodge 2.H.N.
	K.L.G. F.80
	Champion L7.
	or L10.S.

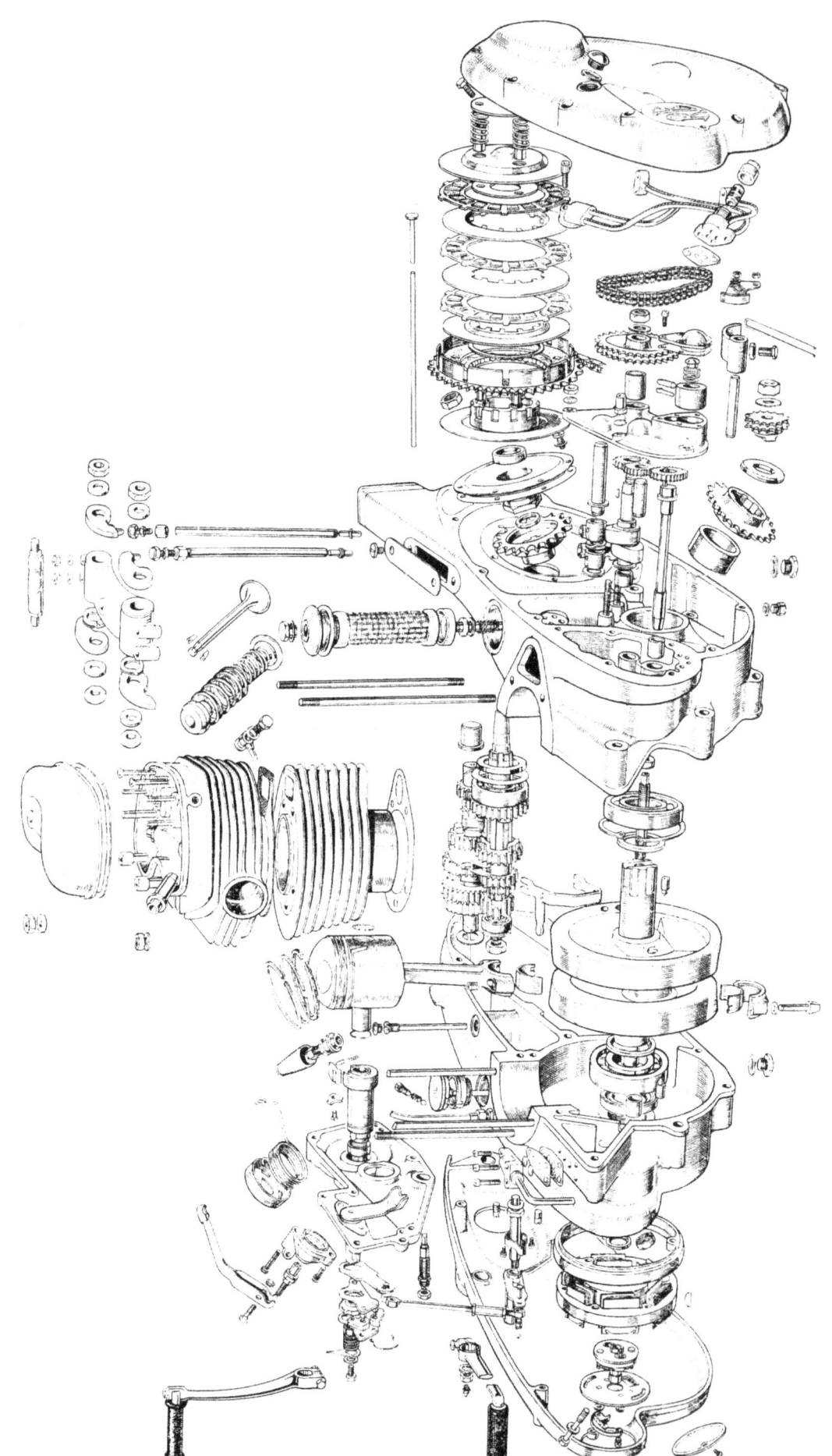

EXPLODED VIEW OF 250 c.c. ENGINE
Fig. 1

SECTION B16
Engine Specification

1. Engine

The engine is of unit construction, the gearbox and oil tank being integral with the crankcase. It has a single vertical four-stroke cylinder with separate head, totally enclosed overhead valve gear and a one-piece high-strength cast iron crankshaft.

The design of the engine is such that, except for the crankshaft and connecting rod, it can be dismantled without removal from the frame.

2. Cylinder Head

The "250 Clipper" and "Crusader 250," with Airflow fairing employ cast iron cylinder heads, whilst aluminium cylinder heads are fitted to the standard "Crusader 250," "Crusader Sports," "Super 5," "250 Trials," "Continental" and "350 Bullet." All of these cylinder heads are generously finned to ensure adequate cooling, and large bore induction ports are incorporated, of three different diameters, the smallest for the "250 Clipper" and "Crusader 250," the medium for the "Crusader Sports" and "250 Trials," and the largest for the "Super 5," "Continental" and "350 Bullet." These ports are streamlined and blended into the valve seating. The valve rockers are mounted on the top of the cylinder head and are enclosed by an aluminium cover secured by a single nut.

3. Cylinder

The cylinder barrel is of cast iron, with internal tunnels enclosing the push rods. The bore is nominally 70 mm. and the stroke 64·5 mm., giving a cubic capacity of 248 c.c. The 70 mm. bore by 90 mm. stroke barrel gives a capacity of 346 c.c.

4. Piston

The piston is cast from low-expansion aluminium alloy, heat-treated and form-turned oval.

There are three piston rings, the top two of which are compression rings. Both are taper ground and the top one is chromium plated. The third one is for oil control and is slotted.

Compression ratios:
Earlier Models:
"250 Clipper" ... ... 7·5 to 1
"Crusader 250" ... ... 8 to 1
"Crusader Sports" ... ... 8·5 to 1

Later Models:
"250 Clipper", "Crusader 250", "Crusader Sports",
"250 Trials" ... ... 8·75 to 1
"Super 5" ... ... 9·75 to 1
1963 Models·
"250 Clipper," "Crusader Sports," "Super 5," "Continental" and "250 Trials" ... 9 to 1
"350 Bullet" ... ... 7·5 to 1

5. Connecting Rod

The connecting rod is produced from a stamping of Hiduminium RR 56 light alloy. The little end bearing is of alloy direct on to the gudgeon pin. In case of wear after long service the little end can be bored out and fitted with a bronze bush, but this is rarely necessary. The big end bearing, on all 250 c.c. models, consists of a pair of white-metalled steel liners, which are renewable, running on the cast iron throw pins of the crankshaft. The detachable bearing caps are bolted to the connecting rods by means of high tensile bolts.

The 350 c.c. engine has a one piece light alloy connecting rod, with a replaceable plain big end bearing. (See Section D, Fig. 2.)

6. Crankcase

The crankcase is die-cast from light alloy in two halves, being split vertically. The crankcase casting also incorporates the gearbox, oil tank and primary chaincase.

7. Crankshaft and Flywheel

The crankshaft for all 250 c.c. models is cast in one piece with the flywheel, from high-quality cast iron and is carefully balanced at 75/25%.

The main journals are ground, and the big end journals are ground and hand-lapped.

The crankshaft for the "350 Bullet" is the "built-up" type, employing two separate flywheels, one with an integral driving shaft, the other with integral timing shaft. The crankpin is secured to the flywheels with two large nuts. (See Section D, Fig. 2.)

8. Main Bearings

The crankshaft runs in a roller bearing on the generator side and a ball bearing on the driving side.

The shaft is fitted with an oil seal on the generator end to prevent oil leakage from the crankcase into the generator cover.

The "350 Bullet" employs an additional plain outrigger bearing on the driving side. (See Section D, Fig. 2.)

9. Camshaft

The camshaft is machined from case hardened steel and is chain-driven at half-engine speed from the timing sprocket on the crankshaft. The cam profiles on the "250 Clipper" and "Crusader 250" are produced with silencing ramps to ensure silent running.

The camshaft employed on the "Crusader Sports," "Super 5," "Continental," "350 Bullet," and "250 Trials," differs from that fitted to the "250 Clipper" and "Crusader 250" models in having a greater rate of lift and different opening and closing points. There are no silencing ramps on these models.

10. Valves

The inlet valves are machined from stampings of special Silicon Chrome Valve Steel, and those

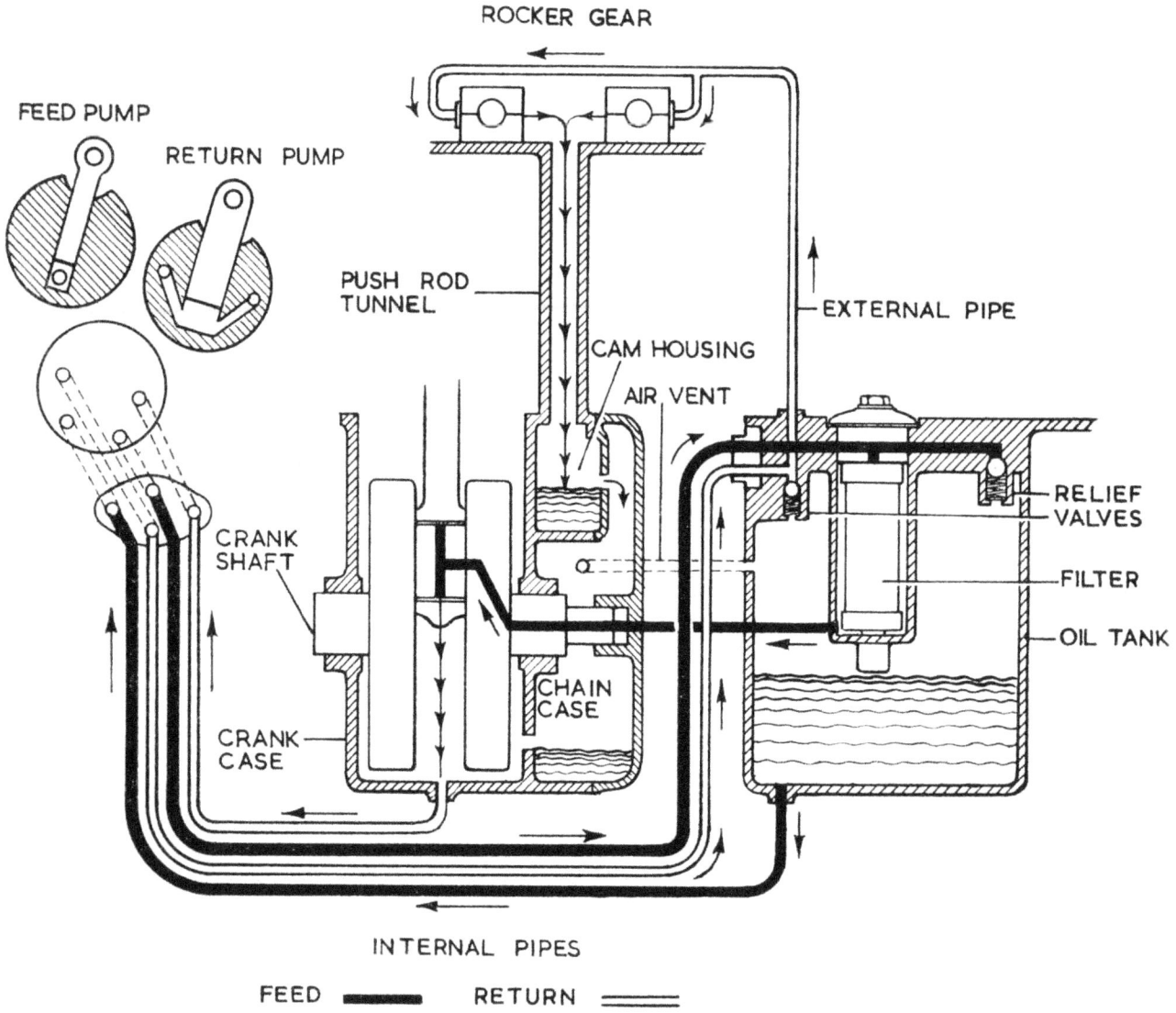

OPERATION OF LUBRICATION SYSTEM—EARLY MODELS

Fig. 2

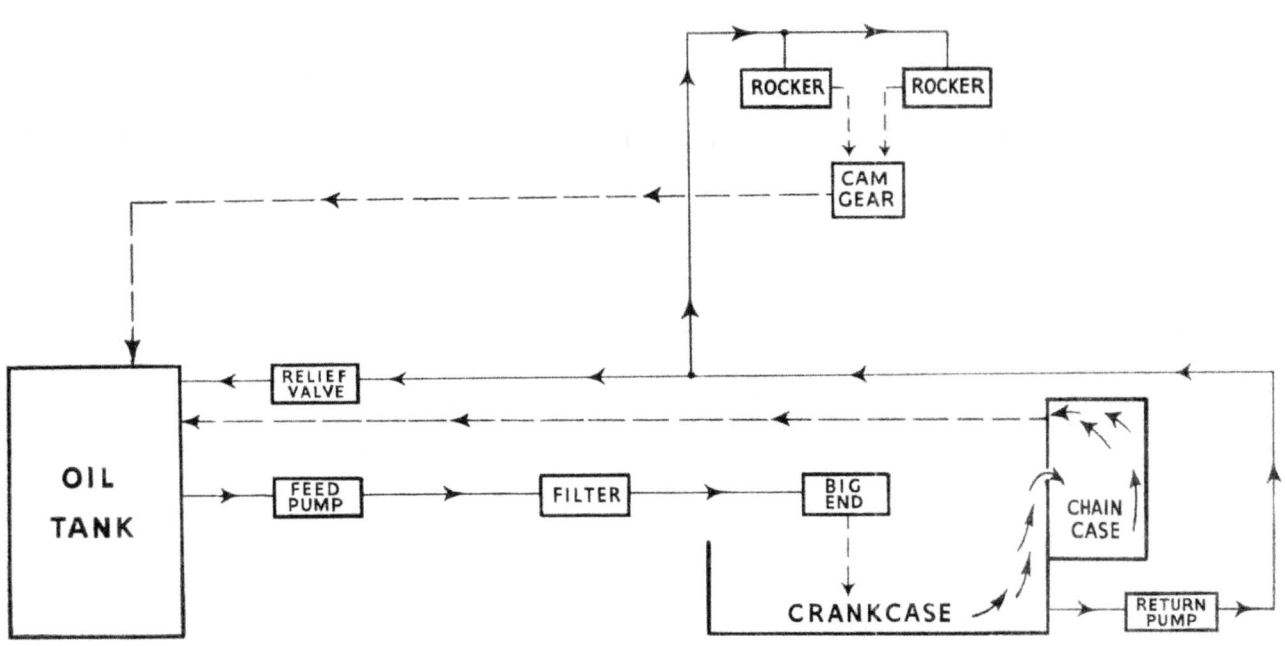

SCHEMATIC DIAGRAM OF LUBRICATION SYSTEM—LATER MODELS
Fig. 3

fitted to the "Crusader Sports," "Super 5," "Continental," "350 Bullet," and "250 Trials" have heads of greater diameter than those fitted to the "250 Clipper" and "Crusader 250."

The exhaust valves are of Austenitic Steel, and those used in the cast iron cylinder head are "Brightray" faced to ensure long service under the higher temperatures involved.

The profile of the inlet valve and that of its seat in the cylinder head are specially designed to give a smooth flow of gas and to eliminate pockets as the valve beds in. (See Section C, Fig. 4.)

11. Valve Gear

The valves are operated from the cams by means of followers, tubular push rods and overhead rockers. To minimise the effect of thermal expansion on the tappet clearance steel push rods are used in conjunction with cast iron cylinder heads and aluminium rods with aluminium heads. On earlier engines one-piece rockers were used in split sintered iron bearings. Later engines have built up rockers running in aluminium bearings. Two compression springs are fitted to each valve. Those fitted to the 350 Bullet "Continental," "Super 5" and Crusader Sports engines are shorter but stronger than those fitted to "250 Clipper" and "Crusader 250" models. On all models adjustment is made by means of adjusting screws at the top of the push rods after removing the cylinder head cover.

12. Timing Drive

The camshaft is located in the camshaft housing, which is cast in with the driving-side crankcase and runs in oil-retaining compo bushes. It is chain driven at half engine speed from the timing sprocket on the crankshaft, and the tightness of the chain can be adjusted by means of a chain tensioner inside the near-side chaincase cover.

The ignition timing is effected by the contact breaker, which is on a common shaft with the oil pump and is gear-driven from the camshaft at half engine speed through two steel pinions with a steel idler pinion.

13. Ignition and Lighting System

Coil ignition and lighting are supplied from a 6-volt battery, which is charged through a rectifier from a Lucas A.C. alternator located inside the generator cover.

The alternator has a solid rotor with six permanent magnets revolving within a six-pole wound laminated stator. The rotor is mounted on the end of the crankshaft and the stator is bolted to the generator-side crankcase.

The arrangement is such that, in case of battery failure, the ignition can be supplied direct from the alternator.

(See Section G.)

14. Carburetters

"250 Clipper" and "Crusader 250":
Amal type 375/16. Monobloc $\frac{7}{8}$ in. bore.

"Crusader Sports" and "250 Trials":
Amal type 376/216. Monobloc $\frac{15}{16}$ in. bore.

"Super 5," "Continental":
    Amal type 376/283. Monobloc 1 1/16 in. bore.
"350 Bullet":
    Amal type 376/297. Monobloc 1 1/16 in. bore.
(See Section F.)

15. Air Cleaner

The air cleaner is Vokes Micro-Vee felt and gauze dry filter, 5 in. in diameter and housed in a compartment of the toolbox.

An air cleaner is fitted to all export models and to the home market "Crusader 250," and "250 Trials," but not to the home market "250 Clipper," "Crusader Sports," "Super 5," "Continental" and "350 Bullet."

16. Lubrication. (See Figs. 2 and 3)

Lubrication is by the Royal Enfield Dry-Sump System, which is entirely automatic and positive in action. The oil tank is integral with the crankcase, ensuring the full rate of circulation immediately the engine is started and rapid heating of the oil in cold weather.

The oil pump is of the duplex type positively driven at half engine speed and having two pistons, one for pumping oil under pressure to the big end and the other for returning the oil from the crankcase back to the tank and to the valve rocker gear. The return pump has a capacity of approximately three times that of the feed pump, which ensures that oil does not accumulate in the crankcase.

The pumps are of the oscillating disc type and both pistons are located in the same disc but they are not interconnected and can be regarded as two separate pumps.

The operation of the pumps themselves is explained on page 5. (See Figs. 4a and 4b.)

The feed pump sucks oil from the tank through a pipe in the chaincase and delivers it through another pipe to the filter and thence through an internal passage drilled in the primary chaincase to a central hole in the crankshaft.

From here the oil passes along drilled holes in the crankshaft, assisted by the centrifugal action caused by the rotation of the engine to the big end. The cylinder and piston and the crankshaft main bearings are lubricated by oil splashed off the big end bearing, the oil finally collecting in the small sump at the bottom rear of the crankcase.

From here lubrication differs between early and later models as follows:

Early Models (see Fig. 2)

Earlier models have the top of the oil filter connected to a pressure control valve of the spring loaded ball type, which is screwed into the top of the crankcase, and this valve discharges into the oil tank.

The return pump sucks the oil from the crankcase through a third pipe in the chaincase and delivers it through a fourth pipe to a drilled passage in the top of the crankcase near the filter. From there most of the oil passes through a second valve back to the oil tank but the back-pressure caused by this valve forces some of the oil in the drilled passage through an external pipe connected to a union on the top of the crankcase to the rocker bearings on the cylinder head.

The oil which passes through the rocker bearings lubricates the valve stems and pushrods and flows down the pushrod tunnel into the camshaft housing. Here it lubricates the cam followers, the cams and the gear train which drives the contact breaker and pump.

The oil level in the camshaft housing is controlled by a hole through which the oil overflows into the primary chaincase, lubricating the timing chain and primary chain.

Another hole between the bottom of the primary chaincase and the crankcase maintains the level of oil in the chaincase, the surplus flowing into the crankcase sump to be picked up by the oil return pump.

Later Models (see Fig. 3)

Later models have dispensed with the relief valve, which is situated in the top of the crankcase of earlier models, the spring loaded oil pump discs now entirely controlling oil pressure.

The return pump sucks the oil from the crankcase through a third pipe in the chaincase and delivers it through a fourth pipe to a drilled passage in the top of the crankcase near the filter. From there most of the oil passes through a spring loaded ball valve back to the oil tank but the back-pressure caused by this valve forces some of the oil in the drilled passage through an external pipe connected to a union on the top of the crankcase to the rocker bearings on the cylinder head.

The oil which passes through the rocker bearings lubricates the valve stems and push rods and flows down the push rod tunnel into the camshaft housing. Here it lubricates the cam followers, the cams and the gear train which drives the contact breaker and pump.

The oil level in the camshaft housing is controlled by a hole through which the oil overflows into the oil tank. Oil from the crankcase, passing through the main journal bearing and through the pressure equalising hole situated above the main bearing, lubricates the primary chain. The oil level in the primary chaincase is governed by surplus oil being flung by the chain into a weir situated in the top rear portion of the case; a hole from the weir drains the oil back to the oil tank.

OIL PUMP DIAGRAMS

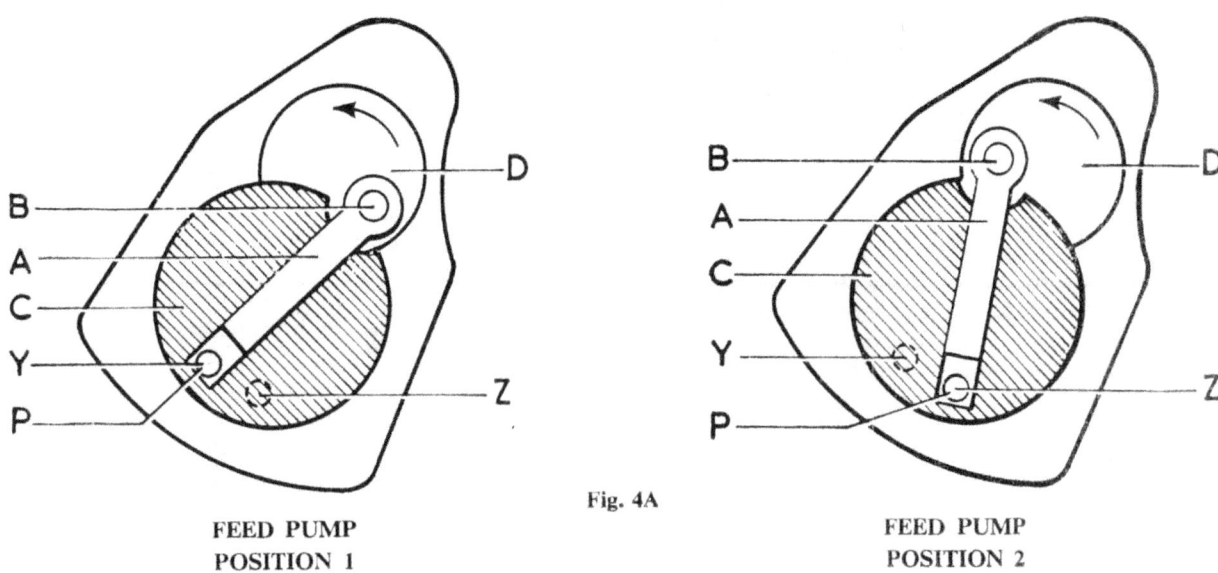

Fig. 4A

FEED PUMP POSITION 1

FEED PUMP POSITION 2

The ports in the housing are connected as follows :
Y — suction from the oil tank
Z — delivery to the big end.

Position 1. The plunger A is being drawn out of the back cylinder hole of the disc C by the action of the peg B on the end of the pump spindle D. The port P in the disc C registers with the suction port Y in the housing so that oil is drawn into the cylinder from the oil tank.

Position 2. The plunger A is being pushed into the cylinder hole in the disc C. The port P in the disc now registers with the delivery port Z in the housing so that oil is forced out of the cylinder to the filter and thence to the big end.

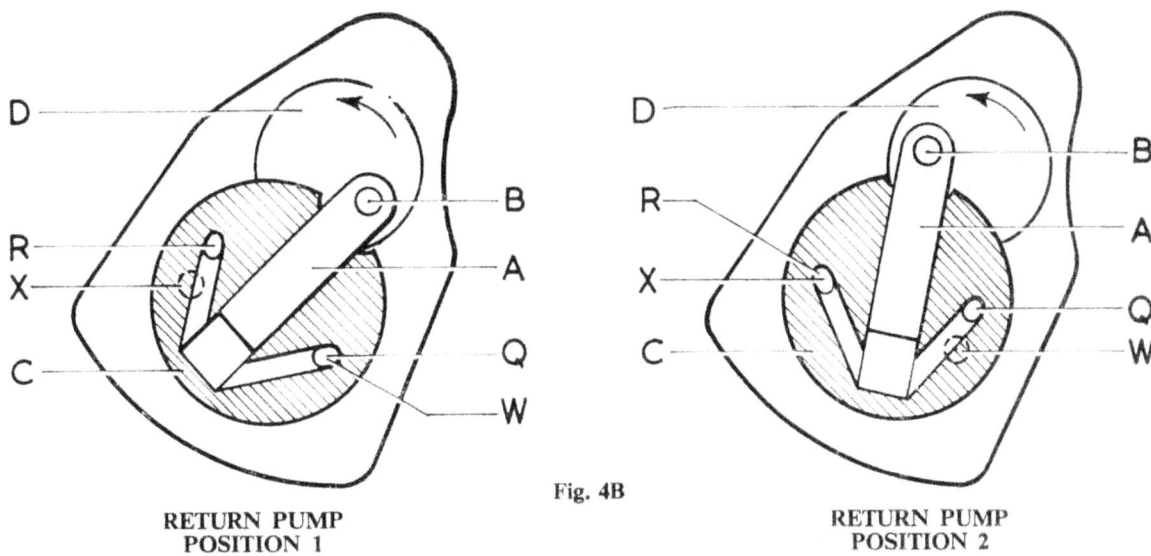

Fig. 4B

RETURN PUMP POSITION 1

RETURN PUMP POSITION 2

The ports in the housing are connected as follows :
W — suction from the crankcase.
X — delivery to the oil tank and rockers.

Position 1. The plunger A is being drawn out of the front cylinder hole in the disc C by the action of the peg B on the end of the pump spindle D. The port Q in the disc C registers with the suction port W in the housing so that oil is drawn into the cylinder from the crankcase sump.

Position 2. The plunger A is being pushed into the cylinder hole in the disc C. The port R in the disc now registers with the delivery port X in the housing so that oil is forced out of the cylinder back to the oil tank and the rocker gear.

All "Super 5," "Continental" and "350 Bullet" models, and later type "250 Clipper," "Crusader Sports," and "250 Trials" models employ an additional filter, through which the oil passes on its way from the crankcase to the return pump. This filter is situated inside the primary chain case. (See Section C, Fig. 1).

17. Breather

The efficient operation of the breather is of paramount importance to the performance of the engine because it acts as a non-return valve between the crankcase and the outside atmosphere, causing a partial vacuum inside the crankcase and the rocker box on the cylinder head.

This partial vacuum stops the passage of oil down the valve guides and prevents other oil leaks which could be caused by a pressure building up in the crankcase. Equalising holes are drilled between the chaincase and the crankcase and between the chaincase and the top of the oil tank.

Early Models

The breather consists of a flattened oil resisting rubber tube located on the front of the crankcase between the engine bearer plates.

Later Models

Later models have a metal tube extending from a flange which is attached by three screws to the top of the crankcase in front of the cylinder.

The underside of the flange has three overlapping circular recesses, the middle one communicating with the breather pipe and the two outer ones with the crankcase. These outer recesses contain one thin steel disc in each, which are free to rise and fall with the pressure or depression in the crankcase. A thin steel base plate, with two vent holes of smaller diameter than the discs fitted below the breather flange, prevents the discs wearing the aluminium surface of the crankcase.

18. Primary Drive

The primary drive from the engine to the gearbox is by an endless chain from a sprocket mounted on splines on the crankshaft to the clutch sprocket, which is incorporated in the clutch itself, and is mounted on the gearbox mainshaft.

The correct tension of the chain is maintained by an adjustable slipper with a chilled cast iron bearing surface accessible when the chaincase cover is removed. An inspection cover is provided in the chaincase so that the chain tension can be checked without the removal of the chaincase cover.

19. Clutch

There are four types of clutch (see Section E). All are of the conventional plate type, having pressure plates on the driven part and friction plates on the driving part, including the sprocket which is lined on both sides with friction material.

The friction material used gives smooth operation and freedom from slipping in the presence of oil.

20. Gearbox

The gearbox is built into the back part of the crankcase and can be completely dismantled with the engine in the frame.

It has foot control with an indicator on the top of the crankcase. All gears are in constant mesh, changes being effected by robust dog clutches. The kick-start mechanism is incorporated in the gearbox.

A full description of the operation of the gearbox is given in Section E.

Gear ratios: "Crusader 250" (earlier models):
1st Gear	...	16·96 to 1
2nd Gear	...	10·44 to 1
3rd Gear	...	7·83 to 1
4th Gear	...	5·80 to 1

Gear ratios: "250 Clipper", "Crusader 250" (later models) **and "Crusader Sports":**
1st Gear	...	18·0 to 1
2nd Gear	...	11·05 to 1
3rd Gear	...	7·80 to 1
Top Gear	...	6·14 to 1

Gear ratios : "Super 5" and "Continental" :
1st Gear	...	17·4 to 1
2nd Gear	...	12·82 to 1
3rd Gear	...	9·57 to 1
4th Gear	...	7·52 to 1
Top Gear	...	6·02 to 1

Gear ratios : "250 Trials" (earlier models):
1st Gear	...	27·83 to 1
2nd Gear	...	20·37 to 1
3rd Gear	...	13·71 to 1
Top Gear	...	8·02 to 1

Gear ratios : "250 Trials" (later models):
1st Gear	...	32·0 to 1
2nd Gear	...	23·5 to 1
3rd Gear	...	15·9 to 1
Top Gear	...	9·45 to 1

Gear ratios : "350 Bullet" :
1st Gear	...	15·1 to 1
2nd Gear	...	9·27 to 1
3rd Gear	...	6·57 to 1
Top Gear	...	5·15 to 1

SECTION C18

Service Operations with Engine in Frame

1. **Removal of the Primary Chaincase Cover (Near Side)**

    First place a tray under the engine to catch the oil which will escape when the cover is removed. The chaincase cover is on the left hand or driving side of the engine.

    Remove the driver's footrests.

    Remove ten screws and draw the cover off.

    In refitting the cover see that the faces are clean and apply jointing compound sparingly.

    Special care must be taken to ensure that the oil seal which is pressed into the cover and which fits over the end of the crankshaft is not damaged and it should be smeared with grease before the cover is refitted.

    See also that the Neoprene seal and tube which connect with the bottom of the oil filter are in their recesses in the chaincase cover.

    The seal should be replaced if worn or damaged.

    The rev. counter drive fitted to the "Continental" primary chain case is best removed by means of the two hexagon headed screws, as although the presence of the drive does not affect removal of the chaincase it is far safer and easier to remesh the rev. counter drive on its own, with the chain case already back in position.

2. **Removal of the Generator Cover (Off Side)**

    Take out the silencer fixing bolt and the pillion footrest, disconnect the front exhaust pipe bracket, and remove the exhaust system complete.

    Remove the kick-start and gear-change levers, the gear indicator pointer and the driver's footrest.

    Remove five screws and the cover can then be drawn off, giving access to the generator and the gear-change mechanism.

3. **Removal of the Rocker Box Cover**

    The rocker box cover can be removed after unscrewing a single central nut. In replacing the cover, see that the gasket is undamaged or, if necessary, fit a new one.

4. **Removal of the Petrol Tank**

    The petrol tank is attached to the frame by a rubber mounted stud at the front, and is clipped at the rear to a rubber sleeve surrounding the top tube. To remove the tank, unscrew one attachment nut, tap out the stud and, after disconnecting the petrol feed pipe, the rear of the tank can be pulled upwards to release the clip and then lifted clear of the frame.

5. **Removal of the Dual Seat and Rear Mudguard**

    The rear mudguard, mudguard carrier and dual seat are removable in one unit after merely slackening off the two nuts on the rear suspension top fixing brackets about $\frac{1}{4}$ in. and pushing the bolts in to release their heads from recesses on the inside of the carrier attachment brackets. Stand behind the machine, grasp the lifting handles on each side and pull the mudguard assembly upwards until the attachment brackets are clear of their respective bolts. Now pull backwards until the clip at the front of the mudguard carrier is free from the backstay bridge tube of the frame, when, after disconnecting the rear light cable, the complete assembly can be removed.

    When replacing, engage the front clip first and drop the assembly into position. When tightening the nuts make sure that the heads of the bolts are right home in the recesses on the inside of the carrier attachment brackets. Re-connect the rear light cable.

6. **Removal of the Tool Box and Air Filter**

    Take off the dual seat and mudguard as described in Subsection 5 and the tool box can then be removed by unscrewing four nuts and bolts, having first disconnected the leads to the battery, coil, rectifier and switch.

7. **Primary Chain Adjustment**

    Access to the primary chain adjuster is gained by removing the primary chaincase cover as described in Subsection 1.

    Beneath the bottom run of the chain is a curved slipper on which the chain rests and which may be raised or lowered by turning the adjusting screw, having first slackened the locknut. A hairpin spring is fitted to the slipper to hold it against the chaincase and prevent bouncing.

    Do not adjust the chain to be dead tight but rotate the engine slowly and, while doing so, test the tension of the top run of the chain by pressing it up and down with the fingers. Adjust the tension so that there is about $\frac{1}{4}$ in. up and down movement at the tightest spot. Re-tighten the lock nut on the adjusting screw, replace the chaincase cover, and put in about ⅓ pint of engine oil.

On some models a screwed plug is provided on the face of the chaincase. When this is removed the chain tension can be checked without removing the chaincase cover.

8. Timing Chain Adjustment

The timing chain adjuster is a curved slipper located by two nuts and studs and is inside the

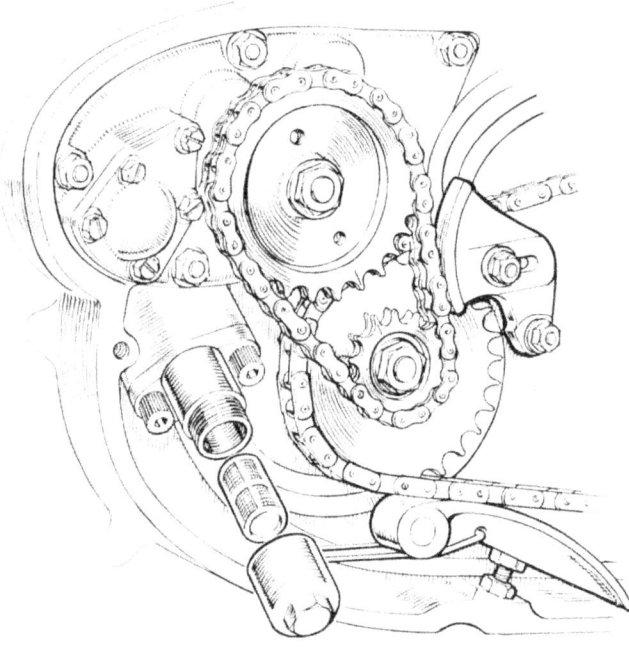

TIMING AND PRIMARY CHAIN ADJUSTMENT AND GAUZE OIL FILTER

Fig. 1

primary chaincase cover which must be removed (see Subsection 1).

To adjust the chain tension slacken the two nuts until the slipper can just be moved and re-tighten it in a position which will allow a lateral movement of about 3/16 in. of the chain on the opposite side. Put about ⅓ pint of engine oil in the chaincase after re-fitting the cover.

9. Valve and Pump Timing

If the drives to the camshaft and the oil pump have been dismantled (See subsections 25 and 26) they must be re-assembled with the timing marks on the sprockets opposite one another in line with the centres of the sprockets and with the dots on the pinion teeth also opposite one another.

Note that, because the idler pinion has one tooth less than the other pinions, the marks will only come opposite every 23 revolutions, but this does not alter the timing once it is set.

For those who wish to check the valve timing, the opening and closing points are given below:

"250 Clipper" and "Crusader 250":
  Exhaust opens ... 80° before B.D.C.
  Exhaust closes ... 30° after T.D.C.
  Inlet opens ... 50° before T.D.C.
  Inlet closes ... 60° after B.D.C.

"Crusader Sports," "Super 5," "250 Trials," "250 Continental" and "350 Bullet":
  Exhaust opens ... 57° before B.D.C.
  Exhaust closes ... 31° after T.D.C.
  Inlet opens ... 27° before T.D.C.
  Inlet closes ... 55° after B.D.C.

The above figures are all given at ·015 in. valve clearance and it is important that this clearance should be used when checking, as the first part of the lift, and the last part of the drop are comparatively slow (particularly on the "250 Clipper" and "Crusader 250" models) and a small variation in clearance considerably alters the opening and closing points. For running, set to the clearance given in Section 10.

10. Valve Adjustment

The rocker clearance is adjusted by means of adjustable cups which are screwed into the upper ends of the push rods and secured by lock nuts.

There are no valve tappets as the cams operate on the push rods through pivoted followers and the clearance must therefore be measured between the rockers and the valve stems.

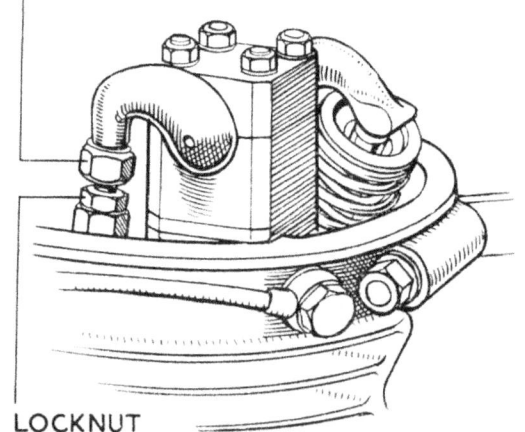

VALVE TAPPET ADJUSTMENT

Fig. 2

In order to obtain access to the push rods and rockers, remove the rocker box cover by unscrewing the central nut (Subsection 3).

Before checking the clearance or making any adjustment, rotate the engine until the piston is at the top of the firing stroke. This will ensure that both valves are closed and that the cam followers are well clear of the silencing ramps on the cams. If the cylinder head has been dismantled, make sure that where valves have detachable end caps these are fitted when reassembling.

The correct clearance between the rockers and the valves with the engine cold is as follows:

Engines with cast iron cylinder heads:
    Inlet   ...   .   ·004 in.
    Exhaust ...   .   ·006 in.

Engines with aluminium cylinder heads:
    Inlet   ... Zero (push rod just free to turn)
    Exhaust ... ... ·002 in.

To make the adjustment hold the push rod end (bottom hexagon) and turn the locknut (middle hexagon) to the right. Screw the push rod cup (top hexagon) to the right to take up clearance or to the left to increase the clearance, at the same time holding the push rod top end (bottom hexagon). Lock the adjustment by tightening the locknut against the push rod end and then recheck the clearance.

Owing to the initial bedding down of the wearing surfaces, the clearance on new engines may require adjustment after the first few hundred miles.

11. Ignition Timing

The contact breaker and automatic centrifugal advance mechanism are found at the front of the crankcase on the generator or right hand side. The advance mechanism and cam are mounted on the pump spindle at the opposite end to the pump and the contact breaker is mounted on a plate which is secured to the crankcase itself by two screws in slotted holes.

The automatic advance mechanism has a range of approximately $12\frac{1}{2}°$, which corresponds to $25°$ of the crankshaft because the contact breaker runs at half the engine speed.

The optimum ignition timing is $30°$ advance ($\frac{7}{32}$ in. before T.D.C.) so that in the fully retarded position the contact points must open when the piston is $5°$ or $\frac{1}{64}$ in. **before** top dead centre.

Access to the contact breaker for adjustment is obtained by the removal of the cap on the generator cover held in position by two screws.

First check the maximum opening of the contact points, which should be ·014–·016 in., and adjust if necessary. The adjustment is made by slackening the two screws holding the contact arm to the plate and setting the contact opening by means of a gauge.

If the contacts are worn or pitted, refer to Section G.

The timing is adjusted by slackening the two screws holding the contact breaker plate to the crankcase and rotating the plate relative to the crankcase.

To set the ignition timing, put the gearbox in top gear and turn the engine by means of the back wheel until the piston is $\frac{1}{64}$ in. before top dead centre on the compression stroke, i.e., with both valves closed. (It may be found convenient to apply the rear brake to hold the engine in this position.) The position of the piston can be determined by means of a wire or rod inserted in the sparking plug hole. Rotate the contact breaker slightly until the contact points are just opening (see below) and then tighten the fixing screws.

Check the timing again and also the maximum opening of the contact points.

There are several methods of determining the point at which the contacts open:—

(i) Switch on the ignition. Looking on the right side of the engine, rotate the cam in a clockwise direction, or the contact breaker plate in counter clockwise direction, until the ammeter needle indicates a discharge. Continue to turn the cam (or contact plate) slowly until the ammeter needle returns to zero, indicating that the points have just opened.

(ii) Remove the sparking plug lead from the cap and tuck it between the fins of the cylinder. Rotate the cam (or contact breaker plate) as above and a spark will be seen at the instant the points open.

(iii) Insert a piece of *thin* tissue paper between the points of the contact breaker and turn the cam (or contact breaker plate) as above until the paper can *just* be pulled out as the points start to open.

If the engine has been dismantled or the contact breaker removed for any reason (see Subsection 26) replace the advance mechanism and cam loosely on the tapered spindle and fit the contact breaker plate with the screws in the middle of the slots. See that the timing marks on the timing and camshaft sprockets and on the timing pinions are in their correct positions (see Subsection 9).

Turn the engine until the piston is $\frac{1}{64}$ in. before top dead centre on the compression stroke, i.e., with both valves closed.

Turn the cam on the spindle in a clockwise direction until the contact points are just opening and then give the cam a sharp tap endways to secure it on the spindle and lock it tightly with the centre fixing screw.

Check the timing again and make the final adjustment by rotating the contact breaker plate as described above.

12. Removal of Carburettor

Disconnect the petrol pipe from the float chamber and remove the two nuts holding the carburettor to the cylinder head.

Where fitted disconnect the air filter sleeve from the carburettor intake, push the sleeve to one side and draw the carburettor back clear of the studs.

Remove the throttle and air slides.

13. Removal of the Cylinder Head

Remove the petrol tank as described in Sub-section 4.

Disconnect the engine steady.

Remove the exhaust pipe.

Disconnect the plug lead and oil pipe.

Push the carburettor back, clear of the studs, after removing the fixing nuts.

Remove the rocker box cover as described in Sub-section 3.

Turn the engine until both valves are closed.

Remove the rockers and bearings completely.

(a) **Early Models:** Remove the four $\frac{1}{4}$-in. nuts on each bearing block, or

(b) **Later Models:** Remove the four $\frac{1}{4}$-in. nuts and the single central $\frac{5}{16}$-in. nut from the bearing housing.

Lift out the push rods. (Note: It is possible to extract the push rods without dismantling the rockers if the cylinder head is lifted slightly first.)

Remove the four sleeve nuts inside the rocker box and the single plain nut near the plug hole. Earlier alloy heads have in addition a single Allen screw situated between the two nuts on the push rod side, and later alloy heads have two Allen screws in the push rod tunnel. After removal of the appropriate nuts and screws, the head may be lifted. To break the carbon seal, tap the head gently with a hide hammer beneath the exhaust and inlet ports. *Do not tap the fins.*

When fitting the head again, first remove the remains of any old compound and make sure that the faces are quite clean. Then apply a thin coating of compound to each side of the gasket. It is advisable to fit a new gasket each time the head is removed.

Place the head on the cylinder barrel, and replace the five washers and nuts, not forgetting the single Allen screw in the earlier alloy head, and the two Allen screws in the later one. Tighten down diagonally from one side to the other to prevent distortion.

Replace the push rods with the adjustable parts upwards. The inlet push rod is the one adjusted to the greater length, and connects the outside follower to the rear rocker.

Refit the rockers and bearings, making sure that the oil feed holes of earlier "250 Clippers," "Crusader 250's" and "Crusader Sports" are at the bottom, and that the caps and bases are in line when tightened down. A sharp tap with a hammer on the end of the rocker will help to ensure this.

When fitting the one-piece rocker housing, to be found on later "250 Clipper," "Crusader 250," and "Crusader Sports" models, and on all "Super 5," "Continental," "350 Bullet" and "250 Trials" models, be sure that it is squarely home on the five studs, then tighten down the nuts evenly.

See that the valve stem caps, where used, are in place.

See that the rocker box gasket is intact. If necessary, fit a new one. Replace the rocker box cover and tighten down the fixing nut.

After the engine has been run long enough to get thoroughly hot, the tightness of the nuts should be rechecked.

After tightening the cylinder head nuts with the engine hot, recheck the rocker clearance at some convenient time when the engine is cold.

14. Removal of the Valves

Remove the cylinder head and rockers (Sub-section 13). Prise away the hardened steel thimbles or end caps where these are fitted. If they have stuck they can be removed by means of a screwdriver.

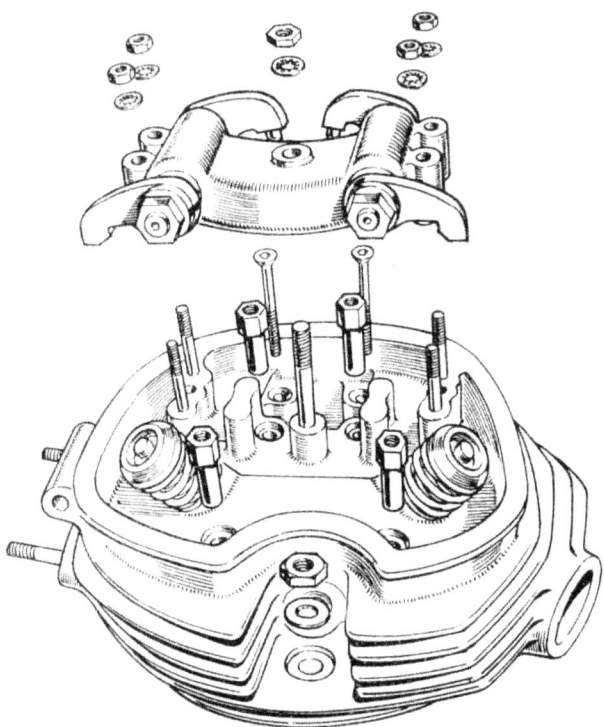

EXPLODED VIEW OF LATER TYPE ROCKER GEAR AND CYLINDER HEAD

Fig. 3

Using a suitable compressing tool, compress the valve springs and remove the split conical collets from the ends of the valve stems.

Slacken back the compressing tool, and release the springs.

Withdraw the valves and place the springs, top spring collars (and bottom collars, if loose), the end caps and split conical collets separately so that they may be re-assembled, each set with the valve from which it was removed.

If either of the valves will not slide easily in its valve guide, remove any slight burrs on the end of the valve stem with a carborundum stone before taking the valve out of the guide. If the burrs are not removed the guide may be damaged.

15. Dismantling the Rockers (later models)

If for any reason the rockers must be dismantled, it is only necessary to remove one nut from each spindle. Draw off the washer and rocker arm and the spindle, complete with the other rocker arm, may be withdrawn.

When reassembling, note that the rocker with the rounded end fits on the pushrod side with a plain washer and nut to secure it.

The broad groove round the rocker spindle should be nearest to the push rod side, and the large double spring washer should be between the rocker bearing and the rocker which bears on the valve.

16. Fitting New Valve Guides

To remove the valve guides from the head, it is necessary to have two special tools, which can easily be made.

The first is a piece of tube with an internal bore of not less than $\frac{7}{8}$ in.

The second is a mandrel about 4 ins. long made from $\frac{9}{16}$ in. diameter bar with the end turned down to $\frac{11}{32}$ in. diameter for a distance of $\frac{1}{2}$ in. (See Section M.)

Support the cylinder head on the tube, which fits over the collar of the valve guide. Using the mandrel, force the guide out of the head with a hand press or by using a hammer.

To fit a new guide, support the head at the correct angle and use a hand press and the same mandrel. If a hand press is not available and the guide is replaced by a hammer, use the mandrel to prevent damage to the guide, which is of cast iron and must be treated with great care.

It is necessary to re-cut the valve seat to the correct profile and to grind-in the valve after a guide has been replaced (see Subsection 20).

17. Removal of the Cylinder Barrel

Remove the cylinder head (see Subsection 13). Lift the barrel off the piston, taking care that any pieces of broken ring do not drop into the crankcase.

Before replacing the cylinder barrel, clean off the joint faces and fit a new paper washer.

18. Removal of the Piston

Remove the cylinder head and cylinder barrel (see Subsections 13 and 17).

With the tang of a file remove the wire circlip retaining the gudgeon pin on the left hand or driving side.

Extract the gudgeon pin using Special Tool No. E.5477A having first marked the pin so that it, and the piston, may be replaced the same way round (the front of the piston is marked).

During this operation put a piece of clean rag in the top of the crankcase to prevent foreign matter from getting in. In particular take care not to drop the circlip in the crankcase.

19. Decarbonising

Having removed the cylinder head, as described in Subsection 13, scrape away all carbon gently and avoid scoring the combustion chamber or the valve seats, taking particular care with an alloy head which is very easily damaged. Be careful, too, not to injure the joint face which beds down on to the head gasket.

Scrape away all carbon from the valve heads and beneath the heads, being careful not to damage the valve faces. In clearing the top of the piston remember that it is made of aluminium alloy and is easily damaged.

If the piston rings are removed, the grooves can be cleaned out and new rings fitted. For cleaning the grooves a suitable tool is a piece of broken ring thrust into a wooden handle and filed to a chisel point.

If the piston ring gaps exceed $\frac{1}{16}$ in. when the rings are in position in the barrel, new rings should be fitted. The correct gap for new rings is ·015–·020 in. The gap should be measured in the least worn part of the cylinder, which will be found to be at the extreme top or bottom of the bore.

While the cylinder and piston are not in position, cover the crankcase with a clean cloth to prevent the ingress of dust and dirt of any kind. Do not, of course, attempt to scrape the carbon from the piston when the mouth of the crankcase is open.

20. Grinding-in the Valves

To grind a valve, smear the seating with a little grinding-in compound, place a light short coil spring over the valve stem and beneath the head, insert the valve into its appropriate guide, press it on to the seat using a tool with a suction

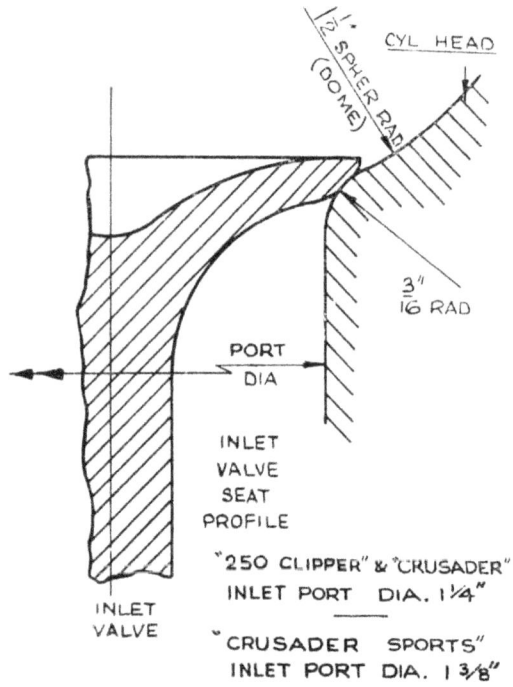

INLET VALVE PROFILE
Fig. 4

cup and grind it on to its seat with a backwards and forwards semi-rotary motion. Alternatively, a tool which pulls on the valve stem may be used.

Frequently lift the valve and move it round so that an even and true seating is obtained. If no light spring is available, the lifting will have to be done by hand. Continue grinding until a bright ring is visible on both the valve and seating.

The face and seat of the exhaust valve is cut at 45° but the profile of the inlet valve is of a special streamlined design as shown in Fig. 4 which eliminates pockets and sharp edges and allows a smooth flow of gas without eddies.

If the valves or their seats are pitted and require re-cutting, care must be taken to reproduce the correct profile.

The cylinder head should preferably be returned to the Works for the inlet valve seat to be re-cut but, if this is not possible, Special Valve Cutting Tools No. E2178, T1891 and Arbor T2053 are available for this purpose. Great care must be exercised in using this tool as it is located off the valve guide and this may be damaged if suitable apparatus is not employed.

The inlet valve face and seat can be cut at 45° in case of expediency but this may have a deleterious effect on the performance of the engine.

21. Re-assembly after Decarbonising

Before building up the engine, see that all parts are scrupulously clean and place them conveniently to hand on a clean sheet of brown paper.

It is advisable to fit a new gasket to the cylinder head and a new paper washer at the cylinder base.

Check the piston ring gaps to find out whether excessive wear has taken place (see Subsection 19).

Smear clean oil over the piston and space the ring gaps, having replaced the rings if these have been removed, lower the piston over the connecting rod and insert the gudgeon pin. Fit the circlip securing the gudgeon pin, making sure that it seats correctly in its groove.

Oil the cylinder bore and lower the barrel over the piston and seat it gently on the gasket.

Drop the push rods down their tunnel into the cups on the cam followers. Note that the shorter rod is the exhaust and is nearest the cylinder.

Fit the cylinder head gasket and replace the cylinder head as described in Subsection 13.

After the engine has been assembled, run it for a brief period at a speed which will ensure that the ignition has been advanced by the

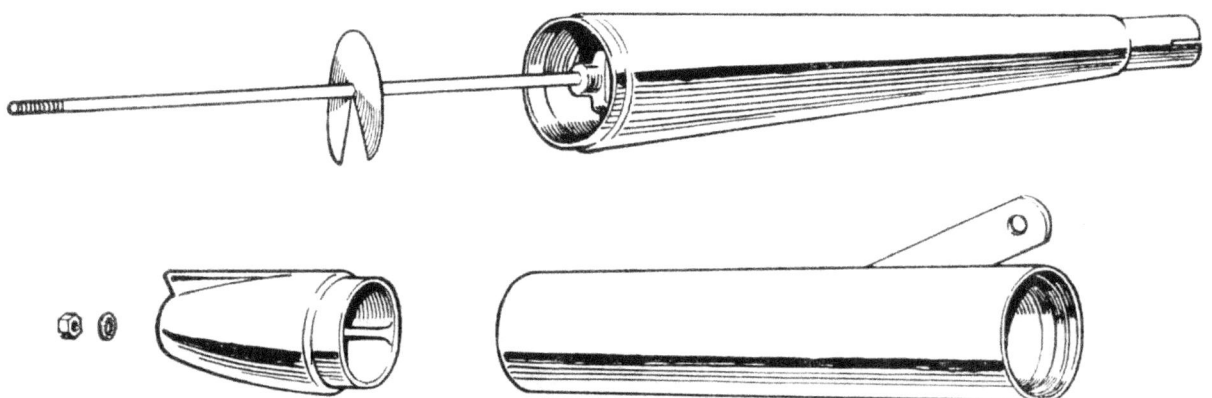

SILENCER FOR ALL LATER MODELS, WITH THE EXCEPTION OF "250 CLIPPER" AND "250 TRIALS"

Fig. 5

automatic advance mechanism. If it is run too slowly, "blueing" of the exhaust pipe may take place.

After the engine has been run for some time and has become thoroughly hot, go over **all** the cylinder head and other nuts to ensure that they are tight.

The silencer fitted to all later models except the "250 Clipper" and "250 Trials" may be dismantled for cleaning before being refitted to the machine.

After removing the $\frac{5}{16}$-in. nut and tab washer in the tail, the tail piece and central body may be drawn off the long central stud located in the front portion of the Silencer. (See Fig. 5.).

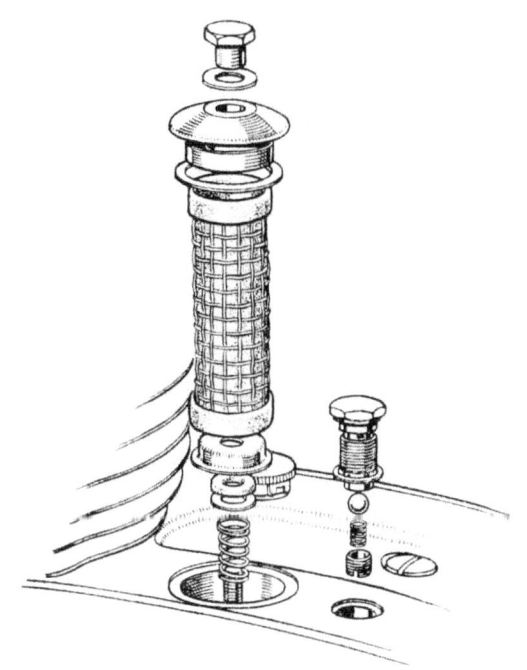

OIL FILTER AND RELIEF VALVE (EARLIER MODELS

Fig. 6

22. Cleaning the Oil Filter

The oil filter is in the oil supply to the big end and is located in the top of the crankcase on the near-side of the engine just behind the cylinder.

The filter element is removed by unscrewing the nut which holds the end cap in position. When re-assembling the filter after cleaning, take care that no grit or other foreign matter is sticking to it.

The felt element should be taken out and washed in petrol after the first 500 miles and after every subsequent 2,000 miles. Fit a new element every 5,000 miles.

All later models: The gauze filter fitted inside the timing case of later "250 Clipper," "Crusader Sports" and "250 Trials," and all "Super 5," "Continental" and "350 Bullet" models, should also be cleaned in petrol after the first 500 miles, and subsequently about every 2,000 miles.

23. Changing the Oil

After the first 500 miles and subsequently about every 2,000 miles, the oil should be drained from the tank and engine sump.

To drain the tank remove the hexagon-headed plug underneath the near-side of the engine. The small screw on the same side of the engine drains the sump.

Recommendations as to the grade of oil to be used are given in detail in the Instruction Book.

24. Removal of the Timing Chain and Sprockets

Take off the primary chaincase as described in Subsection 1 and remove the timing chain tensioner slipper.

Remove the crankshaft sprocket nut and washer.

Withdraw the camshaft sprocket from the tapered camshaft using Special Tool No. E.4870. The timing sprocket on the end of the crankshaft has a parallel bore and can be drawn off easily.

Remove the camshaft sprocket, timing sprocket and chain all together, taking care not to lose the key.

When replacing the sprockets and chain see that the timing marks are opposite one another in line with centres of the sprockets and that the key is in position. Note that the slot in the end of the crankshaft for the timing sprocket is offset so that the sprocket cannot be put on the wrong way round (see Fig. 1).

25. Overhauling the Oil Pump

The oil pump is located in a small chamber cast in the cam housing cover. It is not necessary to remove the latter to dismantle the pump but, if it has been removed it must be re-fitted before the pump is re-assembled.

Remove five $\frac{3}{16}$ in. hexagon headed screws and take off the pump cover.

Withdraw the pump disc, plungers, spring and spring cap.

Check the fit of the plungers in the disc; they should have a minimum of clearance but should be able to be moved in and out by hand.

If, when fitting a new disc or plunger, the plunger is found to be too tight, carefully lap with metal polish until it is just free. If the pump disc is not seating properly or if a new pump disc is being fitted, it should be lapped to the seating with Special Tool No. E.5425, using Carborundum 360 fine paste or liquid metal polish, until an even grey surface is obtained.

Wash all passages, etc., thoroughly with petrol after lapping, in order to remove all traces of grinding paste, and then oil the parts thoroughly

Check the pump disc spring for fatigue by assembling the pump and placing the cover in position without tightening up. It should be held not less than ⅛ in. off its facing if the spring is correct. The free length of the spring when new is ⅝ in.

When re-assembling the pump, fit a new paper gasket if necessary. Jointing compound is not used.

To check the operation of the pump remove the filler cap and oil should be seen returning through the relief valve. A certain amount of air will be mixed with the oil because the capacity of the return pump is greater than that of the feed.

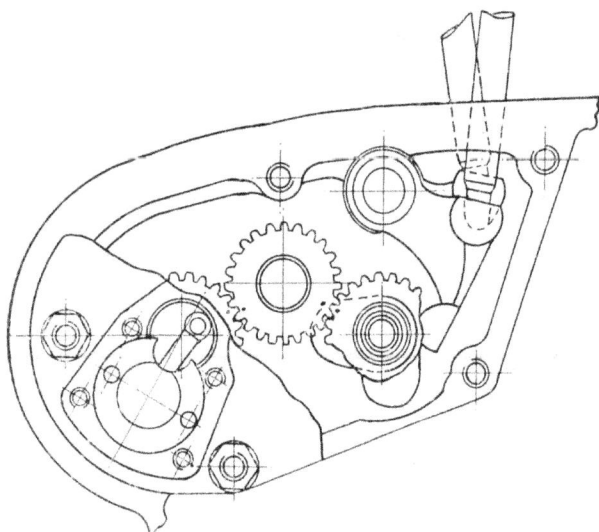

CAM HOUSING WITH COVER REMOVED
Fig. 7

26. Dismantling the Cam Gear

Remove the camshaft sprocket, timing sprocket and chain (Subsection 24).

Remove five ¼ in. nuts and washers securing the cam housing cover.

Remove the cam housing cover.

Withdraw the camshaft, cam followers and idler pinion.

On re-assembly see that the washers are replaced in the correct order on the cam follower spindle thus:
  (i) thrust washer
  (ii) exhaust cam follower
  (iii) spring washer
  (iv) inlet cam follower
  (v) thrust washer

Note that the exhaust cam follower is the longer of the two.

When replacing the camshaft be careful not to omit the ·030 in. thrust washer which goes at the back of the camshaft next to the crankcase.

Engage the pump pinion, idler pinion and camshaft pinion so that the marks are opposite one another. Note that, because the idler pinion has one tooth less than the other pinions, the marks will only come opposite every 23 revolutions, but this does not alter the timing once it is set.

When refitting the cam housing cover see that the faces are clean and apply jointing compound sparingly.

The cam housing cover can be removed without dismantling the oil pump, but the pump must be dismantled before replacing the cam housing cover, in order to fit the pump plungers over the peg on the pump spindle correctly.

27. Removal of the Contact Breaker

Access to the contact breaker for adjustment can be obtained by removing the small circular cover at the front of the generator or off-side cover and secured by two screws.

If it is required to dismantle the contact breaker, however, it is necessary to remove the generator cover (Subsection 2).

Undo the two screws in the slots in the contact breaker plate which can then be removed. This will be easier if the generator stator and retaining ring are first removed (Subsection 31).

Unscrew the fixing bolt in the centre of the spindle and the cam together with the centrifugal weights of the automatic advance mechanism can be drawn off. (See Subsection G2f, fig. 5).

The back plate assembly is mounted on a taper on the spindle and can be removed by inserting a piece of 5/16 in. dia. tapered bar in place of the centre screw and gently rocking it to and fro.

28. Removal of the Primary Drive Chain and Sprockets

The primary drive chain is an endless chain and it is therefore necessary to remove it and the engine sprocket and clutch sprocket together at the same time.

Remove the primary chain case (Subsection 1).

Remove the timing chain and sprockets (Subsection 24).

Remove the primary chain tensioner slipper.

Dismantle the clutch (Section E, Subsection 5).

Draw off both sprockets together with the primary chain.

29. Attention to the Breather

Early Models

The early type breather is located on the front of the crankcase between the front engine plates. It consists merely of a piece of synthetic rubber tube with a flattened end and very little can go wrong with it. If, however, it is found to be faulty it should be replaced with a new one.

Later Models

Being of simple design, this should not require attention, but if it is removed from the crankcase the two thin steel discs must be put back into the two outside recesses and the thin steel base plate placed between the breather flange and the crankcase.

If the breather is not operating efficiently it may cause pressure in the crankcase, instead of a partial vacuum, which may give rise to smoking or over-oiling.

30. Pressure Relief Valves

Early models have a pressure relief valve in the oil feed to the big end.

All models have a pressure relief valve for the rocker gear supply.

Their function is to prevent excessive pressure and their settings are not critical.

They are set before leaving the Works and should not normally require to be disturbed. If, however, it is found necessary to dismantle either, they can be reset as follows.

Early Models

Big End Relief Valve. This is located at the rear of the oil cleaner cap on the top of the crankcase and can be removed complete by unscrewing the hexagon head. It consists of a body containing a $\frac{5}{16}$ in. steel ball and spring held in position by a plug.

It should be set to release at a pressure of about 60 lbs. per sq. in., which will be obtained when the face of the plug is level with the end of the body. Lock the plug with a centre punch if it has been moved.

When replacing the valve see that the fibre washer is in good condition or oil leakage may occur.

All Models

Rocker Feed Relief Valve. The rocker relief valve can be seen if the oil filler cap on the top of the crankcase at the off-side of the engine is removed.

It consists of a $\frac{3}{16}$ in. steel ball, spring and plug screwed into the crankcase casting. The correct pressure is obtained with the plug screwed right home.

If the valve is dismantled, the ball can be removed by means of a small magnet, but great care must be taken not to drop the ball or the other parts into the oil tank.

If this should happen on engines with die-cast crankcases, it is possible to obtain access to the bottom of the oil tank by removing the generator cover and first draining the oil tank before taking off a small brass plate secured by four screws and marked "Do not remove."

If this plate is taken off, care must be taken when replacing it to clean off any old jointing compound and to fit a new paper gasket sealed with fresh compound.

31. Removal of the Generator

Stator. Remove the generator cover (Sub-section 2).

Unplug the connections in the generator lead at the rear of the crankcase.

Slacken the three cable clips inside the top of the crankcase so that the leads are free.

Remove three $\frac{1}{4}$ in. nuts and washers and the stator can then be withdrawn together with the retaining ring.

Rotor. The rotor is keyed on to the end of the crankshaft and can be drawn off after removing one $\frac{3}{8}$ in. nut and washer.

32. Internal Oil Pipes

The internal oil pipes inside the primary chaincase are attached to the crankcase by screws and should not normally be disturbed.

If, however, they have been removed make sure the joint faces are perfectly clean and before replacing them apply jointing compound sparingly so that it does not get into the oil passages.

Section **D6a** *ROYAL ENFIELD WORKSHOP MANUAL* Page 1

SECTION D6a

Service Operations with Engine out of Frame

1. **Removal of the Engine from the Frame**

    Disconnect the battery leads.
    Disconnect the petrol pipe.
    Remove the petrol tank.
    Remove the exhaust pipe.
    Remove the engine steady.
    Remove the rear chain and slide back gaiters.
    Remove the carburettor complete.
    Disconnect the generator leads at the junction plugs.
    Disconnect the contact breaker lead in the toolbox.
    Disconnect the clutch cable on the handlebar.
    Unplug the sparking plug lead.
    Remove the footrests and bar.
    Remove the rev. counter drive from the primary chaincase where fitted.
    Remove the primary chaincase (Section C, Subsection 1).
    Remove the generator cover (Section C, Subsection 2).
    Remove the rear fixing bolt complete with distance piece.
    Support the engine on a suitable block or box.
    Remove the rear engine plates complete with centre stand by taking out two $\frac{3}{8}$ in. bolts.
    Remove the front engine plates.
    Lift the engine out of the frame from the generator side (off side).

2. **Dismantling the Crankcase**

    Having taken the engine out of the frame, drain the oil from the oil tank and from the gearbox by taking out the two hexagon headed drain plugs at the bottom of the crankcase.

    Dismantle the cylinder head, cylinder barrel, piston, cam gear, generator and contact breaker as described in Section C, and the clutch and gearbox as described in Section E.

    On the off (generator) side, undo four $\frac{1}{4}$ in. nuts "A" (Fig. 5, Section E) from studs and one from the through bolt "B," near the bottom between the generator and the gear change lever.

    Undo two $\frac{1}{4}$ in. bolts "C" in the crankcase below the generator cover.

    Remove the off (generator) side half crankcase by tapping gently with a hide hammer behind the contact breaker housing leaving the crankshaft in the near (driving) side half case.

    Press the crankshaft assembly out of the near side half case by means of a hand press or by using Special Tool No. E.6960.

3. **Main Bearings**

    The main bearings consist of a roller bearing on the off (generator) side, and a ball bearing on the near (driving) side. The "350 Bullet" has in addition a plain bearing situated between the ball bearing, and the driving sprocket. Should the bearing require attention or replacement on the 350 c.c. engine, it is recommended that the crankcase, complete with crankshaft, is returned to the works.

    The proceedure for dealing with the 250 c.c. bearings is as follows:

    When the crankcase has been dismantled it will be seen that the ball bearing stays in the near side half crankcase, the outer race of the roller bearing stays in the off side half crankcase and the inner race of the roller bearing and the rollers stay on the shaft.

    To remove the ball bearing, first take out the circlip which holds it in position in the near side half case then heat the case to 100°C. by immersion in hot water or in an oven after which the ball bearing can be pressed or driven out.

    When fitting a new ball bearing heat the case only in the same way and drop the bearing in, taking great care to keep the bearing square with the bore. Do not forget to fit the circlip.

    To remove the outer race of the roller bearing from the off side crankcase, first heat the crankcase to 100°C. and then tap the case on a wooden base until the race drops out.

    The inner race and rollers can be drawn off the crankshaft, using a claw-type extractor. On later models flats are provided on the distance piece to accommodate the claws of the extractor.

    When fitting a new roller bearing the outer race is dropped into the off side half crankcase (with the number facing away from the flywheel) after the latter has been heated and the inner race is tapped on to the crankshaft (also with the numbers away from the crankshaft) with a hollow mandrel.

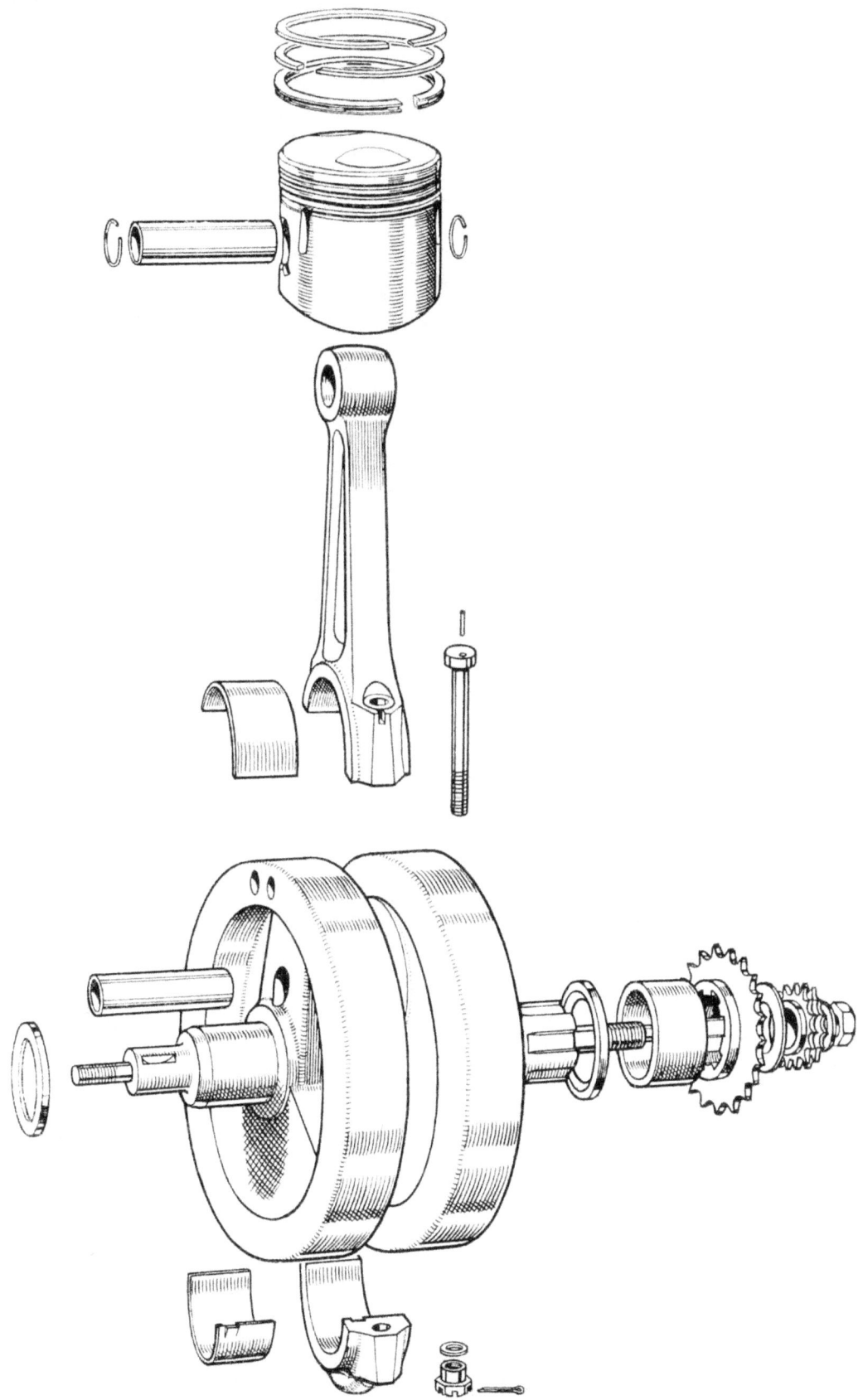

PISTON, CONNECTING ROD AND CRANK ASSEMBLY, EARLIER 250 c.c. ENGINE
Fig. 1

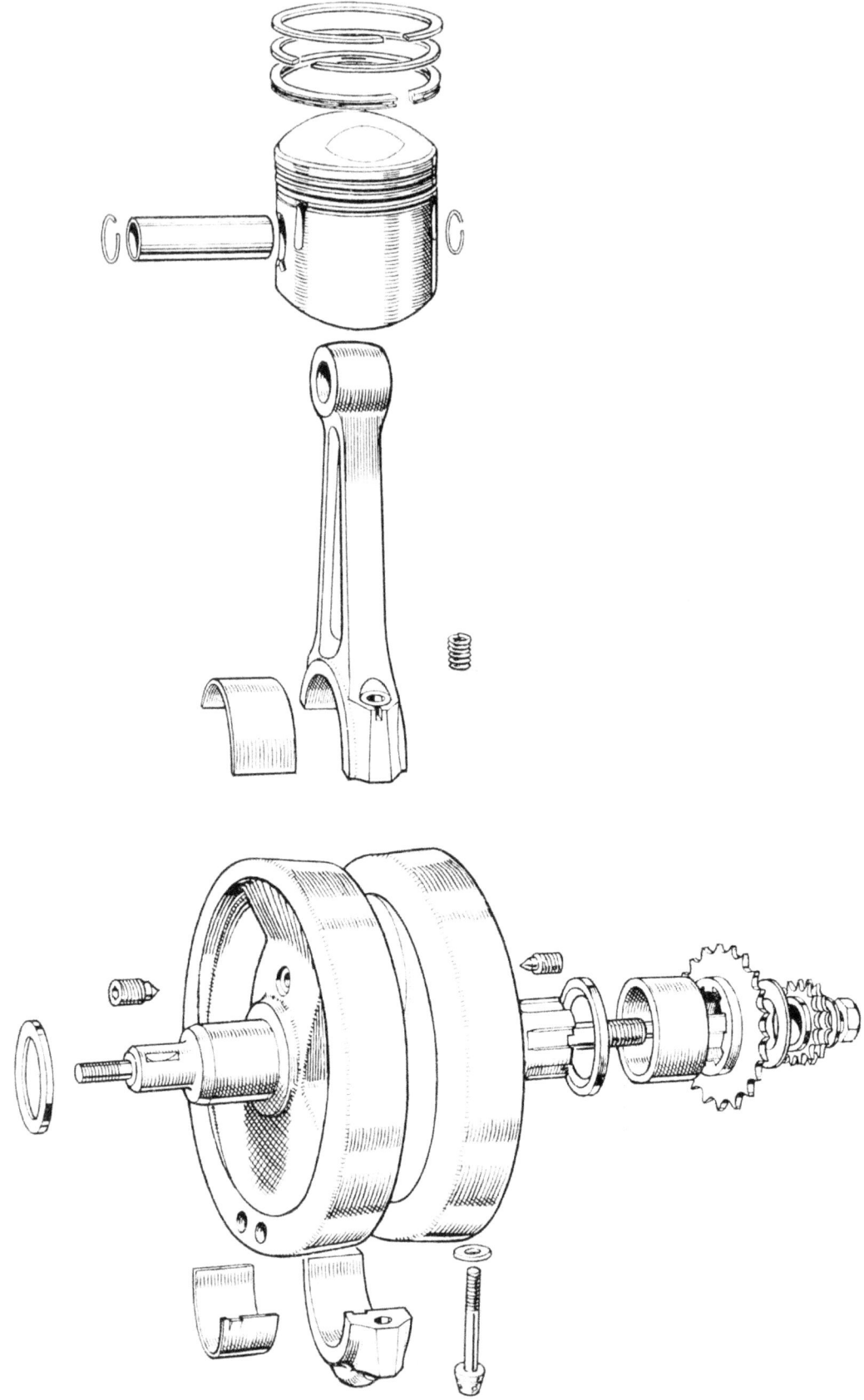

PISTON, CONNECTING ROD AND CRANK ASSEMBLY, LATER 250 c.c. ENGINES
Fig. 2

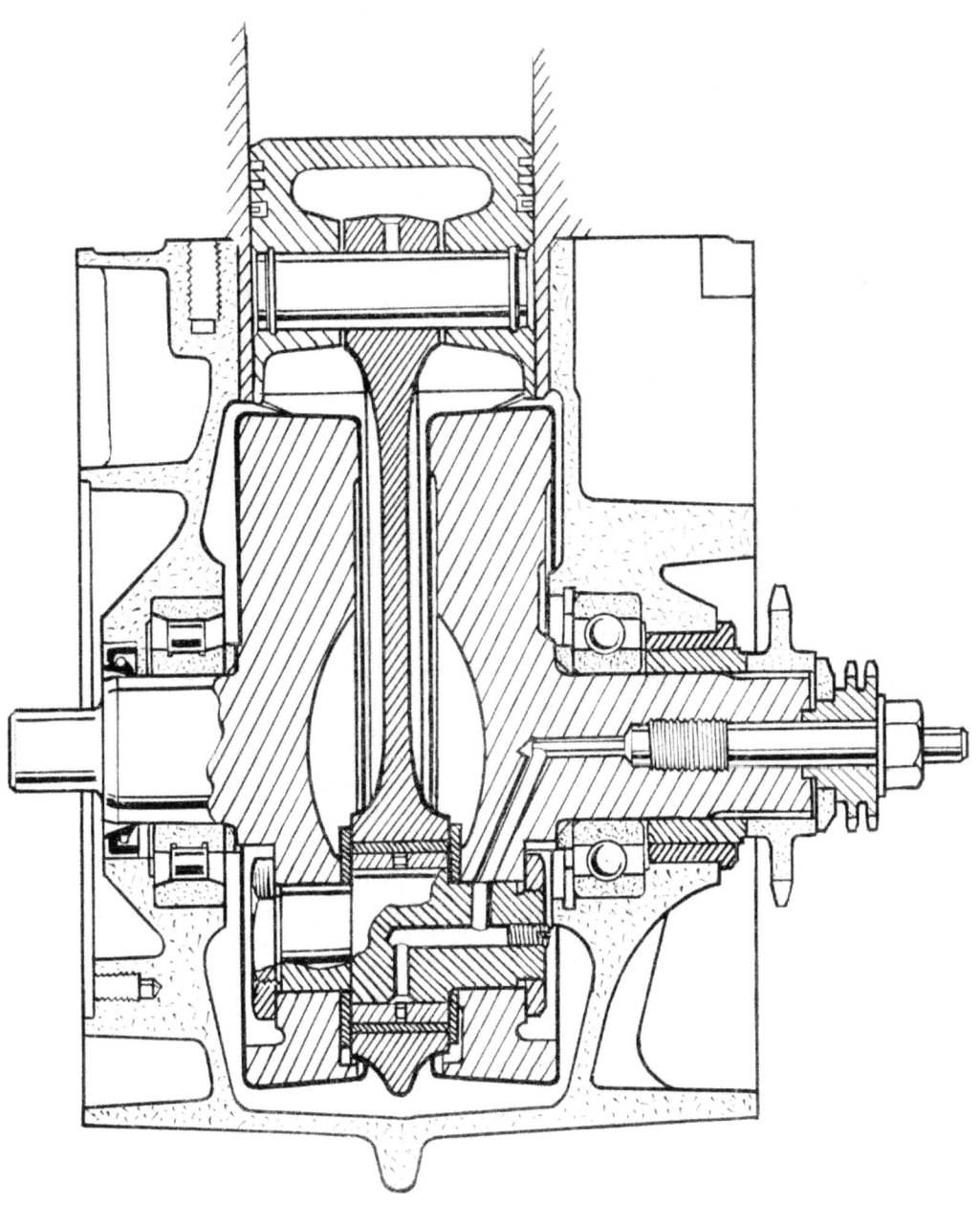

PISTON, CONNECTING ROD AND CRANK ASSEMBLY
350 c.c. ENGINE
Fig. 3

Remember to put the two distance pieces on the shaft first with the chamfer towards the flywheel.

4. Fitting the Connecting Rod, 250 c.c. Engine

The connecting rod is removed from the crankshaft by unscrewing the castle nuts from the big end bolts, having first taken out the split pins.

Before dismantling the big end, however, see that it is marked so that it can be put back the same way round on the crankpin with the cap relatively in the same position.

While the con rod is off the crankshaft, wash all the oil passages thoroughly with petrol, under pressure if possible.

When re-fitting the connecting rod, apply colloidal graphite liberally to the bearing and tighten the bolts progressively with a torque wrench set at 250 in-lbs.

Do not forget to replace the split cotter pins.

White-metalled steel shells are fitted to the connecting rod and these are replaceable.

Fitting the Connecting Rod (350 *c.c. engine*): This is a one-piece connecting rod, with a plain bearing, and the crankshaft must be split at the crankpin for its removal. However, it is recommended that the crankshaft connecting rod assembly be returned to the factory for any servicing necessary.

5. Re-Assembly of the Crankcase

Fit the ball bearing in the nearside crankcase as described in Subsection 3. If the gearbox main bearing has been removed, fit that at the same heating, taking care to put the oil seal in position first, together with a packing shim (if necessary) to prevent the seal from turning. Peen the metal of the crankcase with a punch or small chisel to prevent the gearbox bearing from moving in its housing.

Fit the inner race of the roller bearing and the distance piece to the generator end of the crankshaft as described in Subsection 3.

Fit the outer roller race into the offside crankcase as described in Subsection 3 and while still hot fit the crankshaft oil seal and the contact breaker spindle oil seal, pressing them in flush with the casing. Be sure that the seals are fitted the right way round, i.e., with the open side towards the flywheel.

Lay the nearside half crankcase flat on two blocks (or on a block with a hole in it) and press the crankshaft into it with a hand press, having first put the distance piece on to the shaft (chamfer side towards the flywheel).

If a hand press is not available, the shaft can be held in soft jaws in a vice, near or driving side upwards, and the nearside crankcase drawn on to it by means of Special Tool No. E.6977, which consists of a slave stud which screws into the end of the shaft and a sleeve which fits over the shaft end and is drawn on by a nut on the slave stud.

Turn the nearside crankcase and the crankshaft over and see that the two $\frac{1}{2}$ in. dia. hollow dowels are in position at the front and rear of the case. The front dowel fits into a counterbore in the front engine plate bolt hole and the rear dowel fits over the $\frac{1}{4}$ in. stud at the rear of the crankcase.

Place the offside crankcase over the shaft and studs, having first applied jointing compound to the joint faces and grease to the oil seals. The latter is most important as the synthetic rubber may tear when the engine is started if fitted dry.

Fit and tighten the seven $\frac{1}{4}$ in. crankcase nuts and washers on the off side crankcase, four being on studs, one on the through bolt and two on the bolts below the generator cover.

6. Crankpin Oil-way

The oil-way in the crankpin tends to choke with sludge and foreign matter during the course of usage. Ultimately, under adverse conditions, the oil-way may be completely choked, thus cutting off the supply of oil to the big end bearing. Whenever the engine is dismantled, the opportunity should be taken to clean all foreign matter from this oil-way. This is done by removing the sleeve which passes through the centre of the crankpin on the earlier models, or by unscrewing the light alloy plugs on the later models.

SECTION E11
Gearbox and Clutch

1. Description of the Clutch

Early Models

The clutch is built into the clutch sprocket and is mounted on the gearbox mainshaft which projects through into the primary chaincase.

There are four driven plates which are plain and three driving plates, giving six friction surfaces.

The driven plates comprise the clutch centre backplate, two plain plates on splines on the clutch centre and the clutch front plate.

The driving plates comprise the clutch sprocket itself which has a Klingerite ring riveted to each side and two pierced plates which rotate with it and which are fitted with cork inserts.

The clutch plates are held in contact, when driving, by three coil springs in the case of the "250 Clipper" and "Crusader 250" models, and six coil springs in the case of the "Crusader Sports," and are released when the springs are compressed by a pad and rod which passes through the centre of the gearbox mainshaft.

Later Models

All later models retain a clutch basically similar to the earlier models, but incorporating five driven plates which are plain, and four driving plates giving eight friction surfaces.

The splined sections on the clutch sprocket, and the clutch centre are longer, and the clutch front plate has a shallower recess for the withdrawal pad than the early type.

On some models the plates are not pierced but have friction material bonded to their surfaces.

All later models have three pressure springs.

350 c.c. Model

This clutch employs six driven plates, which comprise the clutch centre back plate, four plain plates and the clutch cover plate.

There are five driving plates including the clutch sprocket, each with friction material bonded to their surfaces. Three pressure springs are used.

2. Description of the Gearbox

The gearbox itself is cast as part of the crankcase, but forms a separate compartment housing the mainshaft, mainshaft sleeve, layshaft and gears.

On early engines the gearbox "breathes" through a small hole in the filler plug and on later ones through a hole in the gearbox cover, connecting the top of the gearbox to the generator compartment on the offside.

Four-speed Gearbox

(See Fig. 2 for operation).

The clutch sprocket A is mounted on the end of the mainshaft B which passes through the mainshaft sleeve C on the end of which is the final drive sprocket D.

At the other end of the mainshaft B is a pinion E which engages with a pinion F on the layshaft G. At the other end of the layshaft G is a pinion H engaging with a pinion J which runs free on the mainshaft sleeve C.

The mainshaft sleeve C has splines on which slides a double pinion KL. This double pinion KL engages with two pinions M and N which are free to rotate or slide on the layshaft G.

The double pinion KL has dogs at each end which can engage with dogs on the pinion E or on the pinion J.

The pinions M and N have internal dogs which can engage or slide over projecting dogs P and Q on the layshaft G.

The double pinion KL and the pinions M and N all slide together and are moved by the operator

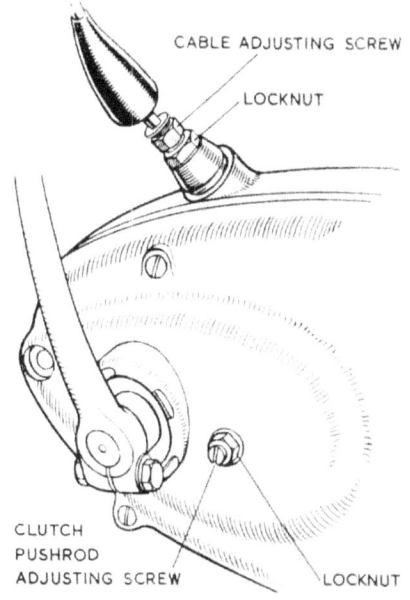

CLUTCH ADJUSTMENTS
Fig. 1

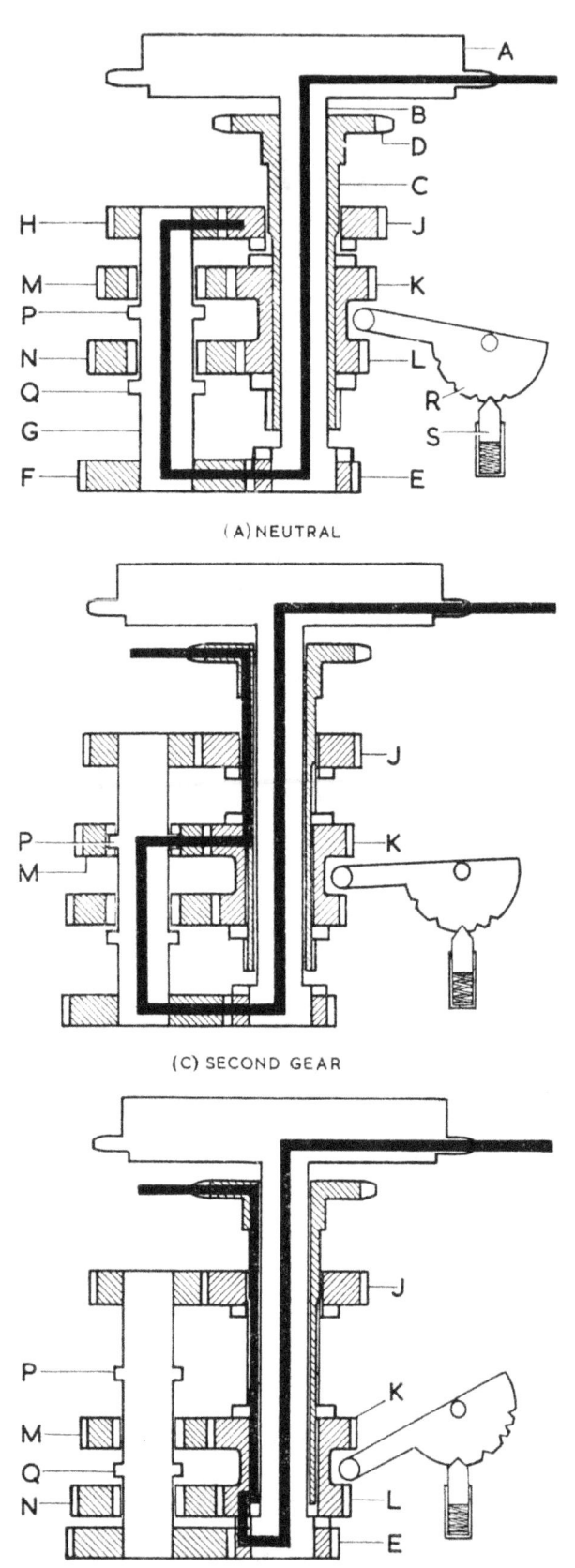

(A) NEUTRAL (B) FIRST GEAR (C) SECOND GEAR (D) THIRD GEAR (E) TOP GEAR

Fig. 14A—Neutral. None of the dogs is engaged so that the mainshaft B and pinions E, F, H, J are rotating but the mainshaft sleeve C and the final drive sprocket are stationary.

Fig. 14B—Bottom Gear. The sliding pinions K, L, M, N have moved over so that the dogs on K engage with the dogs on the pinion J. This causes the double pinion KL, the mainshaft sleeve C and the sprocket D to rotate with the pinion J which is being driven from the mainshaft through the layshaft G. The dogs P and Q are not engaged.

Fig. 14C—Second Gear. The sliding pinions have moved so that the dogs on J are disengaged but the dogs P on the layshaft engage with the pinion M. The drive from the mainshaft and layshaft then passes through pinions M and K to the splines on the mainshaft sleeve and the pinion J is free on the sleeve.

Fig. 14D—Third Gear. The sliding pinions have moved further over so that the dogs Q on the layshaft engage with the pinion N which drives the pinion L and thus the mainshaft sleeve, the pinion M being free on the layshaft.

Fig. 14E—Top Gear. The sliding pinions have now moved right over so that both sets of dogs P and Q on the layshaft have disengaged but the dogs on the double pinion KL have engaged with those on the pinion E and the mainshaft and sleeve rotate together giving a one to one drive through the gearbox from the clutch sprocket to the output sprocket the pinions M, N, J being free to rotate.

OPERATION OF GEARS
Fig. 2

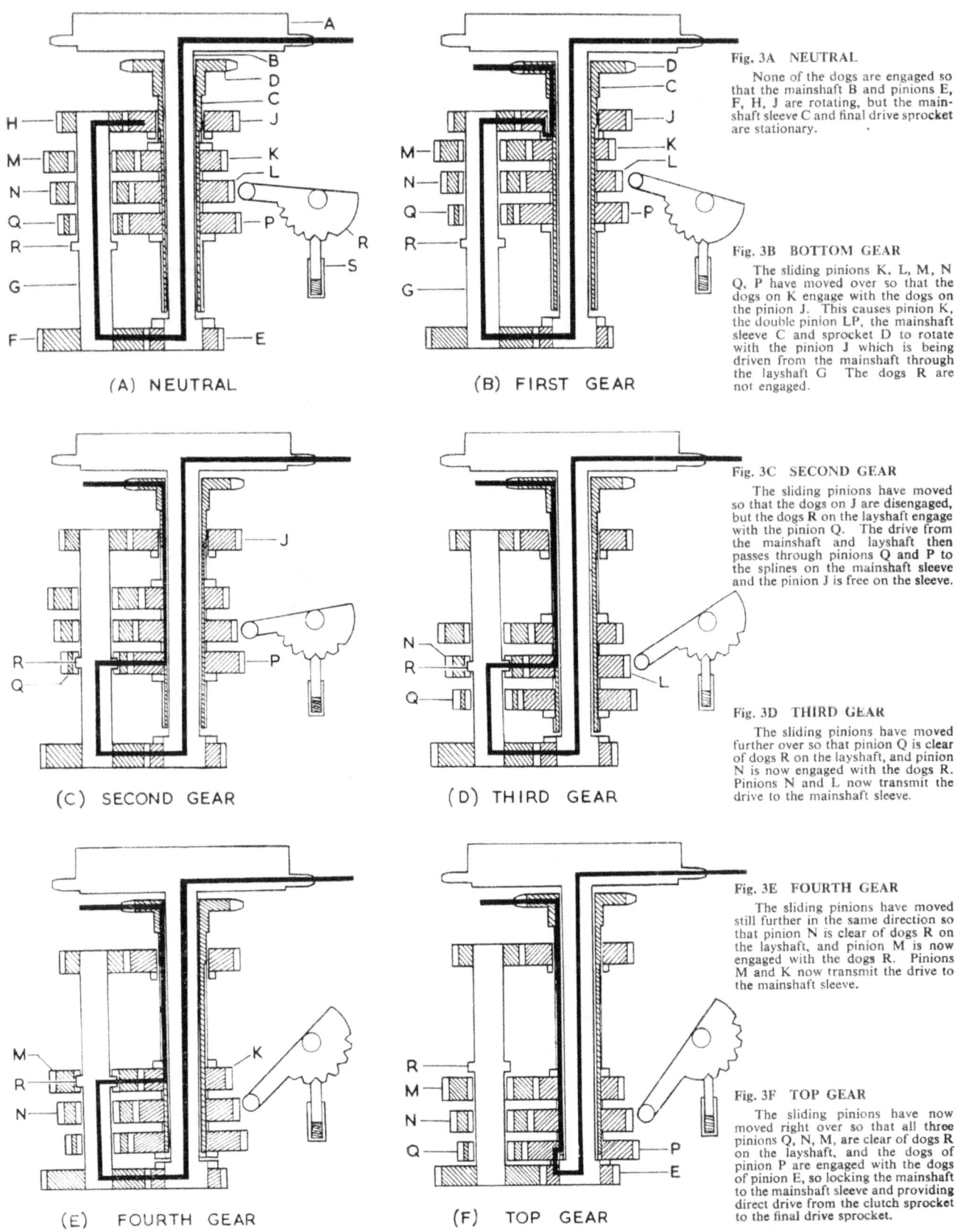

Fig. 3A NEUTRAL

None of the dogs are engaged so that the mainshaft B and pinions E, F, H, J are rotating, but the mainshaft sleeve C and final drive sprocket are stationary.

Fig. 3B BOTTOM GEAR

The sliding pinions K, L, M, N Q, P have moved over so that the dogs on K engage with the dogs on the pinion J. This causes pinion K, the double pinion LP, the mainshaft sleeve C and sprocket D to rotate with the pinion J which is being driven from the mainshaft through the layshaft G. The dogs R are not engaged.

Fig. 3C SECOND GEAR

The sliding pinions have moved so that the dogs on J are disengaged, but the dogs R on the layshaft engage with the pinion Q. The drive from the mainshaft and layshaft then passes through pinions Q and P to the splines on the mainshaft sleeve and the pinion J is free on the sleeve.

Fig. 3D THIRD GEAR

The sliding pinions have moved further over so that pinion Q is clear of dogs R on the layshaft, and pinion N is now engaged with the dogs R. Pinions N and L now transmit the drive to the mainshaft sleeve.

Fig. 3E FOURTH GEAR

The sliding pinions have moved still further in the same direction so that pinion N is clear of dogs R on the layshaft, and pinion M is now engaged with the dogs R. Pinions M and K now transmit the drive to the mainshaft sleeve.

Fig. 3F TOP GEAR

The sliding pinions have now moved right over so that all three pinions Q, N, M, are clear of dogs R on the layshaft, and the dogs of pinion P are engaged with the dogs of pinion E, so locking the mainshaft to the mainshaft sleeve and providing direct drive from the clutch sprocket to the final drive sprocket.

OPERATION OF FIVE-SPEED GEARS
Fig. 3

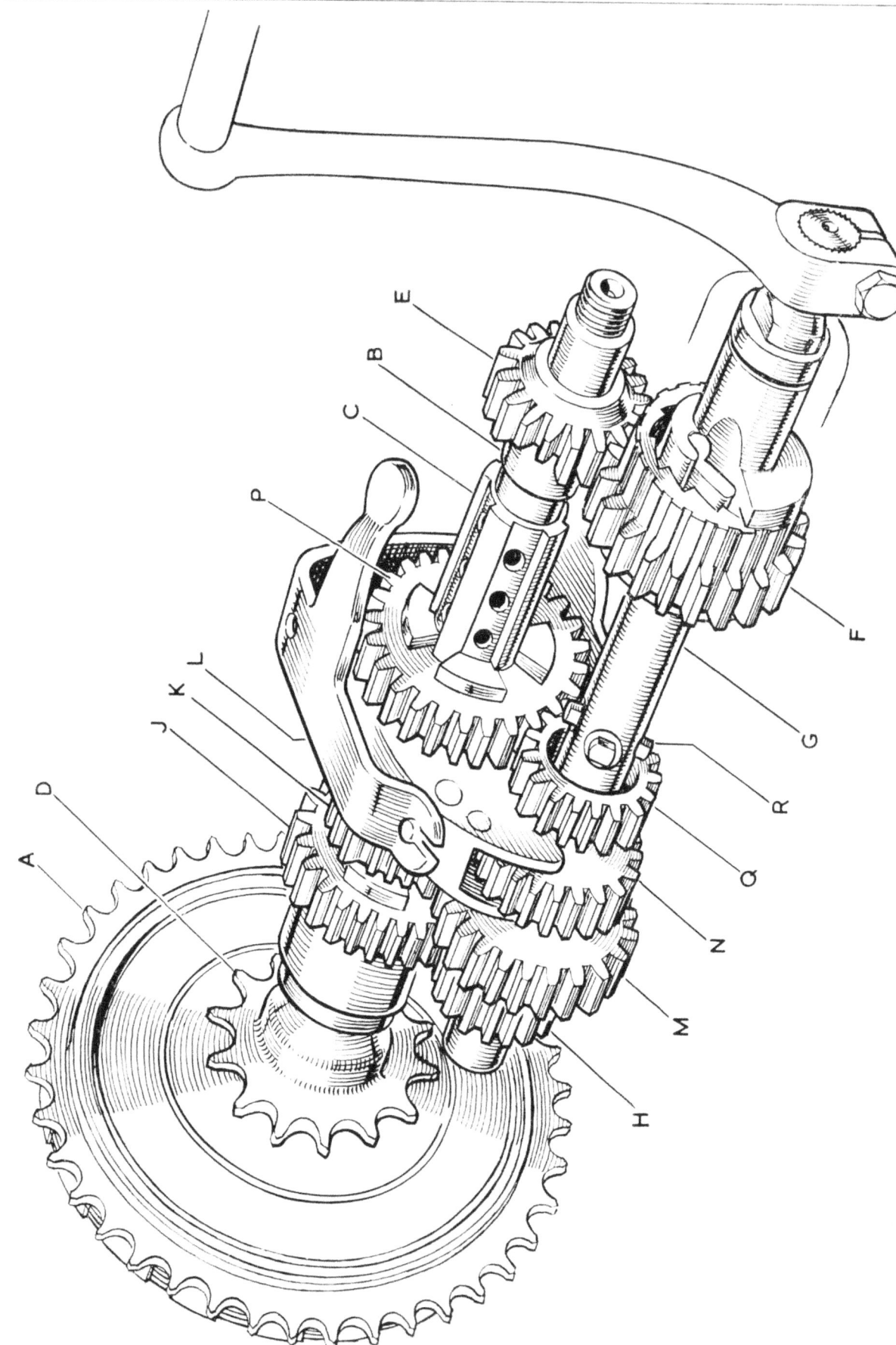

ARRANGEMENT OF FIVE-SPEED GEARS
Fig. 4

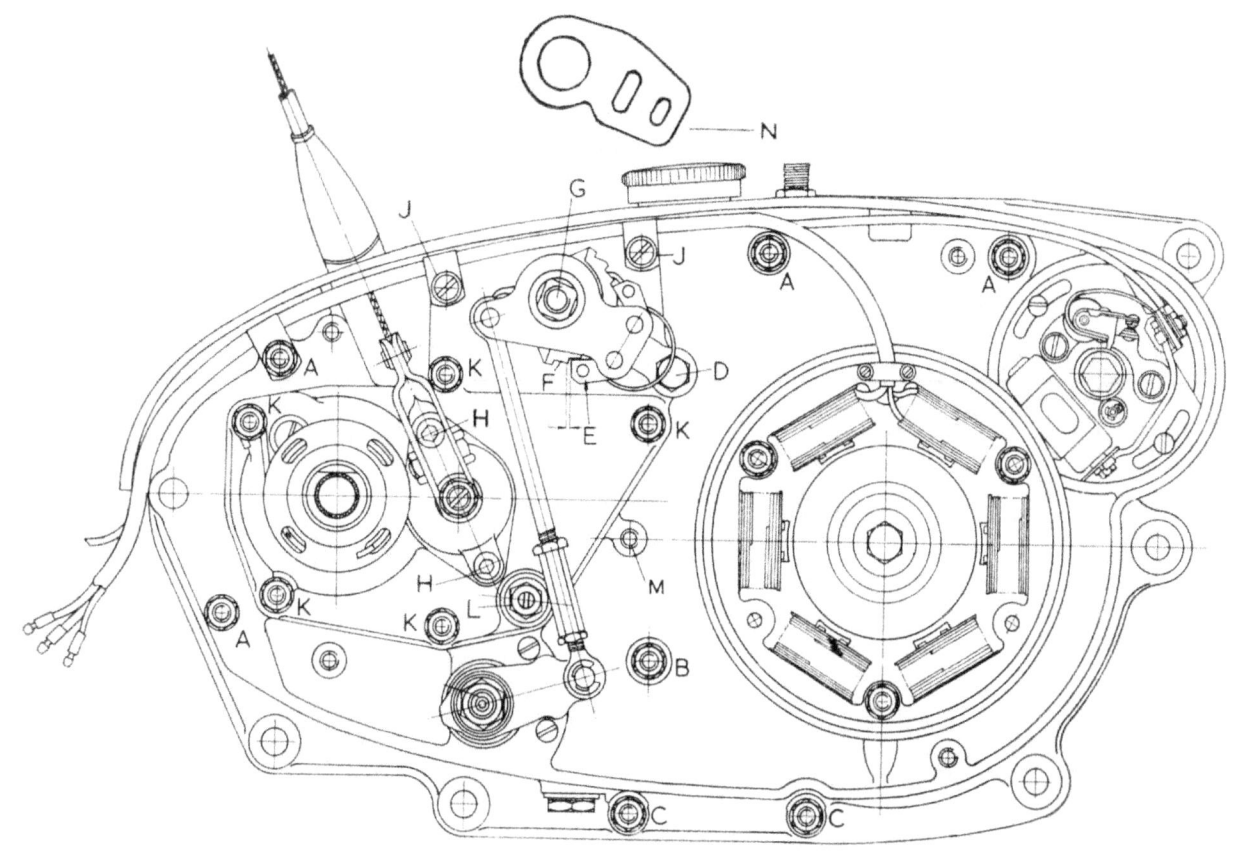

ENGINE WITH GENERATOR COVER REMOVED
Fig. 5

fork R. The latter is located by a spring plunger S engaging with a notched plate which is part of the operator arm R.

The kickstart lever is connected to the pinion F on the layshaft by a ratchet mechanism which automatically disengages when the lever is released.

Five-speed Gearbox

The positions of the clutch sprocket, main shaft, mainshaft sleeve, final drive sprocket, layshaft, operator fork and kickstart mechanism are similar to the four-speed gearbox, but the number and arrangement of the pinions differ as can be seen in Fig. 4. The operation of the gearbox is shown diagrammatically in Fig. 3.

3. Adjustment of the Clutch

Slide back the plastic cover where the clutch cable enters the top of the crankcase. This will expose the clutch cable adjuster (see Fig. 1).

Slacken the locknut and screw in the adjusting sleeve so that there is slack in the clutch cable.

Slacken the locknut on the clutch pushrod adjusting screw which is protruding through the generator-, or off-side, cover in line with the gearbox main shaft and immediately in front of the kickstart spindle.

Turn the slotted adjusting screw until it begins to tighten up, then slacken it back one complete turn. This will ensure that the clutch operating lever inside the cover is in its best working position.

Screw out the clutch cable adjusting sleeve on the top of the crankcase until there is not less than $\frac{1}{16}$ in. free movement of the clutch cable when the clutch lever on the handlebar is operated.

Tighten the locknut and replace the plastic sleeve.

Owing to the initial bedding down of the clutch friction material, it may happen that the clearance in the clutch control is taken up during the first few hundred miles with a new machine and will require adjustment soon after delivery.

4. Adjustment of the Gear-Change Mechanism

To obtain access to the gear-change mechanism, the generator cover must be removed as described in Section C, Subsection 2.

(a) To adjust the Selector Pawls. Slacken the $\frac{1}{4}$ in. pin D (see Fig. 5) and move the backplate so that it is in the central position in the slot, i.e., so that the pawls lie flat on the ratchet teeth.

(b) To adjust the Selector Rod. Slacken the locknuts on the turnbuckle on the selector rod.

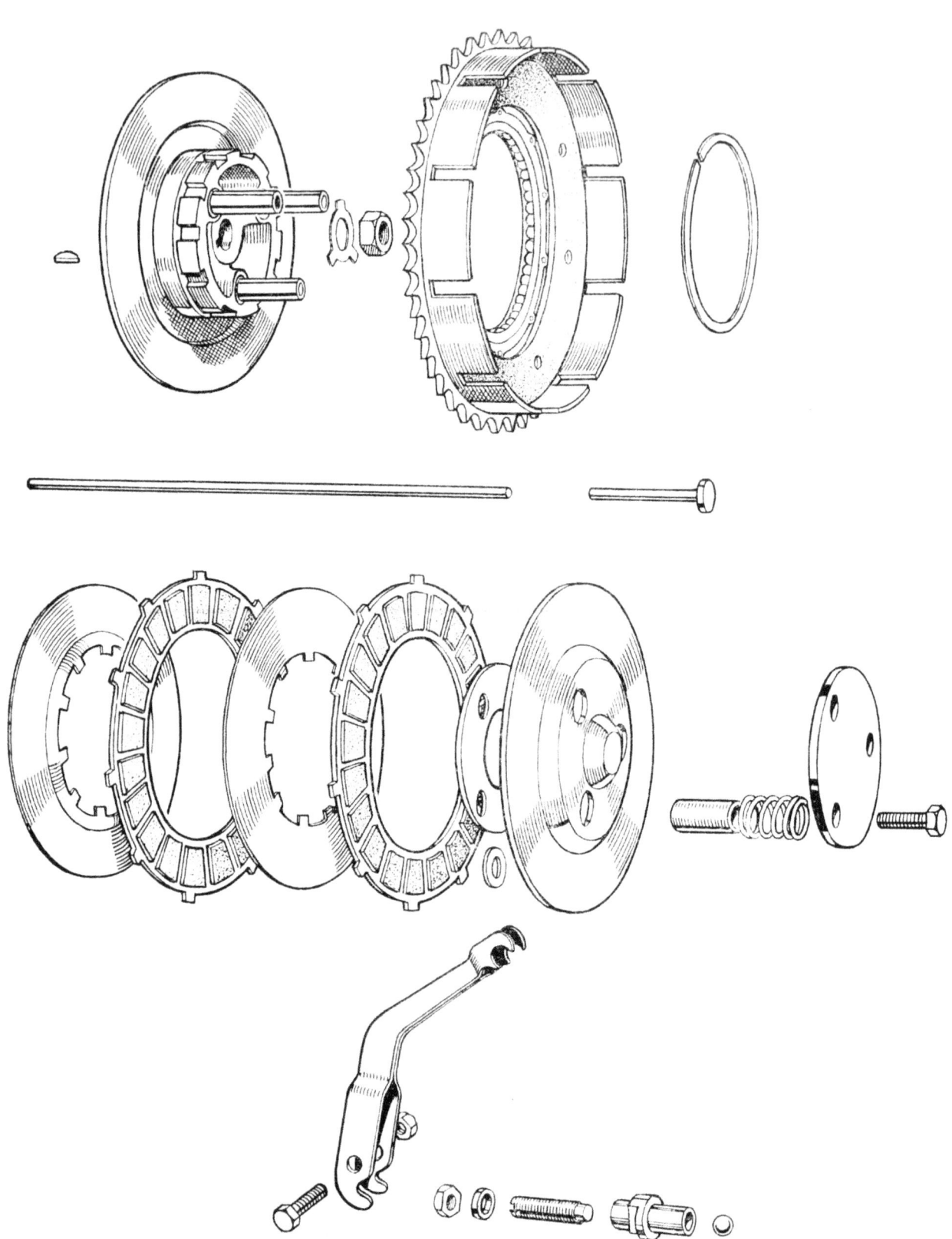

EXPLODED VIEW OF CLUTCH—EARLY "CRUSADER 250" AND "250 CLIPPER"
Fig. 6

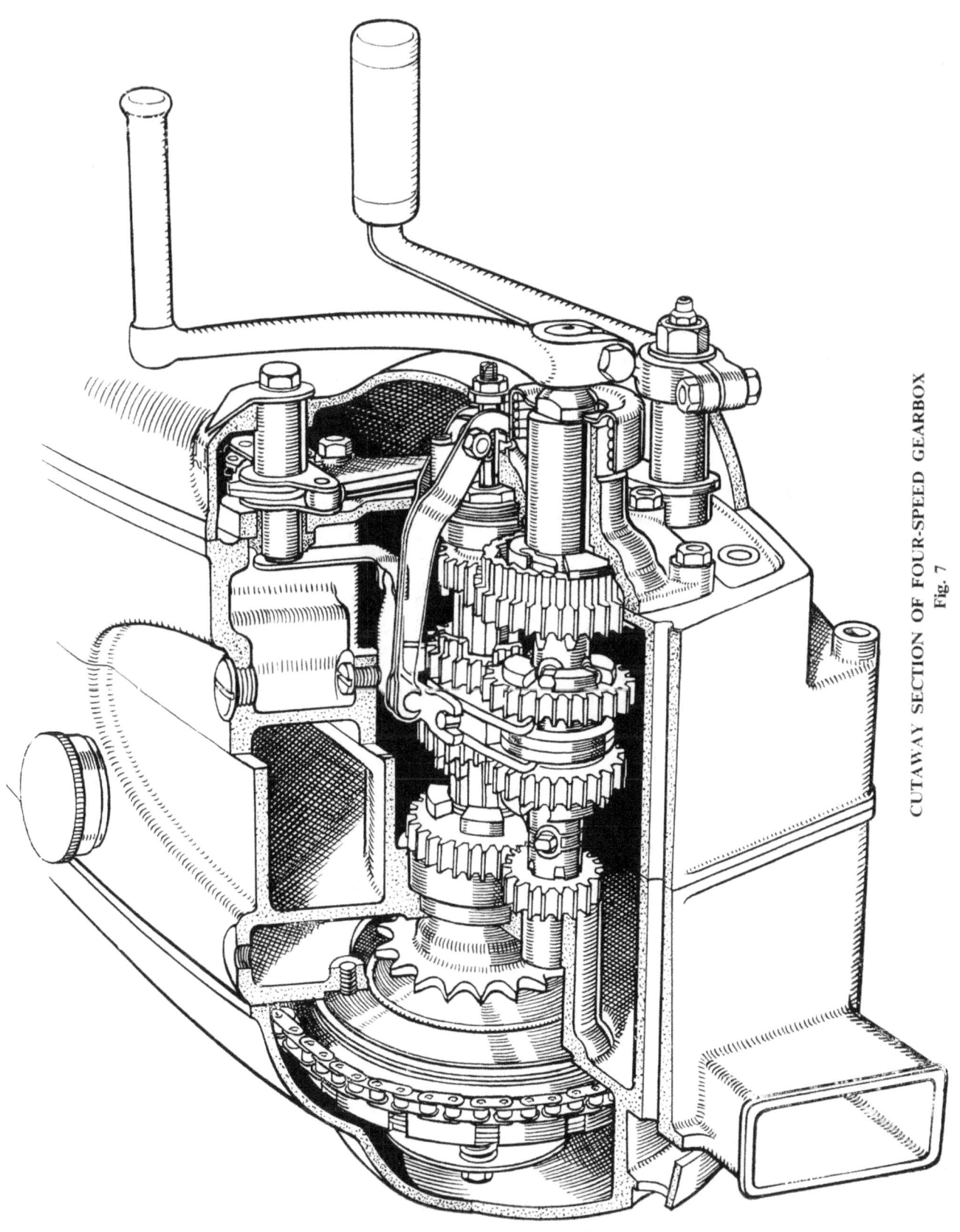

CUTAWAY SECTION OF FOUR-SPEED GEARBOX
Fig. 7

The top and bottom nuts have right and left hand threads respectively.

Put the gear box into third gear and adjust the turnbuckle so that when the pawl carrier plates are in the mid position there is equal clearance between the ends of the two pawl faces and the ratchet teeth (lower pawl and ratchet tooth shown as E and F respectively in figure 5).

(c) Modified Gear Change Mechanism as fitted to later 1962 models. Adjust as indicated, then slacken the nut K on the stud immediately below the set pin D. Fit foot control pedal if necessary, engage top gear and, **holding the pedal hard down, swivel** the outer control stop plate N (illustrated separately in figure 5) downwards until the pawl pin is at the top of the centre slot; tighten the nut K on its stud, locking the stop plate in position. Before finally replacing the generator cover, check all gears and make any final adjustment on the link rod.

5. Dismantling the Clutch

Remove the primary chaincase (Section C, Subsection 1).

Put the gearbox in top gear.

Undo three $\frac{1}{4}$ in. hexagon-headed pins and all the plates, springs and distance pieces can then be removed.

Remove chain adjuster pad.

Remove the circlip retaining the clutch sprocket and the latter can then be removed. If the engine sprocket is to be removed, the clutch sprocket, engine sprocket and chain must all be removed at the same time (see Section C, Subsection 28).

Remove the clutch operating pad.

Turn back the tab on the centre washer and remove the nut.

Pull off the clutch centre with Special Tool No. E.5414. The clutch centre is on a taper on the shaft and care should be taken not to lose the key.

6. Reassembly of the Clutch

The reassembly of the clutch is the reverse of Subsection 5 but care must be taken to put the plates, etc., back the right way round and in the right order as follows (see Fig. 6):

Replace the clutch centre on the taper (not forgetting the key). Tighten the centre nut and bend up the tab of the tab-washer. Then replace the clutch sprocket and circlip, making sure that the latter is right home in the groove.

The above applies to all three types of clutch.

From here proceed as follows for plate assembly:

Early 250 *Models*
 Plain dished plate (centre outwards).
 Cork plate.
 Plain plate.
 Cork plate.

Later 250 *Models*
 Plain dished plate (centre outwards).
 Cork plate.
 Plain plate.
 Cork plate.
 Plain dished plate (centre inwards).
 Cork plate.

350 c.c. Model
 Plain dished plate (centre outwards).
 Cork plate.
 Plain plate.
 Cork plate.
 Plain plate.
 Cork plate.
 Plain dished plate (centre inwards).
 Cork plate.

Now proceed for all models as follows:
 Clutch plate retaining ring (3 in. dia. with three $\frac{3}{8}$ in. holes).
 Three distance washers (if fitted).
 Three distance tubes.
 Clutch operating pad (and rod if it has been removed).
 Front plate (5 in. dia. with three $\frac{1}{2}$ in. holes).
 Three springs. (Early "Crusader Sports": six springs.)
 Flat outer plate (3 in. dia. with three $\frac{1}{4}$ in. holes).
 Three $\frac{1}{4}$ in. hexagon headed pins.
 Adjust the clutch cable (Subsection 3).
 To facilitate the fitting of the three $\frac{1}{4}$ in. pins, first use two longer pins so that the springs can be compressed and the first pin started. Then replace the two long pins in turn by the correct ones.

7. Removal of the Final Drive Sprocket

Remove the primary chaincase cover (Section C, Subsection 1).

Dismantle the clutch as described in Subsection 5.

Remove the primary chaincase back cover secured by six screws behind the clutch, having first removed the key from the gearbox main shaft and taking care not to damage the rubber oil-seal which is located in the back cover.

Remove the set screw locking the sprocket nut.

Remove the sprocket nut, taking care not to dislodge the felt oil-seal inside the nut. The sprocket can then be drawn off the splines on the main shaft.

Note. If the gearbox is to be completely dismantled, the final drive sprocket should be removed **before** taking off the gearbox cover on the opposite side.

Before replacing the final drive sprocket, smear the boss of the sprocket liberally with grease where it enters the oil-seal and be careful not to damage the rubber of the seal.

When replacing the sprocket nut, see that the felt oil-seal inside it is intact and that the end of the set screw does not protrude through the back of the sprocket.

Thoroughly clean the joint-face of the back cover, and the face on which it seats, to remove any old jointing compound. Fit a new paper gasket and apply jointing compound to both sides.

Grease the main shaft where the rubber oil-seal fits over it and note that the holes in the back cover are not spaced symmetrically.

8. Dismantling the Gearbox.

It is important to note, before commencing to dismantle the gearbox, that the layshaft and sliding pinions can be removed without dismantling the clutch and final drive sprocket, in which case the main shaft and main shaft sleeve are left in position.

Also, the main shaft can be removed when the clutch is taken off but without removing the final drive sprocket and main shaft sleeve.

If, however, the main shaft is to be removed the clutch must be removed BEFORE the gearbox cover on the off side is taken off and if the main shaft sleeve is to be removed the final drive sprocket must also be removed BEFORE the gearbox cover is taken off.

The following instructions are for the **COMPLETE** dismantling of the gearbox, but this may not be entirely necessary, as explained above.

Remove the generator cover (Section C, Subsection 2).

Disconnect the clutch cable.

Drain the oil from the gearbox by removing the drain plug on the off side.

Dismantle the clutch as described in Subsection 5.

Remove the final drive sprocket as described in Subsection 7.

Remove the small circlip at the lower end of the connecting link, below the turnbuckle on the foot change mechanism.

Slide off the selector mechanism, using two screwdrivers.

Remove two Allen screws H (Fig. 5) and take off the main shaft end-cap together with the clutch operating lever. (This is not necessary if the clutch is removed.)

Remove the main shaft nut (**LEFT HAND THREAD**) and the oil thrower. Note that the recess in the oil thrower faces outwards. (This is not necessary if the clutch is removed.)

Remove two cheese-headed screws J (with wiring clips) near the top of the crankcase.

Remove five ¼ in. nuts K, and washers, securing the gearbox cover.

Remove the gear locating plunger L (see Fig. 5).

Slide the cover off, with the kick-start mechanism and the selector arm, and with the main shaft if the clutch has been removed.

The layshaft complete with gears, and the 2nd and 3rd gear sliding pinions of the four-speed gearbox, or the 2nd, 3rd and 4th gear sliding pinions of the five-speed gearbox, can then be withdrawn.

9. Re-Assembling the Gearbox

When re-assembling the gearbox, reverse the procedure given in Subsection 8.

Take care that the gear-change fork engages correctly and see that the distance shim is in position on the layshaft behind the kick-start pinion before replacing the gearbox cover.

If the main shaft nut has been removed, see that the oil thrower is replaced the right way round, i.e. with the recess facing outwards.

Replace the gear locating plunger L. Screw the plunger in as far as it will go and then screw it back one turn and tighten the locknut, keeping the screwdriver slot on the plunger vertical.

On some models the plunger is not guided and the housing is then screwed in as far as it will go.

Fill the gearbox to the correct level with engine oil. **Grease of any kind should not be used.** To check the oil level, remove the screw M (Fig. 5).

10. The Kick-Start Mechanism

If the kick-start mechanism has been dismantled, take care to replace the parts in the same order and to put the return spring back in the same position as before. If it is too tight, it will break when the kick-start pedal is pressed right down.

Take care not to damage the rubber seal which fits in a groove on the kick-start shaft or oil leakage into the generator cover will result.

SECTION F4
Amal Monobloc Carburetter

1. General Description

The Amal Monobloc Carburetter has been introduced as an improvement on the earlier standard needle type. In general it gives better petrol consumption, combined with improved starting and acceleration from low speeds and a small increase in maximum speed.

The float chamber is integral with the mixing chamber and contains a pivoted barrel-shaped float operating on a nylon fuel needle. There is a considerable leverage ratio between the float and the needle and, in consequence, flooding is rare unless there is dirt on the needle seating.

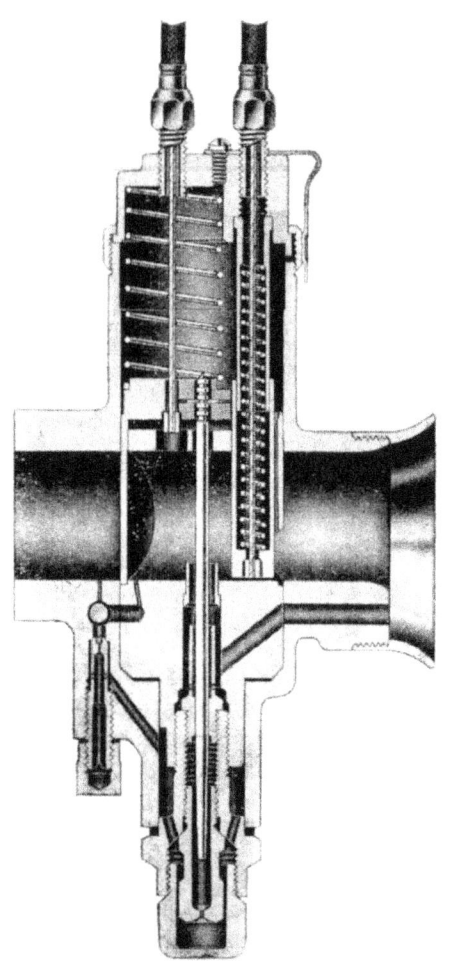

SECTION THROUGH MIXING CHAMBER, SHOWING AIR VALVE AND THROTTLE CLOSED

Fig. 1

The supply of air to the engine is controlled by a throttle slide which carries a taper needle operating in the needle jet. The needle is secured to the throttle slide by a spring clip fitting in one of five grooves and the mixture strength throughout a large proportion of the throttle range is controlled by the position of this needle in the slide and by the size of the jet in which it works. There is, however, a restricting or main jet at the bottom of the needle jet and the size of this controls the mixture strength at the largest throttle openings. At very small throttle openings petrol and air are fed to the engine through a separate pilot system, which has an outlet at the engine side of the throttle. The air supply to this pilot system is controlled by the pilot air screw and the slow running of the engine can be adjusted by means of this screw and a stop which holds the throttle open a very small amount. The throttle slide is cut away at the back and the shape of this cut-away controls the mixture at throttle openings slightly wider than that required for slow running. There is a compensating system to prevent undue enriching of the mixture with increasing engine speed, this system consisting of a primary choke surrounding the upper end of the needle jet through which air is drawn in increasing quantities as the depression in the main choke increases. This air supply and the supply to the pilot system are taken from two separate ducts in the main air intake to the carburetter so that all the air passing to the engine can be filtered by fitting an air cleaner to the main carburetter air intake.

Two small cross holes in the needle jet, at a level just below the static level in the float chamber, permit petrol to flow into the primary choke when the engine is not running or when it is running at very low speeds, thus forming a well of petrol which will be drawn into the engine on starting or accelerating from low speeds. At moderately high engine speeds the level of petrol in the float chamber falls slightly and in consequence no more fuel flows through the cross holes in the needle jet so that the petrol well remains empty until the engine slows down or stops.

A handlebar controlled air slide is provided to enrich the mixture temporarily when required.

2. Tuning the Carburetter(s)

The throttle opening at which each tuning point is most effective is shown in Fig. 2. It should be remembered, however, that a change of setting at any point will have some effect on the setting required at other points; for instance, a change of main jet will have some effect on the mixture strength at half throttle which, however, is mainly controlled by the needle position. Similarly an alteration to the throttle cut-away may affect both the needle position required and the adjustment of the pilot air screw. For this reason it is necessary to tune the carburetter in a definite sequence, which is as follows:

First—Main Jet. The size should be chosen which gives maximum speed at full throttle with the air control wide open. If two different sizes of jet give the same speed the larger should be chosen for safety as it is dangerous to run with too weak a mixture at full throttle.

Second—The pilot air screw should be set to give good idling. Note that the pilot jet is detachable and two sizes are available, 25 c.c. and 30 c.c. If the pilot air adjusting screw requires to be screwed out less than half a turn the larger size pilot jet should be used; if the air screw requires to be screwed out more than 2-3 turns fit the smaller size of pilot jet.

PHASES OF AMAL MONOBLOC CARBURETTER THROTTLE OPENINGS

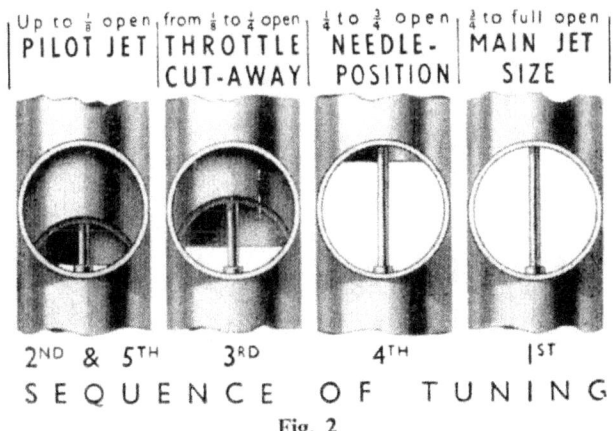

SEQUENCE OF TUNING
Fig. 2

Third—The throttle valve should be selected with the largest amount of cut-away which will prevent spitting or misfiring when opening the throttle slowly from the idling position.

Fourth—The lowest position of the taper needle should be found consistent with good acceleration with the air slide wide open.

Fifth—The pilot air screw should be checked to improve the idling if possible. When setting the adjustment of the pilot air screw this should be done in conjunction with the throttle stop. Note that the correct setting of the air screw is the one which gives the fastest idling speed for a given position of the throttle stop. If the idling speed is then undesirably fast it can be slowed down by unscrewing the throttle stop a fraction of a turn.

It will be noted that of the four points at which adjustments are normally made, i.e., pilot air screw, throttle cut-away, needle position and main jet size, the first and third do not require changing of any parts of the carburetter. Assuming that the carburetter has the standard setting to suit the particular type of engine any small adjustments occasioned by atmospheric conditions, changes in quality of fuel, etc., can usually be covered by adjustment of the pilot air screw and raising or lowering the taper needle one notch. If, however, the machine is used at very high altitudes or with a very restricted air cleaner a smaller main jet will be necessary. The following table gives the reduction in main jet size required at different altitudes:

Altitude, ft.	Reduction, %
3,000	5
6,000	9
9,000	13
12,000	17

In the case of carburetters for engine running on alcohol fuel considerably larger jets are needed. In most cases a No. 113 needle jet will be required and the main jet size will require to be increased by an amount varying from 50% to 150% according to the grade of fuel used.

If the engine is run on fuel containing a small proportion of alcohol added to the petrol, a rough and ready guide is that the main jet should be increased by 1% for every 1% of alcohol in the fuel. In most cases alcohol blends available from petrol pumps do not contain sufficient alcohol to require any alteration to the carburetter setting.

The range of adjustment of the taper needle and the pilot air screw are determined by the size of the needle jet and of the pilot outlet respectively. Standard needle jets have a bore at the smallest point of ·1065 in. and are marked 106. Alternative needle jets ·1055 in., ·1075 in., ·109 in. and ·113 in. bore are available and are marked 105, 107, 109 and 113 respectively.

The standard pilot outlet bore is ·025 in. but in some cases larger size pilot outlets are used. Since the pilot outlet is actually drilled in the body of the carburetter it is necessary to have a carburetter with the correct size pilot outlet if the best results are to be obtained.

The accompanying table shows the standard settings for Amal Monobloc Carburetters used on Royal Enfield motor cycles.

Both instruments used for the twin carburetter models are identical in all respects but for the float chamber arrangement, which is as follows:

The carburetter which supplies the left-hand cylinder has an integral float chamber which

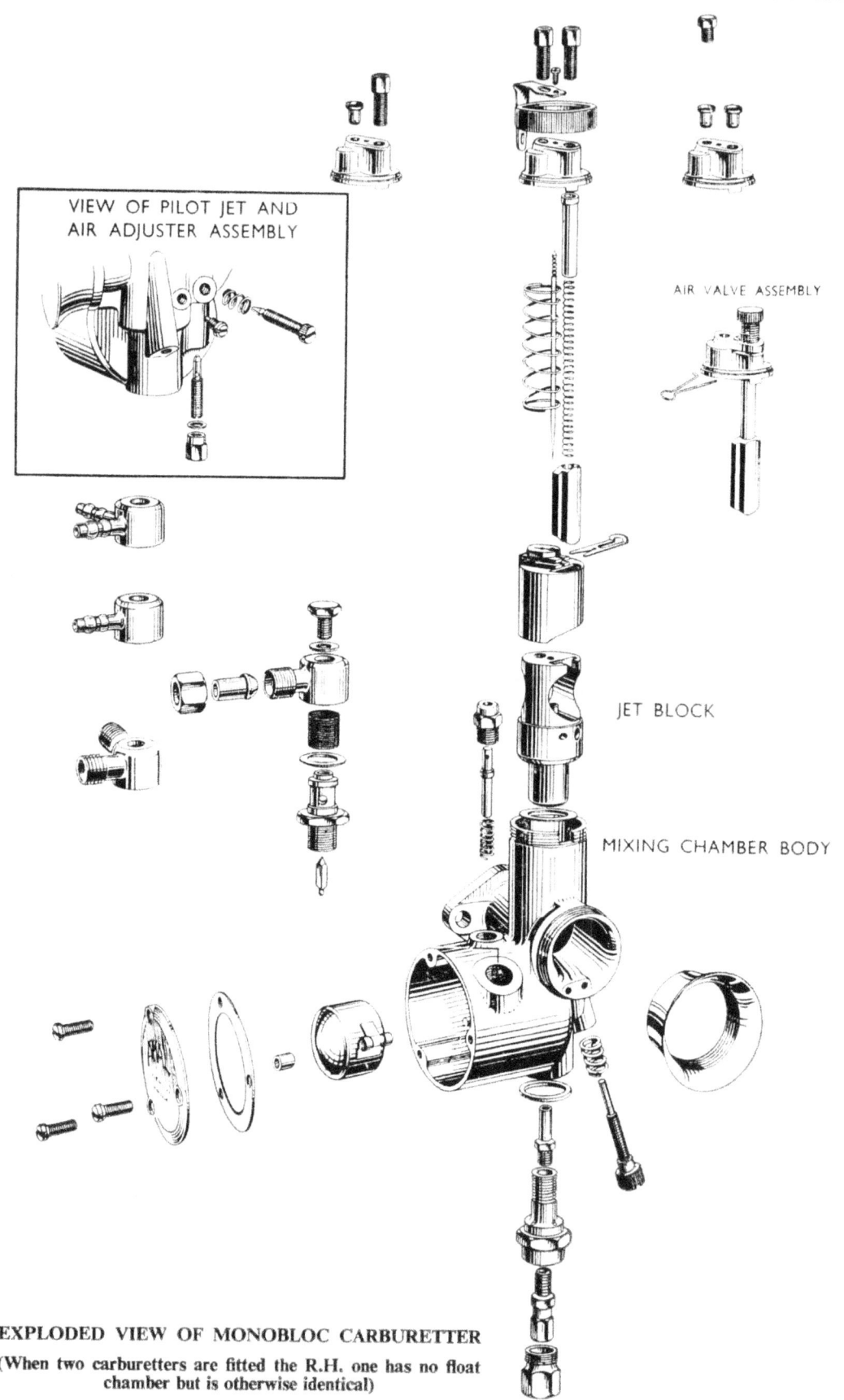

EXPLODED VIEW OF MONOBLOC CARBURETTER
(When two carburetters are fitted the R.H. one has no float chamber but is otherwise identical)

also controls the fuel supply via a connecting pipe to the right-hand instrument which does not have a float chamber in unit with it.

It is important that the pilot air screws of both carburetters are in identical positions, relative to one another, the same applying to the throttle valves when seated on their stops. This is essential for an even smooth tickover and low-speed running. The speed of the tickover is regulated by these four adjuster screws. For an instant pick-up, both throttle valves must commence to rise from their stops simultaneously, when the twist grip is rotated. This is obtained by adjusting the twin control cables. Each main jet needle must be in the third groove.

Both air slides, operated from a single handlebar lever, must open and close identically, as failure to do this may result in one slide not opening fully, with a resultant loss of power.

It is most important that all of these adjustments are carried out in a thorough and careful manner if the maximum power and smoothness is to be obtained.

The "ears" to be found on the leading edges of the battery and toolbox lids are to shield the carburetter air intakes and so prevent misfiring at maximum revs.

3. Dismantling Carburetter

The construction of the carburetter is clearly shown in Fig. 3.

If the float chamber floods, first make sure that there is no dirt on the fuel needle seating. Owing to the use of a nylon needle and the leverage ratio between float and needle, flooding is very unlikely with this type of carburetter unless dirt is present or, of course, the float is punctured.

If it is necessary to remove the jet block note that this is withdrawn from the upper end of the mixing chamber after unscrewing the jet holder. Be careful not to damage the jet block when removing or refitting it. Note that the large diameter of the jet block pulls down on to a thin washer.

A single strand of an inner control cable is useful for clearing the small passages in the jet block and care must be taken not to enlarge these by forcing the wire through them. Compressed air from a pipe line or a tyre pump is preferable. A choked main jet should be cleared only by blowing through it.

4. Causes of High Petrol Consumption

If the petrol consumption is excessive first look for leaks either from the carburetter, petrol pipe, petrol tap(s) or tank. If coloured petrol is in use this will readily indicate the presence of any small leaks which otherwise might pass unnoticed. If the petrol system is free from leaks, carefully set the pilot adjusting screw as described in Subsection 2 to give the correct mixture when idling. Running with the pilot adjusting screw too far in is a common cause of excessive petrol consumption. If the consumption is still heavy try the effect of lowering the taper needle in the throttle slide by one notch. Do not fit a smaller main jet as this will not affect consumption except when driving on nearly full throttle or may make the mixture too weak at large throttle openings, thus causing overheating. Remember that faults in other parts of the machine can have a marked effect on petrol consumption. Examples of this are binding brakes, chains too tight or out of line and, in particular, under-inflated tyres.

Settings of AMAL Monobloc carburetters on ROYAL ENFIELD motor cycles

Machine	Carburetter Type No.	Choke Bore in.	Main Jet c.c.	Needle Jet	Needle Position	Throttle Valve	Pilot Jet c.c.
"250 Clipper" 1955 (late), 1956, 1957 and 1958 (early)	375/10	$\frac{25}{32}$	120	105	3	375/4	25
"Crusader 250" 1957-1962 "250 Clipper" Late 1958-1963	375/16	$\frac{7}{8}$	120	105	3	375/3½	25
1964	375/58	$\frac{7}{8}$	95	105	3	375/3½	25
"Crusader Sports" 1959-1963 and "250 Trials" 1962 onwards	376/216	$\frac{15}{16}$	150	106	3	376/3½	25
"Crusader Sports" 1964	376/313	$\frac{15}{16}$	130	106	3	376/3½	25
"Super 5" 1962 onwards and "Continental" 1963	376/283	$1\frac{1}{16}$	180	106	4	376/3½	25
1964	376/311	$1\frac{1}{16}$	170	106	4	376/3½	25
"350 Bullet" 1955 (late)-1958 "350 Clipper" 1958-1962 "Works Replica" 1958-1961	376/29	1	180	106	3	376/3½	25
"350 Bullet" 1959-1962	376/215	$1\frac{1}{16}$	190	106	3	376/4	30
"350 Bullet" 1963	376/297	$1\frac{1}{16}$	180	106	3	376/3½	25
1964	376/312	$1\frac{1}{16}$	160	106	3	376/3½	25
"500 Bullet" 1956-1958	389/9	$1\frac{1}{8}$	200	106	2	389/3½	30
"500 Bullet" 1959-1962	389/34	$1\frac{3}{16}$	*220	106	3	389/3½	30
"Meteor Minor" 1958-1961 "Meteor Minor Sports" 1960-1962 "500 Sports Twin" 1963 onwards	376/92	$1\frac{1}{16}$	250	106	2	376/3½	30
"Super Meteor" 1956-1962 "Constellation" 1963 onwards	376/41	$1\frac{1}{16}$	240	106	3	376/3½	30
"Constellation" 1960-1962	L/H 376/242 R/H 376/243	$1\frac{1}{16}$	320	106	3	376/4	25
"Interceptor" 1963	L/H 389/85 R/H 389/86	$1\frac{1}{16}$	380	106	3	389/3½	25
1964	L/H 389/205 R/H 689/205	$1\frac{3}{16}$	380	106	3	389/3½ 689/3½	25

* No 250 Main Jet if no Air Cleaner fitted.

SECTION G2f

Lucas A.C. Lighting-Ignition System

1. General

The Lucas A.C. Lighting-Ignition System comprises seven main components:

(1) Alternator with magnet rotor.
(2) Bridge-connected rectifier.
(3) Ignition coil.
(4) Contact breaker unit with automatic timing control.
(5) Lighting switch.
(6) Ignition switch.
(7) 6-volt battery.

Under normal running conditions electrical energy in the form of rectified A.C. passes through the battery from the alternator, the rate of charge depending on the position of the lighting switch. When no lights, or only the pilot lights, are in use the alternator output is sufficient only to supply the ignition coil and to trickle charge the battery. When the lighting switch is turned to the "HEAD" position the current increases proportionately.

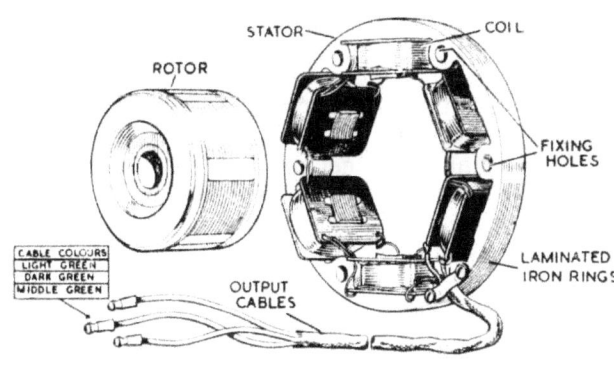

Fig. 1

1 (a). Alternator Model RM13 and RM18

The alternator (see Fig. 1) has an outside diameter of 5 in. and is suitable for motor cycles up to 250 c.c. having headlamp bulbs not exceeding 30 watts. The alternator comprises two main components, a stator and a rotor. The stator is built up from iron laminations and carries three pairs of series-connected coils insulated from the laminations. The rotor has a hexagonal steel core, each face of which carries a permanent magnet keyed to a laminated pole tip. The pole tips are riveted circumferentially to brass side plates, the assembly being cast in aluminium and machined to give a smooth external finish. The stator and rotor can be separated without the need

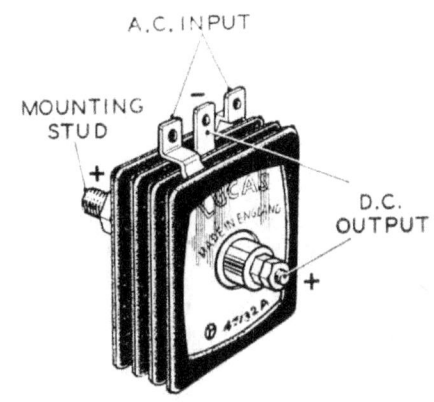

RECTIFIER

Fig. 2

to fit magnetic keepers to the rotor poles. As the rotor turns rapid and repeated reversals of flux take place in the coil cores. These lines cut through the turns of the coil and induce alternating voltages in that coil. External connections are taken to these coils from a bridge-connected rectifier (see Fig. 2).

1 (b). Circuit Details

The alternator stator carries three pairs of series-connected coils, one pair being permanently connected across the rectifier bridge network. The purpose of this latter pair is to provide some degree of charging current for the battery whenever the engine is running.

Connections to the remaining coils vary according to the position of the lighting and ignition switch controls, as shown schematically in Fig. 3.

In the "OFF" and "PILOT" positions two pairs of coils are disconnected and only the third pair is in use. Current flows from these through the rectifier and battery, taking one of two alternative paths (indicated by the arrows on the rectifier

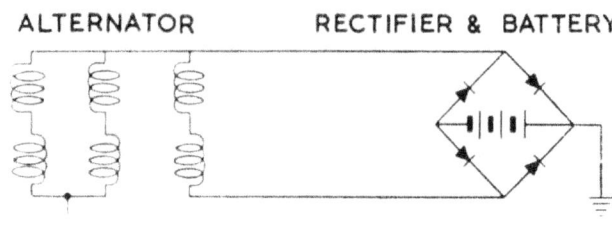

LIGHTING SWITCH AT "OFF" & "PILOT"

LIGHTING SWITCH AT "HEAD"
INTERNAL CONNECTIONS OF ALTERNATOR

Fig. 3

diagram) according to the instantaneous polarity at the alternator coils. Thus the rectifier acts as an electrical non-return valve converting the A.C. current from the alternator into uni-directional current, which trickle charges the battery as well as energising the ignition coil. In the "HEAD" position the alternator output is increased by connecting all three pairs of coils in parallel, thus providing current for the headlight, tail and speedometer lights in addition to the ignition and a trickle charge to the battery.

1 (c). Emergency Starting

An emergency starting position is provided on the ignition switch. This switch is for use if the battery has become discharged and a normal start cannot be made. In the switch position "EMG" the alternator is connected directly to the ignition coil and this allows the engine to be started independently of the battery (see Fig. 4). During the closed period of the contact points, pulses of uni-directional current pass from the upper end of the two left alternator coils (Fig. 4) through the top right hand plate of the rectifier and the contact points back into the left hand alternator coils. If the opening of the contact points is timed to coincide with one of these pulses there will be sufficient energy present in the system to overcome the impedance of the primary winding of the ignition coil and the voltage of the battery, thus causing a pulse of current to pass through the primary of the ignition coil and so create sufficient voltage in the secondary winding to provide a good spark at the plug. The advantage of this system is that the primary of the ignition coil is short-circuited during the closed period of the contact

breaker so that no unwanted sparks can occur on the compression stroke of the engine. Note that, if the battery is removed, the emergency start will not function unless the lead normally connected to the battery negative terminal is earthed. The emergency start system functions better with a discharged battery than with a fully charged one.

Proper functioning of the emergency starting feature is dependent on accurate ignition timing being observed and correct contact breaker gap being maintained. After starting has been effected the ignition switch should be turned to the normal running "IGN" position.

With the later type ignition switch, it is necessary to push in the key and then turn in an anti-clockwise direction for the emergency start position.

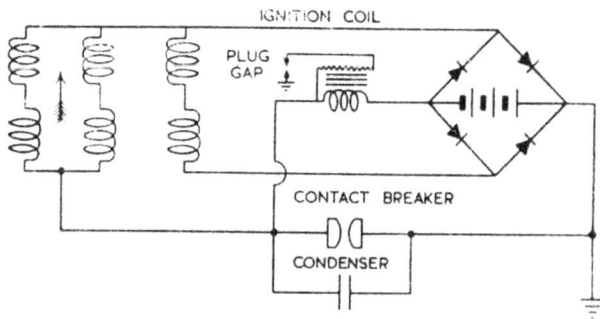

Fig. 4

1 (d). Direct Operation

Short journeys without the battery can be made with the switch in the "EMG" position. To do this, the cable normally connected to the battery negative terminal must be connected to an earthed point on the machine. If lights are required when the battery is disconnected, use only the headlights and keep the engine speed low to prevent excessive voltage rise.

2. Routine Maintenance

The alternator and rectifier require no maintenance apart from ensuring that all connections are clean and tight.

If the rotor, stator, engine crankshaft, or stator locating ring have been disturbed, the air gap between the rotor and stator should be checked. If a feeler gauge at least ·008 in. thick cannot be passed between the rotor and each of the stator poles the alignment should be checked.

The nuts which clamp together the rectifier plate assembly must not under any circumstances be slackened. They have been carefully set during manufacture to give correct rectifier performance. A separate nut is used to secure the rectifier to the frame of the motor cycle.

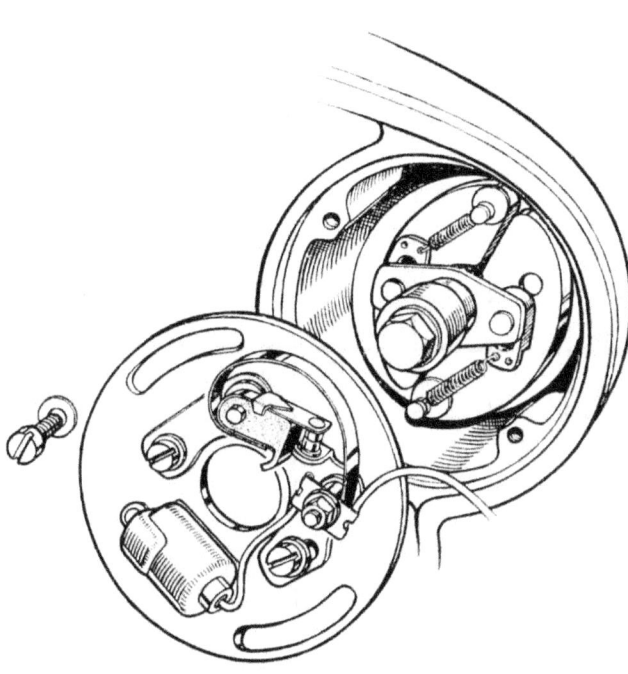

CONTACT BREAKER

Fig. 5

2 (a). Ignition Coil

The ignition coil should be kept clean and the terminals kept tight.

2 (b). Contact Breaker Unit Model CA1A

(See Fig. 5). *Lubrication every* 3,000 *miles*.

(i) Remove the metal cover and smear thin oil on the cam. On no account must oil or grease be allowed to get on or near the contacts.

(ii) Lubricate the automatic timing control mechanism using thin machine oil.

Cleaning every 6,000 *miles*.

Examine the contact breaker. The contacts must be free from grease and oil. If they are burnt or blackened, clean with a fine carborundum stone or a very fine emery cloth. Wipe away any dirt or metal dust with a clean petrol-moistened cloth.

Cleaning of contacts should be carried out with the moving contact removed. To remove this, slacken the terminal screw and withdraw the rocker arm complete with contact and spring.

Before replacing the arm lightly smear the pivot with grease. When refitting the contact breaker arm spring make sure that it is below the fibre washer, i.e. between the fibre washer and the wiring tag from the condenser.

2 (c). Contact Breaker Setting

The contact breaker setting should be checked after the first 500 miles running and subsequently every 6,000 miles. To check the gap, turn the engine over slowly until the contacts are seen to be fully open and insert a 0·014—0·016 in. feeler gauge between the contacts.

If the gap width is correct the gauge will be a sliding fit. To adjust the setting, set the engine in the position giving maximum contact opening. Slacken the two screws securing the contact carrier plate to the back plate. The contact carrier plate swivels around the rocker arm pivot and can be adjusted until the correct gap is obtained.

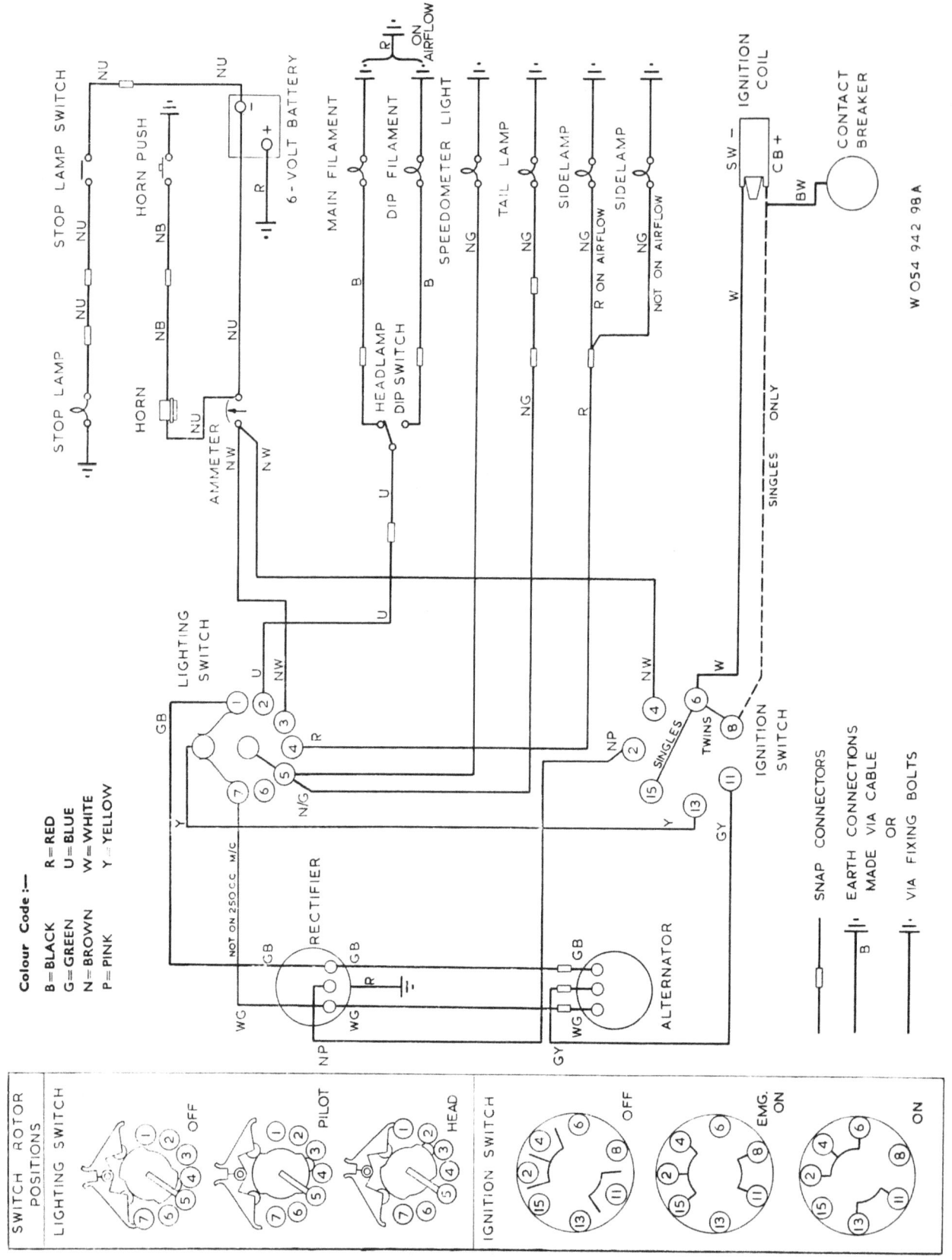

WIRING DIAGRAM
Fig. 6

SECTION G4a
Battery Model PUZ7E

1. General

The model PUZ7E (see Fig. 1) is a "dry-charged" battery and is supplied without electrolyte but with its plates in a charged condition. When the battery is required for service it is only necessary to fill each cell with sulphuric acid of the correct specific gravity. No initial charging is required, but the battery must be left to stand at least one hour after filling before putting the machine into service **and then adjusting the acid level if necessary.**

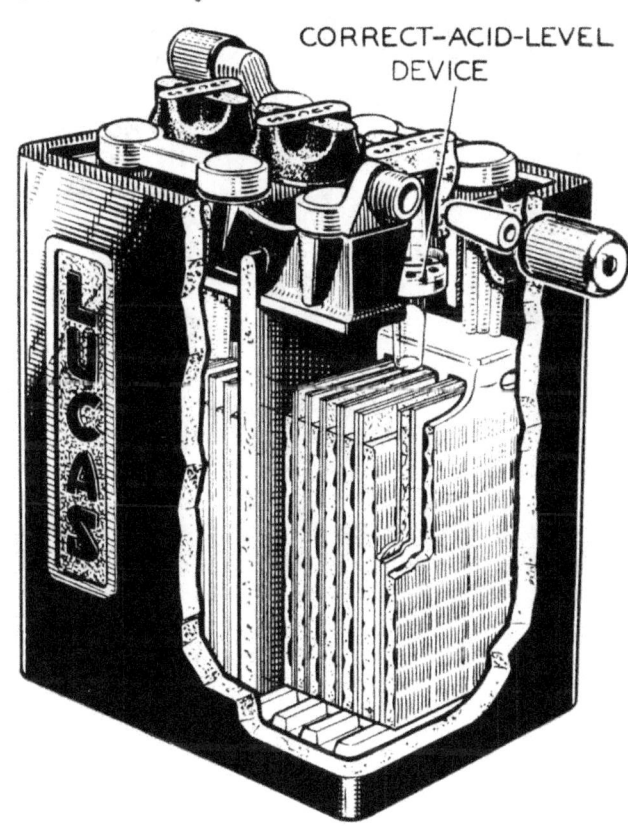

CORRECT-ACID-LEVEL DEVICE

Fig. 1

2. Preparation for Service

The electrolyte is prepared by mixing together distilled water and concentrated sulphuric acid, using lead-lined tanks or suitable glass or earthenware vessels. Slowly add the acid to the water, stirring with a glass rod. Never add water to the acid, as this causes dangerous spurting of the concentrated acid. The specific gravity of the filling electrolyte depends on the climate in which the battery is to be used.

Specific gravity of electrolyte for filling 'dry-charged' batteries:

Climates below 90°F. (32°C.)	Climates above 90°F. (32°C.)
Filling, 1·270	Filling, 1·210

The approximate proportions of acid and water to obtain these specific gravities:

To obtain specific gravity (corrected to 60°F.) of:	Add 1 vol. of 1·835 S.G. acid (corrected to 60°F.) to:
1·270	2·9 vols. of water.
1·210	4·0 vols. of water.

Heat is produced by the mixture of acid and water, the electrolyte should be allowed to cool before pouring it into the battery.

The specific gravity of the electrolyte varies with the temperature. For convenience in comparing specific gravities, they are always corrected to 60° F., which is adopted as a reference temperature.

The method of correction is as follows:—

For every 5°F. below 60°F., deduct ·002 from the observed reading to obtain the true specific gravity at 60°F. For every 5°F. above 60°F add ·002 to the observed reading to obtain the true specific gravity at 60°F.

The temperature must be that indicated by a thermometer having its bulb actually immersed in the electrolyte and not the ambient temperature.

Fill the cells to the tops of the separators, *in one operation*. The battery filled in this way is 90% charged. When time permits, a short freshening charge for no more than four hours at the normal recharge rate of 1·5 amp. should be made.

3. Routine Maintenance

Fortnightly (or more frequently in hot climates) examine the level of electrolyte in the cells and if necessary add distilled water to bring the level up to the tops of the separators. The use of a Lucas Battery Filler will be found helpful, as it ensures that the correct electrolyte level is automatically maintained and also prevents distilled water from being spilled on the top of the battery (see Fig. 2).

Occasionally examine the terminals, clean and coat them with petroleum jelly. Wipe away all

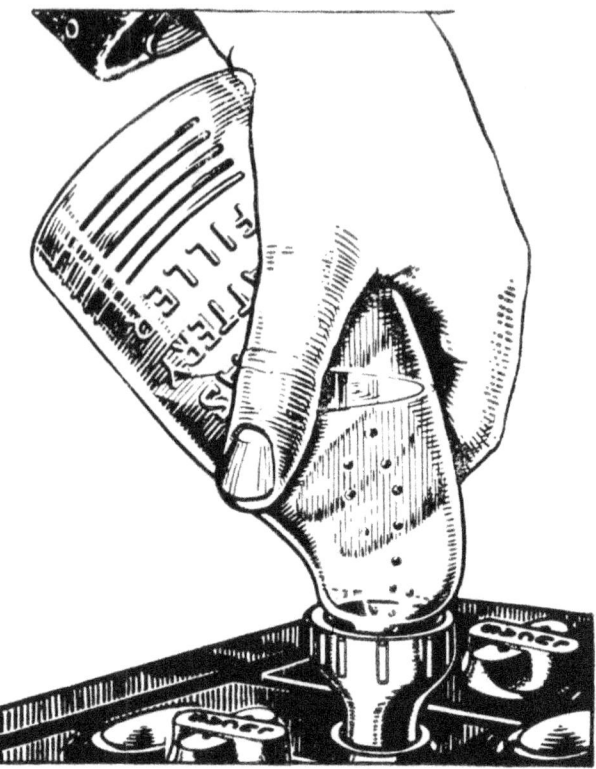

Fig. 2

The following table shows the state of charge at different values of specific gravities:

State of Charge	Temperature under 90°F.	Temperature over 90°F.
Battery fully charged	1·270—1·290	1·210—1·230
Battery about half charged	1·190—1·210	1·130—1·150
Battery fully discharged	1·110—1·130	1·050—1·070

If the battery is discharged, it must be recharged, either on the motor cycle by a period of daytime running or from an external D.C. supply at the normal recharge rate of 1·5 amp.

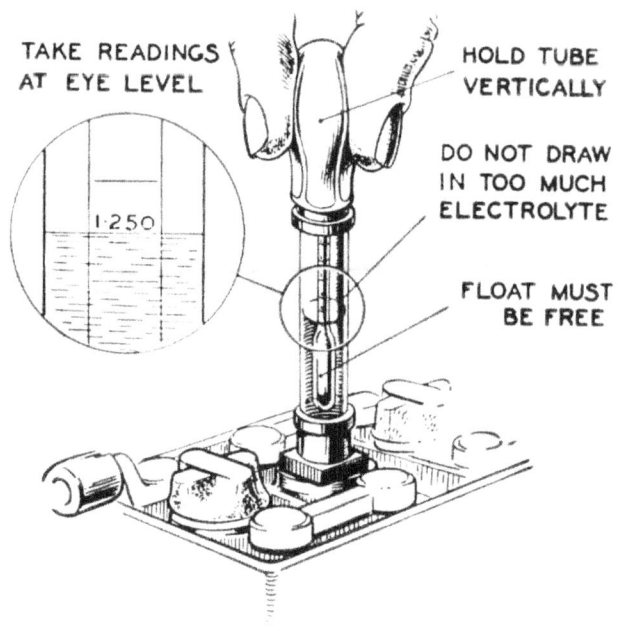

Fig. 3

dirt and moisture from the top of the battery and ensure that the connections are clean and tight.

4. Servicing

If the battery is subjected to long periods of night parking with the lights on, without suitable opportunities for recharging, a low state of charge is to be expected.

Measure the specific gravity of the acid of each cell in turn with a hydrometer (see Fig. 3).

SECTION G4c

Battery Model MLZ9E

Model MLZ9E is a 6-volt unit. The battery container is moulded in translucent polystyrene through which the acid can be seen. A coloured line denoting the maximum filling level is plainly marked on the outside of the container. When the battery is being charged, either on the machine or on the bench, the electrolyte level may rise above this line but will return to it during off-charge periods. During these latter periods, the upper surfaces of the plates are wetted by capillary attraction.

N.B. Unlike normal battery practice, the MLZ9E battery must not be topped up to the separator guard but only to the coloured line.

The top of the container is so designed that when the cover is in position the special anti-spill filler plugs are sealed in a common venting chamber. Gas from the filler plugs leaves this chamber through an elbow-shaped vent pipe union which can be inserted in one of four alternative sealed outlets. Polythene tubing may be attached to the vent pipe union to lead the corrosive fumes away from any parts of the machine where they might cause damage.

Heavy-duty, nut-and-bolt fixing terminals are isolated from the venting chamber.

Internally, the battery consists of three cell packs with separators formed from a dry inert micro-porous material. The use of this material means that a weaker filling acid can be used compared with the acid-diluting wet wood separators formerly employed.

Guards are fitted across the cell packs to protect the top edges of the separators from damage by battery filler nozzles, etc.

Model MLZ9E is supplied dry-charged, the filling and soaking instructions being given at the end of these notes.

Technical Data

(1) Nominal Voltage: 6.
(2) Number of Plates: 9 per cell.
(3) Volume of Electrolyte: 125 c.c. per cell.
(4) Amp. hr. capacity: 12 at 10-hour rate; 13 at 20-hour rate.
(5) Recharge current: 1·5 amperes.
(6) Specific gravity of electrolyte (corrected to 60°F., 15·5°C.) for filling the dry-charged battery:
   (a) In climates ordinarily below 80°F. (26·6°C.) use acid of 1·260 s.g. (corrected to 60°F.).
   (b) In climates ordinarily above 80°F. use acid of 1·210 s.g. (at 60°F).
(7) Preparation of 1·260 and 1·210 s.g. electrolyte:
   (a) To prepare 1·260 s.g. electrolyte, slowly pour ONE PART by volume of 1·835 s.g. SULPHURIC ACID into 3 PARTS of DISTILLED WATER.
   (b) To prepare 1·210 s.g. electrolyte, the required ratio of acid to water is 1 : 4.

N.B. Always add the acid to the water and never vice versa or dangerous spurting may result.

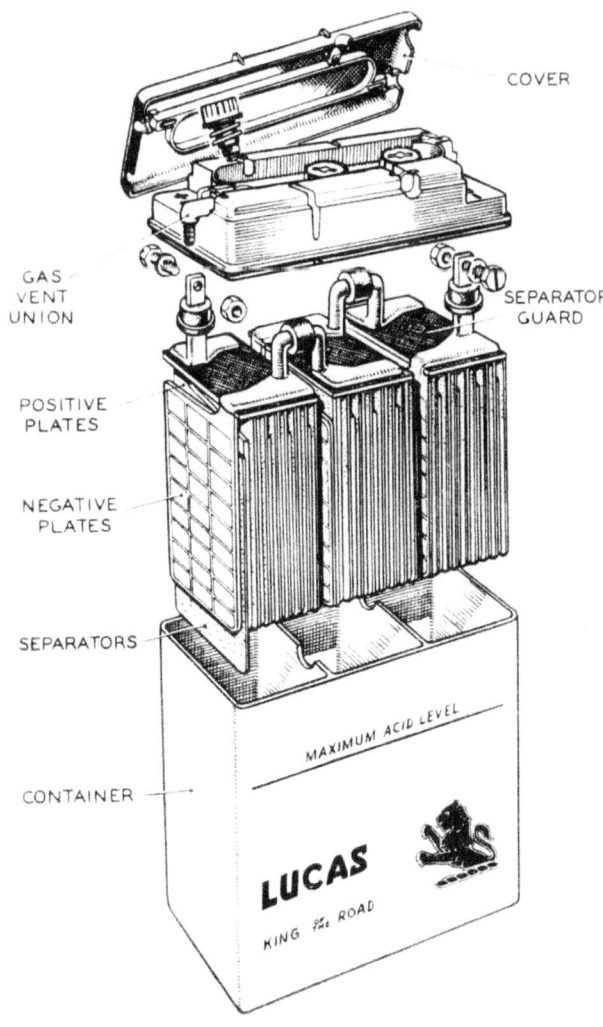

Fig. 1

Filling and Soaking the MLZ9E Battery

Discard the vent hole sealing tapes.

Pour into each cell in one operation pure dilute sulphuric acid of appropriate specific gravity to the coloured line denoting the maximum filling level and allow the battery to stand for one hour. Check the level and syphon off surplus acid from any cell where it has risen higher than the acid level line. Thereafter keep the acid just level with the coloured line by topping up with distilled water.

A discharge can be taken from the battery one hour after it has been filled but, if time permits, it is advisable to first give the battery a four hour freshening charge at the normal recharge rate, i.e., 1·2 amperes.

SECTION G5d
Head and Tail Lamps

1. Headlamp

The "250 Clipper," "Crusader 250," "Crusader Sports" and "350 Bullet" have a Lucas Light Unit MCF 700 built into the Casquette

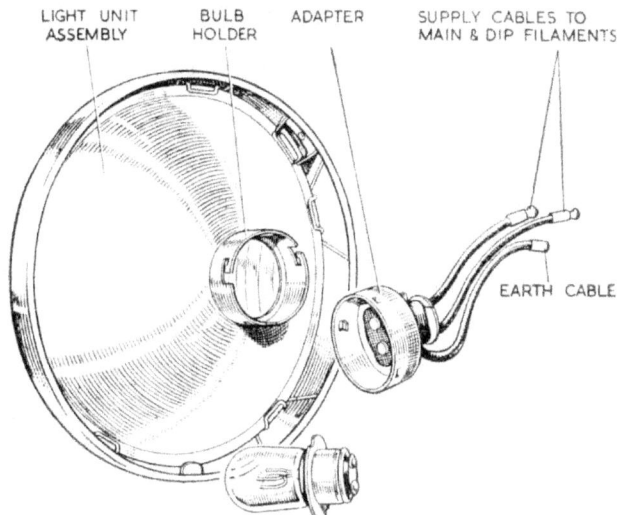

HEADLAMP MCF 700
Fig. 1

Fork Head, which contains twin parking lamps, the ammeter and the switch.

The "Super 5" employs Lucas Light Unit MCF 700 P built into the Casquette with a single parking bulb within the unit, whilst the "Continental" has the MCF 700 P unit built into a separate headlamp, which is mounted on the forks by means of a bracket.

2. Lucas Light Unit

The unit incorporates a combined reflector and front lens assembly (see Fig. 1). This construction ensures that the reflector and lenses are permanently protected, thus the unit keeps its high efficiency over a long period. A "prefocus" bulb is used, the filaments of which are accurately positioned with respect to the reflector, thus no focusing device is necessary.

The bulb has a large cap and a flange, which has been accurately positioned with relation to the bulb filaments during manufacture. A slot in the flange engages with a projection on the inside of the bulb holder positioned at the back of the reflector.

A bayonet-fitting adaptor with spring-loaded contacts secures the bulb firmly in position and carries the supply to the bulb contacts.

The outer surface of the lens is smooth to facilitate cleaning. The inner surface is formed of a series of lenses which determine the spread and pattern of the light beams.

In the event of damage to either the lens or reflector a replacement light unit must be fitted.

3. Replacing the Light Unit and Bulb

Slacken the securing screw at the top of the headlamp rim. Remove the front rim and Light Unit assembly.

Withdraw the adaptor from the Light Unit by twisting it in an anti-clockwise direction and pulling it off. Remove the bulb from its locating sleeve at the rear of the reflector.

Disengage the Light Unit securing springs from the rim and lift out the Light Unit.

Position the new unit in the rim so that the word "TOP" on the lens is correctly located when the assembly is mounted on the headlamp. Refit the securing springs ensuring that they are equally spaced around the rim.

Replace the bulb and adaptor. The bulb must be the Lucas "prefocus" type—6 v. 30/24 watt Lucas No. 312.

Locate the bottom of the Light Unit and front rim assembly in the headlamp shell or in the fixing rim attached to the Casquette fork head. Press the front on and tighten the securing screw at the top of the headlamp.

4. Parking Lights

Access to the parking bulbs is obtained by removing the parking lamp rim (see Fig 2). This is

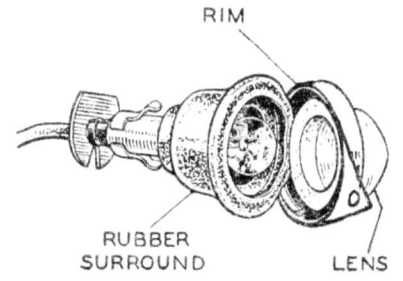

PARKING LIGHT
Fig. 2

forced over the edge of the rubber lamp body and is additionally secured by means of a small fixing screw. After removal of the lamp rim the parking lamp lens can be pulled out of the rubber body, after which the bulb will be accessible.

5. Tail Light

The Lucas lamp, Type 564 (Fig. 3) is a combined stop and tail light and also incorporates a reflector.

Access to the bulb is obtained by removing the two screws which secure the plastic cover.

The correct bulb is Lucas No. 352, 6 volt, 3/18 watt for machines up to 250 c.c., or Lucas No. 384, 6 volt, 6/18 watt for larger capacity machines. The 3 or 6 watt filament provides the normal tail light, while the 18 watt filament is illuminated on movement of the brake pedal.

Care must be taken that the leads to the stop tail lamp are correctly connected, as the use of the 18 watt filament on the normal tail light will not only discharge the battery but could cause trouble from excessive heat affecting the plastic cover. At the same time, the 6 watt filament, if used as a stop-tail light, will be ineffective in bright sunlight or at night when the tail light filament is illuminated.

STOP-TAIL LAMP L.564
Fig. 3

Page 1 — ROYAL ENFIELD WORKSHOP MANUAL — Section **H6**

SECTION H6
Frame

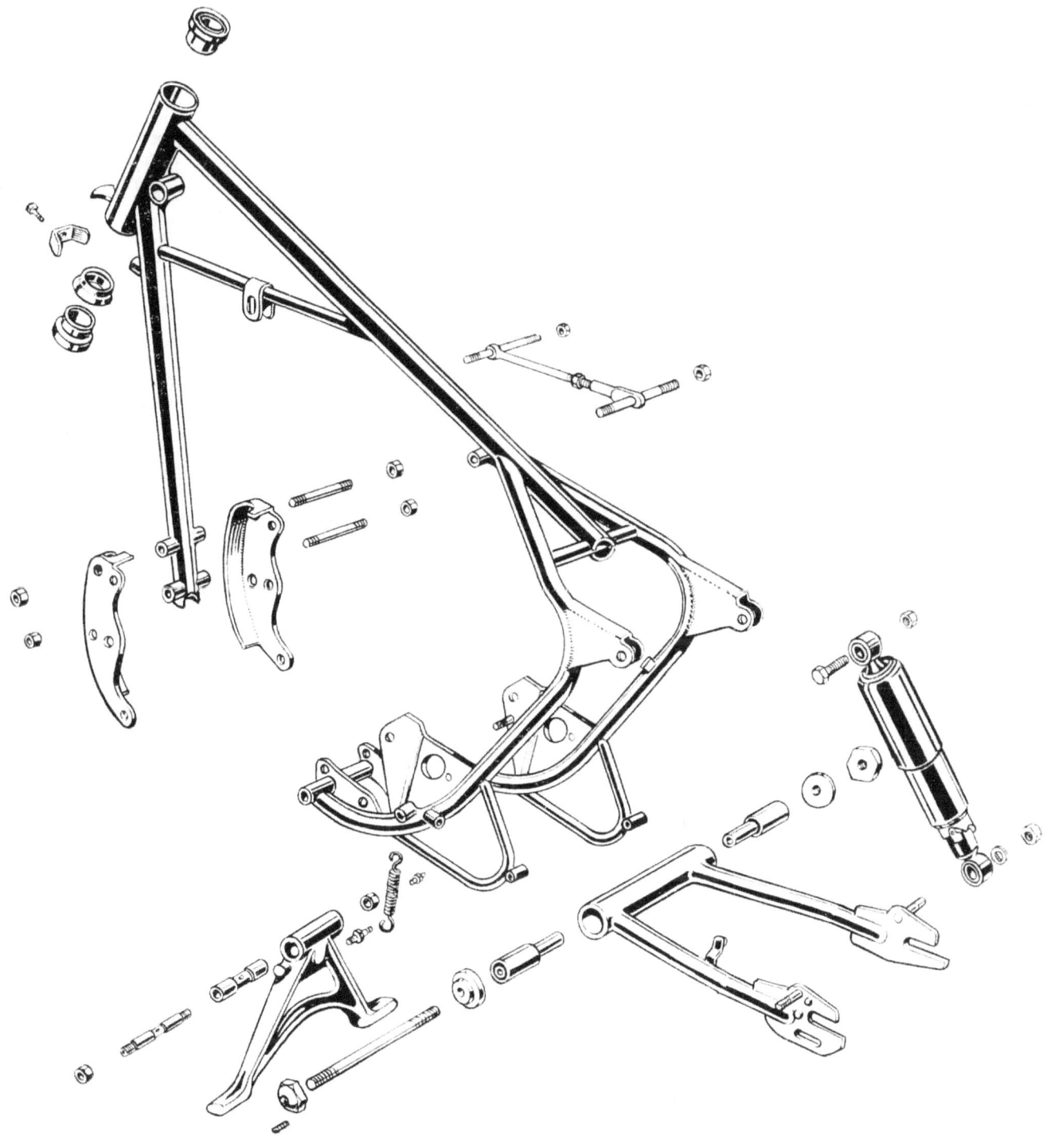

FRAME FOR LATER 250 c.c. AND 350 c.c. MODELS

Fig. 1

1. Description of Frame

The frame is built throughout of cold-drawn weldless steel tubing with welded joints, liners being fitted where necessary for extra strength. The principal frame members are made of chrome-molybdenum alloy steel tubing, which retains its strength and resistance to fatigue after welding.

The swinging arm unit which forms the chainstays pivots on a stout steel tube, which is secured to the main frame by a long bolt passing through the pivot plates. No bushes are fitted, as the cast-iron chainstay bearing housing and hardened surface of the tube are together good bearing metals. Hardened steel thrust washers are provided to deal with side thrust. The torsional rigidity of the swinging arm unit helps to maintain the rear wheel upright in the frame and thus relieves the wheel spindle of bending stresses, to which it is subject with other types of rear suspension.

Later swinging arm units are fitted with two rubber bushes in the bearing housing. The inner sleeves of these bushes extend inwards and butt together. Washers are situated on either side of the bearing housing and a long stud runs through the centre, onto each end of which screws a large nut from the outside of the frame.

2. Steering Head Races

The steering head races, 31302, are the same at the top and bottom of the head lug, but the bottom race is fitted with a pressed steel cover. The races are easily removed by knocking them out with a hammer and drift, and new races can be fitted either under a press or by means of a hammer and a wooden drift.

3. Removal and Replacement of Rear Mudguard Unit

The rear mudguard, mudguard carrier and dual-seat are removable in one unit after merely slackening the two rear suspension top fixing nuts and pushing back the bolts about ⅛ in. to release their heads from the recesses on the inside of the carrier brackets. Stand behind the machine, grasp the lifting handles (if fitted) and pull the mudguard assembly upwards until the attachment brackets are clear of their respective nuts. Now pull backwards until the clip at the front of the mudguard carrier is free from the backstay bridge tube of the frame, when, after disconnecting the rear light cable, the complete assembly can be removed.

When replacing, engage the front clip first and drop the assembly into position. When tightening the nuts make sure that the heads of the bolts are right home in the recesses on the inside of the carrier attachment brackets.

4. Removal of Rear Suspension Unit

First remove the rear mudguard unit as described above. Undo the rear suspension top pivot pin nut and drive out the pivot pin. Then hinging the suspension unit back on the lower pivot pin, remove the lower nut and push the suspension unit off the pivot pin welded to the fork end.

5. Servicing Rear Suspension Units

The Girling units fitted to this machine are sealed, and servicing of the internal mechanism can be carried out only by the manufacturers.

The bottom cup for the suspension spring is adjustable in three positions, the necessary "C" spanner will be found in the tool kit. The bottom position is suitable for a medium-weight rider; the centre position for a heavy rider or a medium weight rider and medium weight passenger; and the top position for a heavy weight rider and heavy weight passenger. The adjustment raises the rear end of the machine to compensate for extra weight so that the normal riding position of the suspension unit is always roughly midway between the two extremes of travel.

The rubber bushes in the top and bottom eyes can easily be renewed and the spring can be removed by pushing down on the top spring cover, so as to release the split collar above it. After removal of the split collar the top cover and spring can be lifted off. When re-assembling, the spring should be greased to prevent rust and squeaking if it should come into contact with either of the covers.

6. Removal of Swinging Arm Chainstays

First remove one of the pivot pin nuts and pull the pivot pin out from the other end. To release the pivot bearing it is necessary to spread the rear portion of the frame, using the frame expander, E.5431, which will spread the frame sufficiently to enable the spigots on the thrust washers to clear the recesses in the pivot plates forming part of the frame.

With the later rubber bushed swinging arms, remove one of the pivot pin nuts and withdraw the pivot pin. The swinging arm can now be removed without resort to the frame expander.

7. Centre Stand

To remove the centre stand, first remove the footrests, footrest bar and distance tube. Remove the two studs holding the small engine plates to the engine-gear unit, disconnect one end of the stand spring, and the stand, together with the engine plates, can be removed from the frame. The stand, stand bearing sleeve and engine plates can now be separated after undoing one of the stand spindle nuts and pushing out the spindle.

8. Wheel Alignment

Note that it is not possible to guarantee that the wheels are correctly aligned when the same notch position is used on both adjuster cams. It is therefore not sufficient to count the notches and use the same position on both sides of the machine. The only way to guarantee that the wheels are in line is to check the alignment from front wheel to back using either a straight-edge or a piece of taut string. The alignment should be checked on both sides of the machine and if the front and rear tyres are of different section, allowance must be made for this.

9. Lubrication

The steering head races, swinging arm pivot bearing and stand pivot bearing should be well greased on assembly. The swinging arm pivot and stand pivot are provided with grease nipples but no nipples are provided for the steering head as experience has shown them not to be necessary. If the steering head bearings are well packed they will last for several years or many thousands of miles. There are no grease nipples for the swinging arm pivot bearings when rubber bushes are fitted.

Recommended greases are Castrolease LM, Mobilgrease MP, Esso Multipurpose grease H, Energrease L2, Shell Retinax "A," or Marfak Multipurpose 2.

10. Removal of Petrol Tank

The petrol tank is attached to the frame by a rubber-mounted stud at the front, and is clipped at the rear to a rubber sleeve surrounding the top tube. To remove the tank, unscrew one front attachment nut, tap out the stud and, after disconnecting the petrol feed pipe, the rear of the tank can be pulled upwards to release the clip and then lifted clear of the frame.

11. Air Cleaner

To obtain access to the air cleaner, first remove the toolbox lid on the right-hand side of the machine. The air cleaner cover, held in place by one central screw, will now be visible. Remove this screw and press inwards the top left corner of the cover, which will pivot outwards at the bottom, enabling it to be removed entirely. To remove the cleaner, hold it by the metal portion and pull to the left, when it will free itself from the rubber sleeve.

The cleaner is intended to be used dry and should not be oiled. It can be cleaned by brushing and blowing with compressed air. As the air to the carburettor passes through the element from outside to inside, the bulk of the dirt will be found on the outer surface of the element.

SECTION J7

Front Fork

With Casquette and Aluminium Alloy Bottom Tubes

"350 Clipper" and "Crusader Sports" 1959 onwards, "Crusader 250" 1957 onwards, "250 Clipper" late 1958 onwards, "250 Trials" 1962 onwards and "250 Continental" and "350 Bullet" 1963 onwards

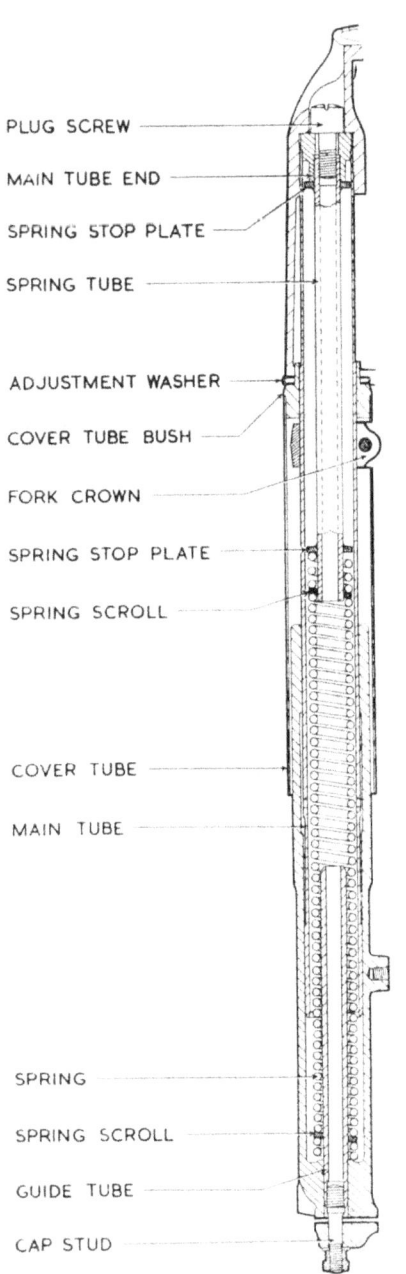

SECTION OF FRONT FORK
Fig. 1

1. Description

Early models

The telescopic fork consists of two legs, each of which comprises a main tube of chrome molybdenum alloy steel tubing which is screwed into the Casquette fork head at the upper end and securely clamped to the fork crown. Sliding over the lower end of the main tube is the cast aluminium alloy fork leg. Into the lower end of this is fitted a tube to which the bottom end of the compression spring is secured, the tube also acting as a guide for the spring. The top end of the spring is secured to a distance tube, which is held to the top of the main tube with a screw. The lower end of the main tube and upper end of the sliding fork leg are protected by a cover tube screwed to the fork crown.

The fork is filled with a light oil (S.A.E.20) to the level of a screw, for lubrication.

Later Models

Fork design and operation is basically as above, and Fig. 1, though the main tube is heavier and the spring is of smaller diameter. The cap stud is integral with the guide tube and the spring stop plate is set further up the spring tube.

A "Casquette" is not employed on the "Continental" model. A different type of fork head is used having no integral headlamp, though it houses the speedometer and rev. counter heads. The "250 Trials" model uses a modified fork with rebound damping (see Subsection 8).

2. Dismantling Fork to Replace Spring

Place the machine on the centre stand, disconnect the front brake control and remove the front wheel and mudguard complete with stay. Unscrew the plug screws in the fork head, when the sliding fork legs, complete with springs and spring distance tubes can be withdrawn from the lower ends of the main tubes. The spring distance tube can now be unscrewed out of the spring and the spring, which is attached at the bottom end in a similar manner to that at the top, can be unscrewed from the sliding fork leg.

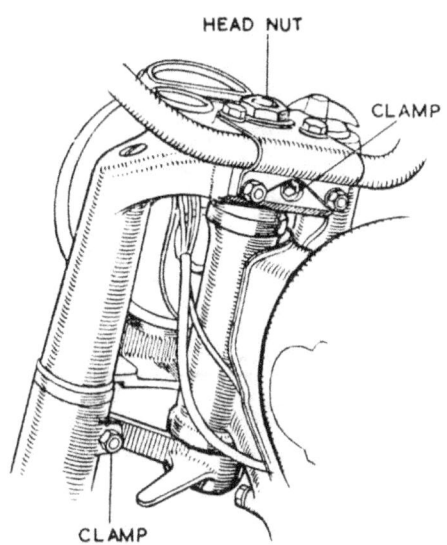

STEERING HEAD ADJUSTMENT
Fig. 2

3. Spring

The spring fitted to the earlier pattern fork measures 16 in. long by $1\frac{3}{32}$ in. diameter. The spring for the later type measures $16\frac{3}{16}$ in. long by $\frac{31}{32}$ in. diameter. Small changes in length are not important but the springs should be changed if they have set more than 1 in.

4. Re-assembly of Parts

No difficulty should be experienced with this. Make sure that the spring is screwed right on to the scrolls at both ends. After assembling the sliding fork legs, springs and spring distance tubes, line up the fork ends in the position in which they will be when the wheel is in position before tightening up the plug screws in the fork head.

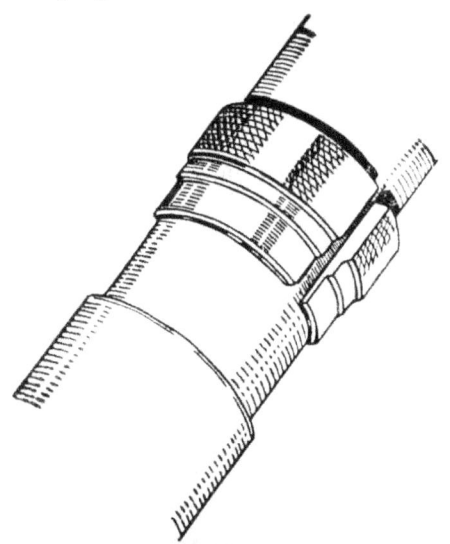

OUTER COVER CENTRALISING BUSHES
Fig. 3

5. Steering Head Races

The steering head bearing consists of two deep groove thrust races each containing nineteen $\frac{1}{4}$ in. diameter balls. The bearing is adjusted by tightening the steering stem locknut after loosening the ball head clip screw and both the fork crown clamp bolts. The head should be adjusted so that, when the front wheel is lifted clear of the ground, a light tap on the handlebars will cause the steering to swing to full lock in either direction, while at the same time there should be only the slightest trace of play in the bearings. Do not forget to tighten the ball head clip screw and fork crown clamp bolts. Before tightening the latter, make sure that the cover tubes are located centrally round the main tubes so that the bottom tube does not rub inside the cover tube. A pair of split bushes (Fig. 3) is useful, to ensure centralisation of the cover tubes.

MAIN TUBE SPANNER
Fig. 4

6. Removal of Complete Fork

The fork, complete with front wheel and mudguard, can be removed from the machine, if necessary, by adopting the following procedure.

The leads to the lighting switch and ammeter should be disconnected from the battery, rectifier, tail lamp, alternator and earth points at their lower ends, or at the plug and socket connectors when these are provided. If it is required to remove the lighting switch and ammeter, these are push fits in the rubber bushes in the fork head. Disconnect the speedometer drive from the speedometer head and remove the two plug screws and loosen the steering head clip bolt and the two fork crown bolts.

Now unscrew the fork main tubes from the fork head by means of a hexagon bar ·500 in.

across flats (Unbrako wrench W.11) or the special tool shown in Fig. 4. At the same time unscrew the steering stem locknut from the top of the steering stem, turning each tube and the nut a turn or two at a time. The main tubes have to be turned in a clockwise direction and the steering stem locknut anti-clockwise. When the nut has been removed from the steering stem and the main tubes have been completely unscrewed from the fork head, the complete fork and wheel with the steering stem can be lifted out of the head lug of the frame.

7. Lubrication

The oil level is determined by a small screw at the back of each sliding fork leg. First place the machine on the centre stand, thus allowing the forks to extend. To fill each fork leg to the correct level remove the plug screws from the fork head and the oil level screws at the back of the sliding fork leg. Pour oil in at the top until it runs out at the level holes. Wait until oil has stopped running and replace level plugs and plug screws.

Recommended grades of oil* are Castrolite, Mobiloil Arctic, Esso Extra 20W/30, B.P. Energol S.A.E. 20W, Shell X-100 20/20W or Havoline 20/20W.

8. "250 Trials" (Fig. 5)

A "Casquette" is not employed on this model but the fork head houses the speedometer. The main fork tubes screw into the steering head and are secured to the fork crown by two clamp bolts. Fitted over the lower end of the main tube is the bottom tube made of high strength aluminium alloy with an integral lug which carries the wheel spindle. At the lower end of the main tube is a steel bush which is a close fit in the bore of the bottom tube. The upper end of the bottom tube carries a bronze bush which is a close fit over the outside diameter of the main tube. The bush is secured to the bottom tube by means of a threaded housing which contains an oil seal. A stud known as the "spring stud" is fitted in the lower end of the bottom tube and a valve port is secured to the lower end of the main tube. As the fork operates oil is forced between the spring stud and the bore of the valve port forming a hydraulic damping system. A compression spring 21 in. long is fitted inside the main tube between the upper end of the spring stud and the upper end of the main tube. The lower end of the main tube and upper end of the bottom tube are protected by a cover secured to the fork crown.

---
* If temperature is above 90°F (32°C) use one of the following :—Castrol XL; Energol S.A.E. 30; Mobiloil A; Esso Extra 20W/30; Shell X-100 30; Havoline 30.

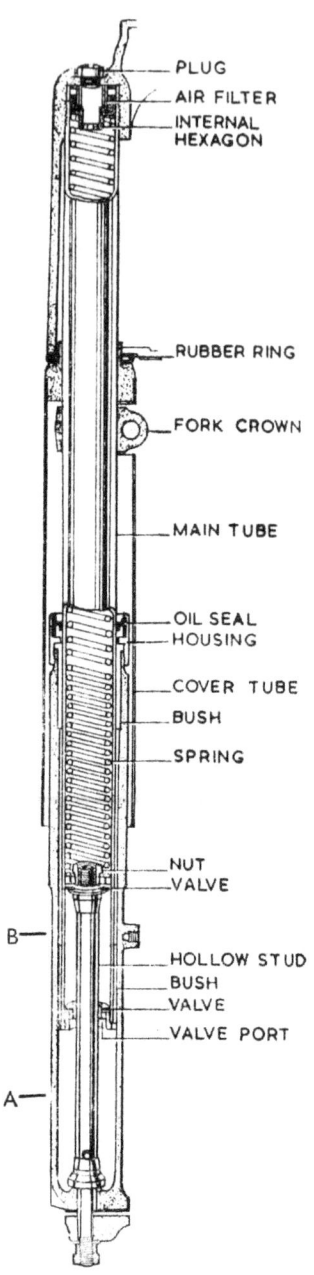

**SECTION OF FORK LEG
"250 TRIALS"**
Fig. 5

The fork is filled with a light oil (S.A.E. 20) to a point above the lower end of the spring so that the damper chamber "B" is always kept full of oil. Upward movement of the wheel spindle forces oil from the lower chamber "A" through the annular space between the spring stud and the bore of the main tube valve port into the damper chamber "B." During this stroke the pressure on the underside of the valve plate causes this to lift so that oil can also pass from "A" to "B" through the eight holes in the valve body. Since, however, the diameter of chamber "B" is less than that of chamber "A" there is not room in "B" to receive all the oil which must be displaced from "A" as the fork operates. The surplus oil passes through the cross hole in the spring stud and up the centre hole in the stud, spilling out through the socket nut which secures the upper end of the spring stud to the bronze guide at the lower end of the fork spring, thus providing a measure of damping.

On the rebound stroke the oil in the damper chamber "B" is forced through the annular space between the spring stud and the bore of the main tube valve port. During this stroke pressure in chamber "B" closes the two disc valves at the upper and lower ends of the chamber so that the only path through which the oil can escape is the annular space between the spring stud and the port. Damping on the rebound stroke is therefore heavier than on the bump stroke. Towards the end of either bump or rebound stroke a small taper portion on the spring stud enters the bore of the valve port, thus restricting the annular space and increasing the amount of damping. At the extreme end of the bump stroke the larger diameter taper on the oil control collar enters the main counterbore of the valve port thus forming a hydraulic cushion to prevent metal to metal contact.

9. Dismantling the Fork to Replace Spring, Oil Seal or Bearing Bushes ("250 Trials")

Place the machine on the centre stand, disconnect the front brake control and remove the front wheel and mudguard complete with stay. Knock the rearmost cap stud upwards into the fork with a soft mallet, which will allow oil to run out of the fork. Pull the fork bottom tube down as far as possible, thus exposing the oil seal housing Unscrew this housing either by means of a spanner on the flats with which it is provided or by using the gland nut hand grips (E.4912). The bottom tube can now be withdrawn completely from the main tube, leaving the bottom tube bush, oil seal housing and oil seal in position on the main tube.

Now unscrew the main tube valve port using "C" spanner (E.5418). The spring stud and spring can now be withdrawn from the lower end of the main tube.

The steel main tube bush can now be tapped off the lower end of the tube, if necessary using the bottom tube bush for this purpose. Before doing this, however, it is advisable to mark the position of the bush with a pencil line so as to ensure reassembling it in the same position on the main tube. The reason for this is that these bushes are finish ground to size after fitting on to the tubes so as to ensure concentricity. After removal of the main tube bush the bottom tube bush, oil seal housing and oil seal can be removed.

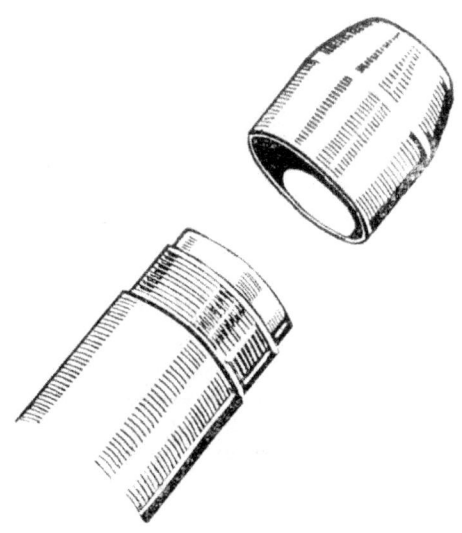

MAIN TUBE SEAL GUIDE
Fig. 6

10. Reassembly of Parts ("250 Trials")

When refitting the oil seal, or fitting a new one, great care must be exercised not to damage the synthetic rubber lip which forms the actual seal. If the seal has been removed from the upper end of the main tube and is refitted from this end a special nose piece (Fig. 6) must be fitted over the end of the tube to prevent the thread from damaging the oil seal.

The spring stud is a tight fit in the hole at the lower end of the bottom tube. Once the stud has been entered in the hole push the bottom tube up sharply against the spring until two or three threads on the stud project beneath the end of the bottom tube. Now fit the nut and washer and pull the stud into position by tightening the nut. If necessary fit the nut first without the washer until sufficient thread is projecting to enable the washer to be fitted.

11. Steering Head Races and Removal of Complete Fork ("250 Trials")

See Subsections 5 *and* 6.

12. Lubrication ("250 Trials")

The lubrication of the fork bearings is effected by the oil which forms the hydraulic damping medium. All that is necessary is to keep sufficient oil in the fork to ensure that the top end of the bottom spring stud is never uncovered even in the full rebound position. The level of oil in the fork can be gauged by removing the top plug screw and inserting a long rod about $\frac{3}{8}$ in. diameter. If slightly tilted this will ledge against the nut at the upper end of the bottom spring stud and indicate the level of oil above the stud. If the fork is empty to start with the quantity required is approximately $7\frac{1}{2}$ fluid ounces in each leg. Use one of the oils recommended in Subsection 7.

SECTION J8

Front Fork

"Crusader Super 5" 1962 onwards

1. Description

The steering stem is integral with the two fork legs, and the steering head is attached by means of an Allen screw into the top of each leg. The internally threaded head adjuster sleeve screws onto the steering stem and is held in position in the head by the clamp bolt, situated horizontally below the handlebars. A separate "Casquette" incorporating the headlamp and instruments is fitted.

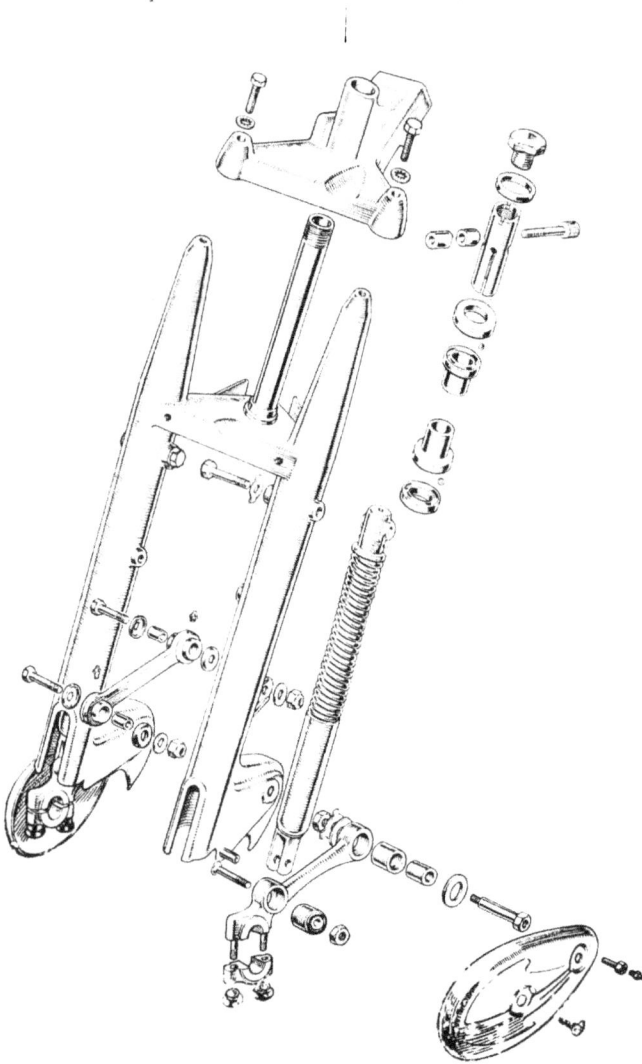

EXPLODED VIEW OF LEADING LINK TYPE FRONT FORK AND STEERING HEAD

Fig. 1

The suspension units are located at their upper ends by set pins situated under the crown, and their lower ends fit onto the links, which in turn pivot from the rear of the fork feet which have moulded side covers secured with a single screw each. A brake anchor arm locates the brake back dlate to the left hand fork leg.

2. Dismantling Fork to replace Suspension Unit

Place the machine on the centre stand, disconnect the front brake cable, and remove the nut and bolt which attaches the brake anchor arm to the left fork leg. Take off the two spindle caps by means of the four cap nuts and remove the wheel.

Remove each moulded side cover by means of the slotted screw and the bolt in the pivot pin. Take out the pin in the rubber bush connecting the suspension unit to the link, and swing the link downwards. After removing the pins adjacent to the steering crown, the suspension units may be withdrawn.

Should it be necessary to remove the link, flatten the tab washer and remove the nut which also secures the lower mudguard bracket onto the inside of the foot. The fulcrum pin may then be withdrawn. When reassembling do not omit the thrust washers on either side of the link and be sure to lock the nut with a NEW tab washer.

Removal of the mudguard is effected by removal of the aforementioned nuts and tab washers and the screws half way up each fork leg.

The later type "Super 5" has its front mudguard secured to the wheel hub assembly, and the mudguard and wheel are removed from the forks complete. In order to remove the tyre or examine the brake linings, the mudguard must be detached by means of the eight set screws. (Two to each mudguard stay.) See Fig. 2.

3. Suspension Units

These units are sealed and require no attention throughout their life. Should there be any deterioration in performance after a very long period of service it is recommended that they should be returned to the factory for exchange units.

4. Re-assembly of Parts

Slide each suspension unit into the fork legs, and secure with the bolts under the steering crown using NEW tab washers to lock them. Swing the links up into position and secure to the bottom of each suspension unit with the countersunk headed bolt and nut. Put back the wheel, couple up the brake anchor arm and cable, and fit the link side covers.

5. Steering Head Races

The steering head bearing consists of two deep groove thrust races, each containing nineteen $\frac{1}{4}$ in. diameter balls. The method of adjustment is as follows:

Take the weight off the front wheel by placing a box or block beneath the crankcase. Loosen the head clamp bolt beneath the handlebars, remove the large central nut and thick washer from the top of the steering head, and tighten down the slotted adjustment sleeve to take up play. Do this carefully, testing until there is the absolute minimum of play but the steering falls over to full lock quite freely when given the slightest push in either direction. Tighten the head clamp bolt and replace the large nut and thick washer. (See Fig. 1.)

6. Removal of Complete Fork

The fork, complete with front wheel and mudguard, can be removed from the machine, if necessary, by adopting the following procedure.

Free the Casquette by removing the two bolts, which screw into the steering crown, and the large central nut from the steering head.

The leads to the lighting switch and ammeter should be disconnected from the battery, rectifier, tail lamp, alternator and earth points at their lower ends, or at the plug and socket connectors when these are provided. If it is required to remove the lighting switch and ammeter, these are push fits in the rubber bushes in the fork head. Disconnect the speedometer drive from the speedometer head, and the drive from the revolution counter head, where fitted. The front brake cable must also be released.

Remove the bolts which secure each fork leg to the steering head. Slacken the steering head pinch bolt, and screw out the slotted sleeve, until the steering stem is released. The whole assembly can then be removed.

7. Lubrication

The suspension units cannot be topped up with oil, and require no attention.

On models provided with grease nipples for the link fulcrum pins and brake anchor arm, these points should be lubricated with a grease gun every 500 miles.

Use one of the following greases in the gun:

Castrolease LM, Shell Retinax A Grease, Energrease L2, Mobilgrease M.P., Esso Multipurpose Grease H or Marfak Multipurpose 2.

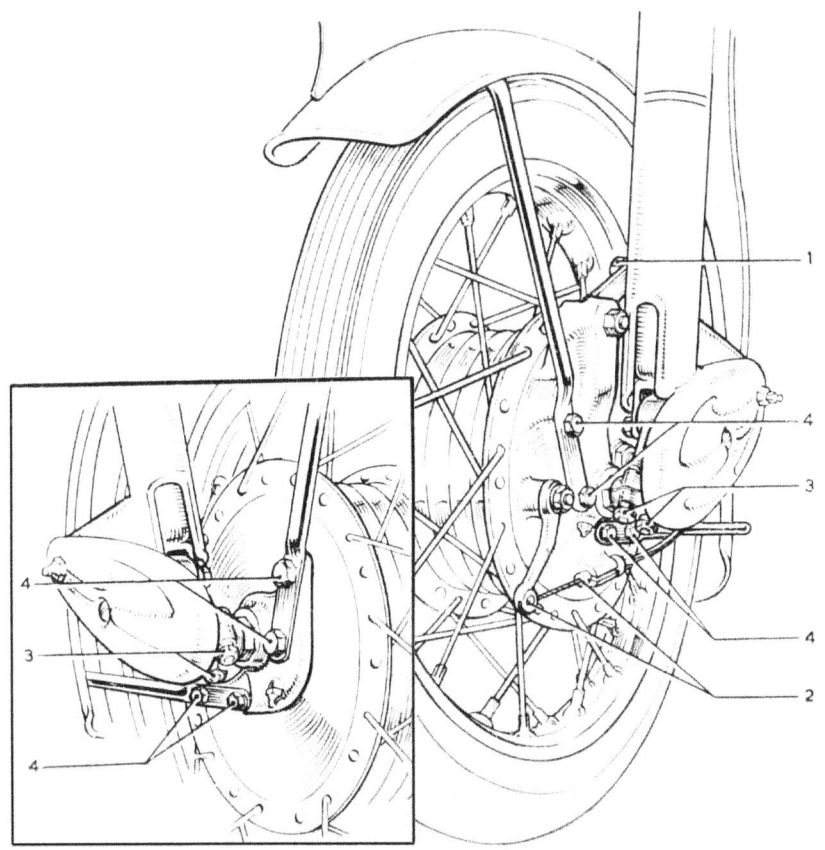

"SUPER 5"
(LATER MODELS)

FRONT WHEEL AND MUDGUARD ARRANGEMENT

Fig. 2

1. Brake anchor arm nut.
2. Brake cable.
3. Wheel spindle cap nuts.
4. Mudguard attachment screws.

SECTION K4

Front Wheel
With Single 6 in. Brake

1. Removal from Fork

To remove the front wheel from the fork place the machine on the centre stand with sufficient packing (about 2 in.) beneath each side of the stand to lift the wheel clear off the ground when tilted back on to the rear wheel. Slacken the brake cable adjustment and disconnect the cable from the handlebar lever and from the operating cam lever on the hub. Unscrew the four nuts securing the fork leg caps and allow the wheel to drop forward out of the front fork. Make sure that the machine stands securely on the rear wheel and centre stand—if necessary place a weight on the saddle or a strut beneath the fork to ensure this.

2. Removal of Brake Cover Plate Assembly

Lock the brake "on" by pressure on the operating lever and unscrew the cover plate nut. The cover plate assembly can then be withdrawn from the brake drum.

3. Removal of Brake Shoes for Replacement, Fitting New Linings, etc.

The brake shoes can be removed after detaching the return springs. Brake linings are supplied either in pairs ready drilled complete with rivets, or ready fitted to service replacement brake shoes. When riveting linings to shoes secure the two centre rivets first so as to ensure that the linings lie flat against the shoe. Standard linings are Ferodo AM2 which are drilled to receive cheese headed rivets.

A number of early "Crusader 250" models were fitted with brake linings bonded to the shoes. These should be returned for servicing when necessary.

4. Removal of Brake Operating Cam

To remove the operating cam unscrew the nut which secures the operating lever to the splines on the cam. A sharp tap on the end of the cam spindle will now free the lever, after which the cam can be withdrawn from its housing. **Do not try and remove the brake shoe pivot pin; it is cast into the brake cover plate and cannot be removed.**

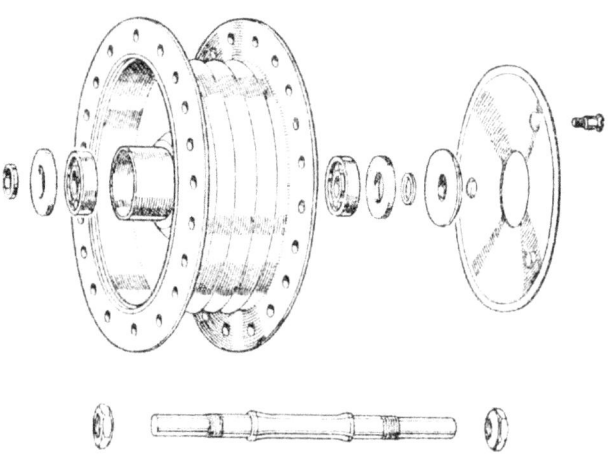

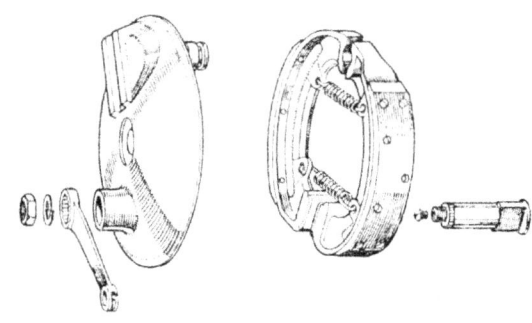

FRONT HUB AND BRAKE
Fig. 1

5. Removal of Hub Spindle and Bearings

To remove the hub spindle and bearings having first removed the brake cover plate, unscrew the retaining nut and remove the dust excluder from the non-brake side of the hub. Now remove the felt washers and the distance washer from the brake side and hit one end of the spindle with a copper hammer or mallet, thus driving it out of the hub, bringing one bearing with it and leaving the other in position in the hub. Drive the bearing off the spindle and insert the latter once more in the hub at the end from which it was removed. Now drive the spindle through the hub the other way, when it will bring out the remaining bearing.

6. Hub Bearings

These are deep-groove single-row journal ball bearings, $\frac{5}{8}$ in. i/d by $1\frac{9}{16}$ in. o/d by $\frac{7}{16}$ in. wide. The Skefko Part No. is RLS5. Equivalent bearings of other makes are Hoffmann LS7, Ransome and Marles LJ $\frac{5}{8}$ in., Fischer LS7.

7. Fitting Limits for Bearings

The fit of the bearings in the hub barrel is important. The bearings are locked on the spindle between shoulders and the distance pieces, which in turn are held up by the nuts on the spindle. In order to prevent endways pre-loading of the bearings it is essential that there is a small clearance between the inner edge of the outer race of the bearing and the back of the recess in either end of the barrel. To prevent any possibility of sideways movement of the hub barrel on the bearings it is, therefore, necessary for the bearings to be a tight fit in the barrel, but this fit must not be so tight as to close down the outer race of the bearing, and thus overload the balls. The following are the manufacturing tolerances which control the fit of the bearings. The figures for the bearings themselves are for SKF. Bearings, but other manufacturers' tolerances are similar.

Bearing o/d, 1·5622/1·5617 in.
Housing bore, 1·5620/1·5616 in.
Bearing bore, ·6252/·6247 in.
Shaft diameter, ·6252/·6248 in.

8. Refitting Ball Bearings

To refit the bearings in the hub, two hollow drifts are required, as shown in Fig. 2. One bearing is first fitted to one end of the spindle by means of the hollow drift; the spindle and bearing are then entered into one end of the hub barrel, which is then supported on one of the hollow drifts. The other bearing is then threaded over the upper end of the spindle and driven home by means of the second hollow drift either under a press, or by means of a hammer, which will thus drive both bearings into position simultaneously.

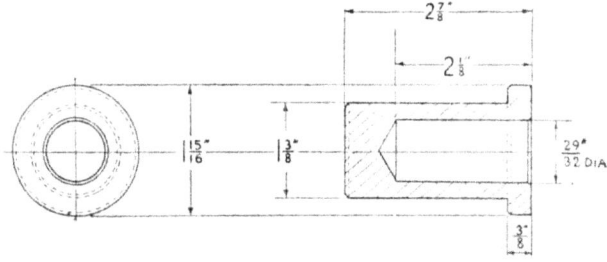

DRIFT FOR REFITTING BEARINGS
Fig. 2

In order to make quite sure that there is clearance between the inner faces of the outer bearing races and the bottom of the recesses, fit the distance washers, cover plate, dust excluder and the nuts on the spindle. Tightening the nuts should not have any effect on the ease with which the spindle can be turned. If tightening the nuts makes the spindle hard to turn this may be taken as proof that the bearings are bottoming in the recesses in the hub barrel before they are solid against the shoulders on the spindle. In this case, the bearing should be removed and a thin packing shim fitted between the inner race and the shoulder on the spindle.

9. Re-assembly of Brake Shoes and Operating Cam into Cover Plate

No difficulty should be experienced in carrying out these operations. Put a smear of grease on the pivot pin and on the operating face of the cam; also on to the cylindrical bearing surface of the operating cam. Fit the operating lever on its splines in a position to suit the extent of wear on the linings and secure with the nut and washer. Note that the position of the operating lever may have to be corrected when adjusting the brake after refitting the wheel. The range of adjustment can be extended by moving this lever on to a different spline. Limit of wear is reached when the cam is turned through nearly 90° with the brake hard on, so that there is a danger that the operating springs cannot return the brake to the off position.

10. Final Assembly of Hub before Replacing Wheel

Before replacing the felt washers which form the grease seals, pack all bearings with grease. Recommended greases are Castrolease LM, Mobilgrease MP, Esso Multipurpose Grease H, Energrease L2, Shell Retinax A, or Marfak Multipurpose 2. The use of H.M.P. greases which have a soda soap base is not recommended, as these tend to be slightly corrosive if any damp finds its way into the hubs.

Make sure that the inside of the brake drum is quite free from oil or grease, damp, etc. Replace the felt washers, distance collars, dust excluder and brake cover plate and securely tighten the spindle nuts.

11. Wheel Rim

The wheel rim is WM2—17 in., plunged and pierced with forty holes for spoke nipples. The spoke holes are symmetrical, i.e., the rim can be assembled to the hub either way round. The rim diameter after building is 17·062 in., the tolerances on the circumference of the rim shoulders where the tyre fits being 53·642/53·582 in. The standard steel measuring tape for checking rims is $\frac{5}{16}$ in. wide, ·011 in. thick, and its length is 53·676/53·616 in.

12. Spokes

The spokes are of the single-butted type, 8-10 gauge, with 90° countersunk heads, thread diameter ·144 in., 40 threads per inch, thread form British Standard Cycle. The inner spokes are $5\frac{11}{16}$ in. long and the outer spokes $5\frac{3}{4}$ in. long. All spokes initially have a bend of approximately 100°. After building the wheel, but before it is finally trued, the spokes are straightened by hitting them with a wooden or hide mallet thus giving them a more acute angle of bend of about 80°. The spokes for the "250 Trials" model are $7\frac{9}{16}$ in. long.

13. Wheel Building and Truing

The spokes are laced one over two, and the wheel rim must be built central in relation to the faces of the nuts on the spindle. The rim should be trued as accurately as possible, the maximum permissible run-out both sideways and radially being plus or minus $\frac{1}{32}$ in.

14. Tyre

The standard tyre is Dunlop 3·25-17 in. Ribbed. When removing the tyre always start close to the valve and see that the edge of the cover at the other side of the wheel is pushed down into the well in the rim.

When replacing the tyre fit the part by the valve last, also with the edge of the cover at the other side of the wheel pushed down into the well.

A 2·75–21 in. tyre is fitted to the 21 in. wheel of the "250 Trials."

If the correct method of fitting and removal of the tyre is adopted it will be found that the covers can be manipulated quite easily with the small levers supplied in the tool-kit. The use of long levers and/or excessive force is liable to damage the walls of the tyre. After inflation, make sure that the tyre is fitting evenly all the way round the rim. A line moulded on the wall of the tyre indicates whether or not the tyre is correctly fitted. If the tyre has a white mark indicating a balance point, this should be fitted near the valve.

15. Tyre Pressures

The recommended pressure for the front tyre is 18 lb. per square inch.

16. Lubrication

Grease the bearings by packing them with grease after dismantling the hub as described above.

Note that the brake cam is drilled for a grease passage but the end of this is stopped up with a countersunk screw instead of being fitted with a grease nipple. This is done to prevent excessive greasing by over-enthusiastic owners. If the cam is smeared with grease on assembly it should require no further attention but in case of necessity, it is possible to remove the screw, fit a grease nipple in its place and grease the cam by this means.

SECTION K5

Front Wheel

With Single 7 in. Brake

1. Removal from Fork

To remove the front wheel from the fork place the machine on the centre stand with sufficient packing (about 2 in.) beneath each side of the stand to lift the wheel clear off the ground when tilted back on to the rear wheel. Slacken the brake cable adjustment and disconnect the cable from the handlebar lever and from the operating cam lever on the hub. Unscrew the four nuts securing the fork leg caps and allow the wheel to drop forward out of the front fork. Make sure that the machine stands securely on the rear wheel and centre stand—if necessary place a weight on the saddle or a strut beneath the fork to ensure this.

The later type "Super 5" has its front mudguard secured to the wheel hub assembly, and the mudguard and wheel are removed from the forks complete. In order to remove the tyre or examine the brake linings, the mudguard must be detached by means of the eight set screws. (Two to each mudguard stay.) See Fig. 2, Section J.

2. Removal of Brake Cover Plate Assembly

Lock the brake "on" by pressure on the operating lever and unscrew the cover plate nut The cover plate assembly can then be withdrawn from the brake drum.

3. Replacing Brake Linings

Brake linings are supplied either in pairs ready drilled complete with rivets, or ready fitted to service replacement brake shoes. When riveting linings to shoes, secure the two centre rivets first so as to ensure that the lining lies flat against the shoe. Standard linings are Ferodo AM2, which are drilled to receive cheese headed rivets.

A number of early "Crusader 250" models were fitted with brake linings bonded to the shoes. These should be returned for servicing when necessary.

4. Removal of Brake Operating Cam

To remove the operating cam unscrew the nut, 10314, which secures the operating lever to the splines on the cam. A sharp tap on the end of the cam spindle will now free the lever, after which the cam can be withdrawn from its housing.

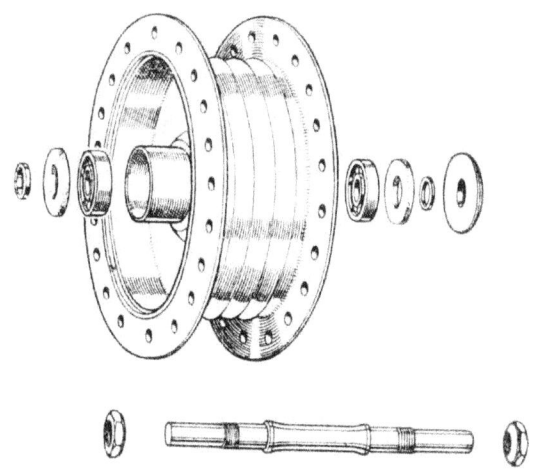

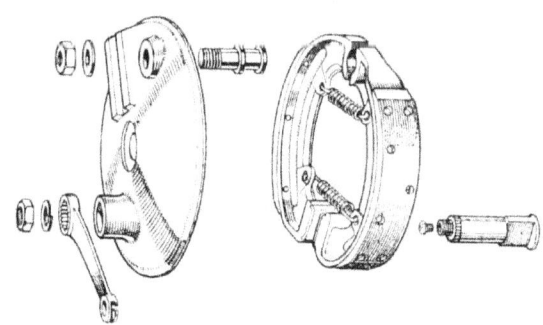

FRONT HUB AND BRAKE
Fig. 1

To remove pivot pin, unscrew nut and tap out pin.

5. Removal of Hub Spindle and Bearings

To remove the hub spindle and bearings, having first removed the brake cover plate, unscrew the retaining nut and remove the dust excluder from the non-brake side of the hub. Now remove the felt washers and distance washers and hit one end of the spindle with a copper hammer or mallet, thus driving it out of the hub, bringing one bearing with it and leaving the other in position in the hub. Drive the bearing off the spindle and insert the latter once more in the hub at the end from which it was removed. Now drive the spindle through the hub the other way, when it will bring out the remaining bearing.

6. Hub Bearings

These are deep-groove single-row journal ball bearings, $\frac{5}{8}$ in. i/d by $1\frac{9}{16}$ in. o/d by $\frac{7}{16}$ in. wide. The Skefko Part No. is RLS5. Equivalent bearings of other makes are Hoffmann LS7, Ransome and Marles LJ $\frac{5}{8}$ in., Fischer LS7.

7. Fitting Limits for Bearings

The fit of the bearings in the hub barrel is important. The bearings are locked on the spindle between shoulder and the distance pieces, which in turn are held up by the nuts on the spindle. In order to prevent endways pre-loading of the bearings it is essential that there is a small clearance between the inner edge of the outer race of the bearing and the back of the recess in either end of the barrel. To prevent any possibility of sideways movement of the hub barrel on the bearings it is, therefore, necessary for the bearings to be a tight fit in the barrel, but this fit must not be so tight as to close down the outer race of the bearing, and thus overload the balls. The following are the manufacturing tolerances which control the fit of the bearings. The figures for the bearings themselves are for SKF Bearings, but other manufacturers' tolerances are similar.

Bearing o/d, 1·5622/1·5617 in.
Housing bore, 1·5620/1·5616 in.
Bearing bore, ·6252/·6247 in.
Shaft diameter, ·6252/·6248 in.

8. Refitting Ball Bearings

To refit the bearings in the hub, two hollow drifts are required, as shown in Fig. 2. One bearing is first fitted to one end of the spindle by means of the hollow drift; the spindle and bearing are then entered into one end of the hub barrel, which is then supported on one of the hollow drifts. The other bearing is then threaded over the upper end of the spindle and driven home by means of the second hollow drift either under a press, or by means of a hammer, which will thus drive both bearings into position simultaneously. In order to make quite sure that there is clearance between the inner faces of the outer bearing races and the bottom of the recesses, fit the distance washers, cover plate, dust excluder and the nuts on the spindle. Tightening the nuts should not have any effect on the ease with which the spindle can be turned. If tightening the nuts makes the spindle hard to turn this may be taken as proof that the bearings are bottoming in the recesses in the hub barrel before they are solid against the shoulders on the spindle. In this case, the bearing should be removed and a thin packing shim fitted between the inner race and the shoulder on the spindle.

9. Reassembly of Brake Shoes and Operating Cam into Cover Plate

No difficulty should be experienced in carrying out these operations. Put a smear of grease on the pivot pin and on the operating face of the cam; also on to the cylindrical bearing surface of the operating cam. Fit the operating lever on its splines in a position to suit the extent of wear on the linings and secure with the nut and washer. Note that the position of the operating lever may have to be corrected when adjusting the brake after refitting the wheel. The range of adjustment can be extended by moving this lever on to a different spline. Limit of wear is reached when the cam is turned through nearly 90° with the brake hard on, so that there is a danger that the operating springs cannot return the brake to the off position.

10. Final Assembly of Hub before Replacing Wheel

Before replacing the felt washers which form the grease seals, pack all bearings with grease. Recommended greases are Castrolease LM, Mobilgrease MP, Esso Multipurpose Grease H, Energrease L2, Shell Retinax A or Marfak Multipurpose 2. The use of H.M.P. greases which have a soda soap base is not recommended, as these tend to be slightly corrosive if any damp finds its way into the hubs.

Make sure that the inside of the brake drum is quite free from oil or grease, damp, etc. Replace the felt washers, distance collars, dust excluder and brake cover plate and securely tighten the spindle nuts.

11. Wheel Rim

The wheel rim is WM2—17 in., plunged and pierced with forty holes for spoke nipples. The

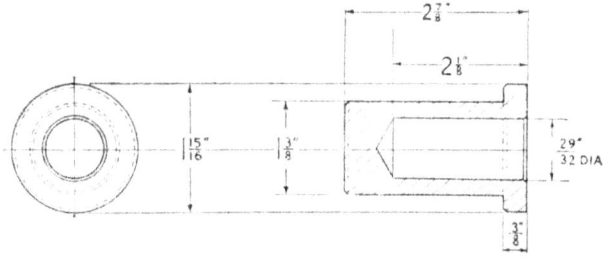

DRIFT FOR REFITTING BEARINGS
Fig. 2

spoke holes are symmetrical, i.e., the rim can be assembled to the hub either way round. The rim diameter after building is 17·062 in., the tolerances on the circumference of the rim shoulders where the tyre fits being 53·642/53·582 in. The standard steel measuring tape for checking rims is $\frac{3}{16}$ in. wide, ·011 in. thick, and its length is 53·676/53·616 in.

12. Spokes

The spokes are of the single-butted type, 8-10 gauge, with 90° countersunk heads, thread diameter ·144 in., 40 threads per inch, thread form British Standard Cycle. All the spokes are initially identical, $5\frac{5}{16}$ in. long with an angle of bend of approximately 100°. After building the wheel but before it is finally trued the spokes from the outside of the spoke flanges are straightened by hitting them with a wooden or hide mallet thus giving them a more acute angle of bend of about 80°.

13. Wheel Building and Truing

The spokes are laced one over two, and the wheel rim must be built central in relation to the faces of the nuts on the spindle. The rim should be trued as accurately as possible, the maximum permissible run-out both sideways and radially being plus or minus $\frac{1}{32}$ in.

14. Tyre

The standard tyre is Dunlop 3·25-17 in. Ribbed. When removing the tyre always start close to the valve and see that the edge of the cover at the other side of the wheel is pushed down into the well in the rim.

When replacing the tyre fit the part by the valve last, also with the edge of the cover at the other side of the wheel pushed down into the well.

If the correct method of fitting and removal of the tyre is adopted it will be found that the covers can be manipulated quite easily with the small lever supplied in the tool-kit. The use of long levers and/or excessive force is liable to damage the walls of the tyre. After inflation, make sure that the tyre is fitting evenly all the way round the rim. A line moulded on the wall of the tyre indicates whether or not the tyre is correctly fitted. If the tyre has a white mark indicating a balance point, this should be fitted near the valve.

15. Tyre Pressure

The recommended pressure for the front tyre is 18 lb. per sq. in.

16. Lubrication

Grease the bearings by packing them with grease after dismantling the hub as described above.

Note that the brake cam is drilled for a grease passage but the end of this is stopped up with a countersunk screw instead of being fitted with a grease nipple. This is done to prevent excessive greasing by over-enthusiastic owners. If the cam is smeared with grease on assembly it should require no further attention but in case of necessity, it is possible to remove the screw, fit a grease nipple in its place and grease the cam by this means.

SECTION L6

Rear Wheel

(Quickly Detachable Type with 6in. diameter Brake and Full-Width Hub)

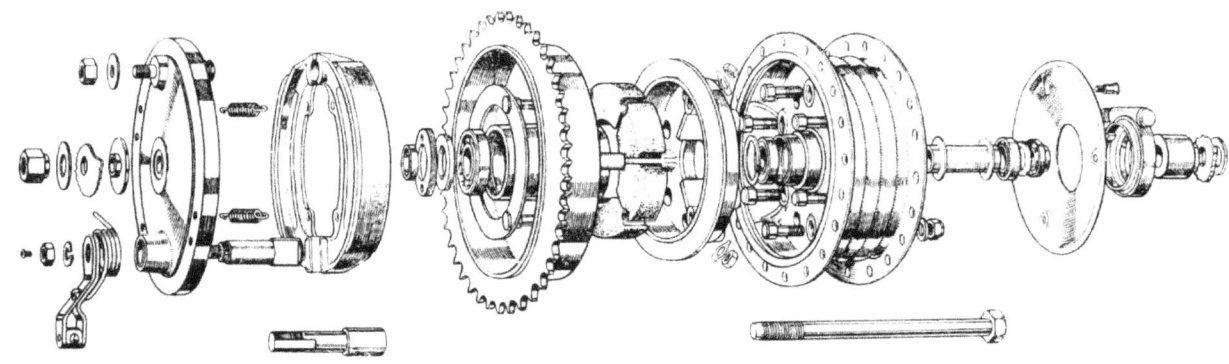

EXPLODED VIEW OF "CRUSADER 250" Q.D. REAR HUB

Fig. 1

1. Description

The main portion of the wheel can be removed from the machine without disturbing the chain or brake, or removing the mudguard. The wheel incorporates the well-known Royal Enfield cush drive and also a 6 in. internal expanding brake.

2. Removal and Replacement of Main Portion of Wheel, for Tyre Repairs, etc.

With the machine on the centre stand unscrew the right-hand spindle nut and withdraw the loose section of the spindle, together with the chain adjuster cam, preferably marking this to ensure that it is replaced in the same position. Now slide the distance collar out of the fork end and lift away the speedometer drive gearbox, which can be left attached to the driving cable. The spacing collar and the felt washer behind it may now be removed to prevent risk of them falling out when manipulating the tyre. If, however, these are too tight a fit in the hub to come out easily they may be left in place. The main body of the wheel can now be pulled across to the right-hand side of the machine, thus disengaging the six driving pins from the cush drive shell. Standing on the left-hand side of the machine, adjacent to the rear mudguard, lean the machine to the left until the wheel can be rolled out between the mudguard and the right-hand fork end.

When replacing the main portion of the wheel reverse the foregoing procedure, taking care, when replacing the speedometer drive gearbox, that the driving dogs inside the gearbox engage with the slots in the end of the hub barrel. The cush drive shell can be prevented from rotating when turning the wheel to engage the six driving pins if the machine is placed in gear or the rear brake is operated. Before tightening the centre spindle make sure that the speedometer drive gearbox is correctly positioned so that there is no sharp bend in the driving cable.

3. Removal and Replacement of Complete Wheel for Access to Brake

Place the machine on the centre stand and remove the rear mudguard unit.* Remove the five screws securing the two parts of the chaincase to the brake cover plate and remove the rear portion of case.† Disconnect the rear driving chain at the spring link and loop the top end of the chain over the tag provided at the top of the fixed portion of the chaincase. Pull on the other end of the chain and allow it to hang from the lower tunnel of the chaincase. This will ensure that the chain is not lost in the case. Unscrew

---

*See Section H6, subsection 3.

†If fitted.

REMOVAL OF Q.D. REAR WHEEL

Fig. 2

the rear brake rod adjusting nut completely and depress the brake pedal so as to disengage the rod from the trunnion in the brake operating lever. Unscrew the brake cover plate anchor nut, and remove this, together with the washer behind it. Unscrew the loose section of the spindle, two or three turns, and the spindle nut, by a similar amount. Mark the chain adjuster cams to ensure replacing in the same position.* Disconnect the speedometer driving cable and slide the wheel out of the fork ends, tilting it so as to disengage the end of the brake shoe pivot pin from the slot in the fork end.

When replacing the wheel make sure that the dogs on the gear in the speedometer drive gearbox are engaged with the slots in the end of the hub barrel. Make sure also that the speedometer drive gearbox is correctly positioned so that there is no sudden bend in the driving cable. When replacing the connecting link in the driving chain, make sure that the closed end of the spring link

points in the direction of travel of the chain. Replace the chain adjuster cams in their original positions or, if necessary, turn each of them the same number of notches to tension the chain and maintain correct wheel alignment. If the chain is adjusted it will be necessary to reposition the front part of the chaincase. This is easily done by slackening the two screws fastening it to the swinging arm chainstay before re-assembling the chaincase to the brake cover plate, then re-tightening the screws. Do not forget to refit the brake rod and adjust the brake so that the wheel turns freely when the brake is off, while at the same time only a small travel of the brake pedal is necessary to put the brake on.

4. Removal of Brake Shoes for Replacement, Fitting New Linings, etc.

Remove the complete wheel as described above, then remove the spindle nut, chain adjuster and the distance collar, thus permitting the complete brake cover plate with operating cam, pivot pin shoes and return springs to be lifted off the hub spindle. The brake shoes can then be removed after detaching the return springs.

---

*Note that the wheel is not necessarily correctly lined up when the same notch position is used on both adjuster cams. Once the position of the cams which gives correct alignment has been found this alignment will, however, be maintained if both cams are moved the same number of notches.

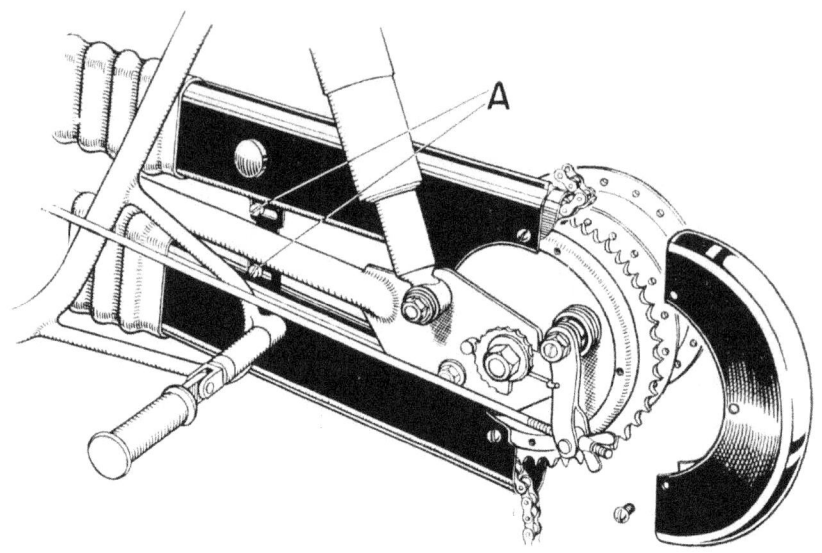

REAR WHEEL ADJUSTMENT
Fig. 3

Brake linings are supplied either in pairs ready drilled complete with rivets or ready fitted to service replacement brake shoes. When riveting linings to shoes secure the two centre rivets first so as to ensure that the linings lie flat against the shoe. Standard linings are Ferodo AM2 which are drilled to receive cheese headed rivets.

A number of early "Crusader 250" models were fitted with brake linings bonded to the shoes. These should be returned for servicing when necessary.

5. Removal of Brake Operating Cam

To remove the operating cam unscrew the nut, which secures the operating lever to the splines on the cam. A sharp tap on the end of the cam spindle will now free the lever, after which the cam can be withdrawn from its housing. **Do not try and remove the brake shoe pivot pin, it is cast into the brake cover plate and cannot be removed.**

6. Cush Drive

The sprocket/brake drum is free to rotate on the hub barrel. Three radial vanes are formed on the back of the brake drum and three similar vanes are formed on the cush drive shell. Six rubber blocks are fitted between the vanes on the

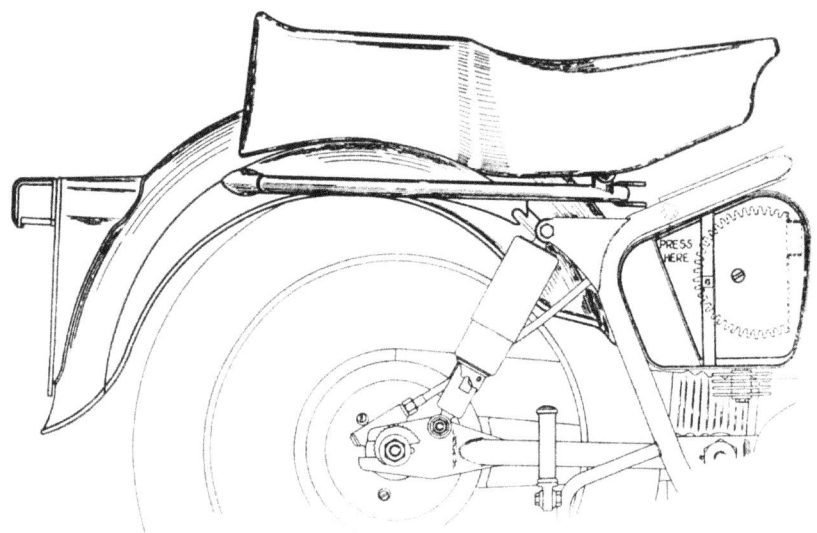

REMOVAL OF REAR MUDGUARD UNIT, ALSO SHOWING AIR FILTER
Fig. 4

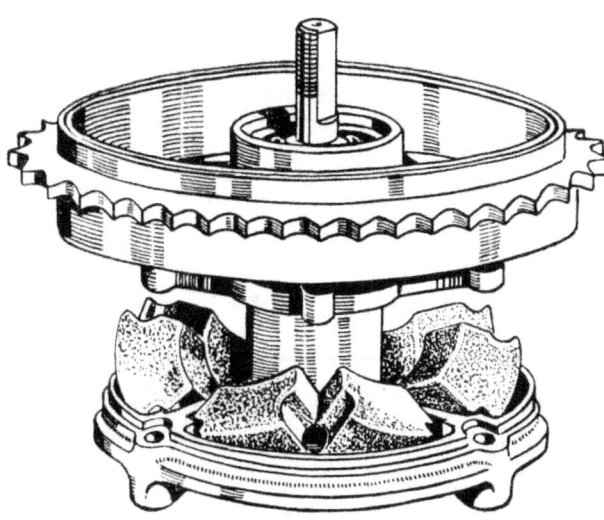

REASSEMBLY OF CUSH DRIVE
Fig. 5

brake drum and those on the cush drive shell, thus permitting only a small amount of angular movement of the sprocket/brake drum relative to the hub barrel and transmitting both driving and braking torques and smoothing out harshness and irregularity in the former.

If the cush drive rubbers become worn so that the amount of free movement measured at the tyre exceeds ½ in. to 1 in. the rubbers should be replaced. To obtain access to them, remove the complete wheel as described above, then unscrew the loose section of the spindle completely. The main portion of the wheel can then be lifted away from the assembly, consisting of the fixed portion of the spindle, sprocket/brake drum complete with brake and the cush drive shell. Now remove the brake cover plate complete with brake shoes as described above, and unscrew the three nuts are the back of the cush drive shell after bending back the locking washers. The three studs are brazed to the lockring and should be driven out of the cush drive shell, each a little at a time to avoid distorting the lockring or bending the studs. The sprocket/brake drum can now be separated from the cush drive shell and the six cush drive rubbers lifted out.

When re-assembling the cush drive the entry of the vanes between the rubbers will be facilitated if the latter are fitted into the driving shell first and then tilted. The rubbers should be liberally painted with soapsuds to facilitate entry of the vanes. Grease the inner face of the lockring before assembling and tighten the three nuts down solid as there is a shoulder on the stud which prevents tightening of the nuts from locking the operation of the cush drive. Do not forget to bend up the tabs of the three locking washers.

When re-assembling the cush drive, coat the inside of the bore of the sprocket/brake drum liberally with grease where it fits over the hub barrel.

7. Removal of Ball Bearings

To remove the ball bearings, take the complete wheel out of the machine and separate the main portion of the wheel from the sprocket/brake drum, cush drive shell assembly as described above. To remove the bearing from the sprocket/brake drum first remove the brake cover plate complete with brake shoe assembly; then remove the distance collar and unscrew the bearing retaining ring with peg spanner. Now screw the loose section of the spindle into the fixed section and drive out the bearing by hitting the hexagon-headed end of the loose section of the spindle.

To remove the bearings from the loose half of the hub barrel, first lift away the distance collar, speedometer drive gearbox, the spacing collar and the felt washer. Remove the bearing retaining circlip from the driving sprocket end of the barrel. Between the two bearings is a spacer slotted at one end to enable a drift to be used on the bearing at that end. Remove this bearing first, then enter the loose section of the spindle into the spacer and drive out the remaining bearing by means of a hammer and drift applied to the hexagon-headed end of the spindle.

8. Hub Bearings

These are deep-groove single-row journal ball bearings, ⅝ in. i.d. by 1 9/16 in. o.d. by 7/16 in. wide. The Skefko Part Number is RLS5. Equivalent bearings of other makes are Hoffmann LS7, Ransome and Marles LJ.5/8 and Fischer LS7.

9. Removal of Hub Driving Pins

To remove the six driving pins from the aluminium full-width hub, first remove the hub

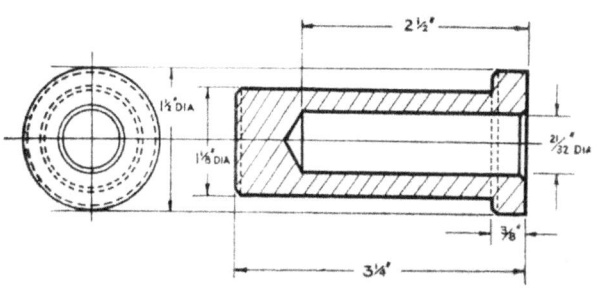

DRIFT FOR REFITTING BEARINGS
Fig. 6

cap after unscrewing the three screws attaching it to the hub. Unscrew the six Simmonds nuts and drive out the pins.

10. Refitting Ball Bearings

To refit the sprocket/brake drum bearing use a hollow drift as shown in Fig. 6. The bearing is first fitted to the fixed section of the spindle; the spindle and bearing are then entered into the sprocket/brake drum and driven home, preferably under a press or using light hammer blows.

The two bearings in the hub barrel are pressed in using the drift part of E.4823. First assemble the bearing into the circlip grooved end of the barrel and fit the circlip. Replace the bearing spacer, the slot in the spacer can be at either end of the hub, and assemble the second bearing, supporting the hub on the inner race of the other bearing. If the drift part of E.4823 is not available it is essential that the last bearing is assembled by applying pressure to both inner and outer races simultaneously to avoid pre-loading the two hub barrel bearings.

11. Re-assembly of Brake Shoes and Operating Cam into Cover Plate

No difficulty should be experienced in carrying out these operations. Put a smear of grease on the pivot pin and on the operating face of the cam; also on to the cylindrical bearing surface of the operating cam if this has been removed. Fit the operating lever and trunnion on its splines in a position to suit the extent of wear on the linings and secure the nut. The range of adjustment can be extended by moving the lever on to a different spline.

12. Final Re-assembly of Hub Before Replacing Wheel

Before replacing the felt washers which form the grease seals, pack all bearings with grease. Recommended greases are Castrolease LM, Mobilgrease M, Esso Multipurpose Grease H, Energrease L2, Shell Retinax A or Marfak Multipurpose 2. These are all medium heavy lime soap or aluminium soap greases. The use of H.M.P. greases, which have a soda soap base is not recommended, as these tend to be slightly corrosive if any damp finds its way into the hubs.

Make sure that the inside of the brake drum is quite free from oil or grease, damp, etc. Replace the felt washers, distance collars, the brake cover plate assembly, speedometer drive gearbox, distance collars and chain adjuster cams, the loose section of the spindle and the spindle nut. The wheel is then ready for re-assembly into the machine.

13. Wheel Rim

The wheel rim is WM2—17 in., plunged and pierced with forty holes for spoke nipples. The spoke holes are symmetrical, i.e., the rim can be assembled to the hub either way round. The rim diameter after building is 17·06 in., the tolerances on the circumference of the rim shoulders where the tyre fits being 53·642/53·582 in. The standard steel measuring tape for checking rims is $\frac{1}{4}$ in. wide, ·011 in. thick, and its length is 53·702/53·642 in.

14. Spokes

The spokes are of the single-butted type, 8-10-in. gauge with 90° countersunk heads, thread diameter ·144 in., 40 threads per inch, thread form British Standard Cycle. The inner spokes are $5\frac{11}{16}$ in. long, and the outer spokes, $5\frac{3}{4}$ in. long. All spokes initially have an angle of bend of approximately 100°. The outer spokes are hit with a hide or wooden mallet after building the wheel but before finally truing it, so as to give a more acute angle of approximately 80°.

15. Wheel Building and Truing

The spokes are laced one over two, and the wheel rim must be built central in relation to the outer faces of the distance collars. The rim should be trued as accurately as possible, the maximum permissible run-out both sideways and radially being plus or minus $\frac{1}{32}$ in.

16. Tyre

The standard tyre is Dunlop 3·25-17 in. Universal tread. When removing the tyre always start close to the valve and see that the edge of the cover at the other side of the wheel is pushed down into the well in the rim. When replacing the tyre, fit the part by the valve last, also with the edge of the cover at the other side of the wheel pushed down into the well.

If the correct method of fitting and removal of the tyre is adopted it will be found that the covers can be manipulated quite easily with the small levers supplied in the tool-kit. The use of long levers and/or excessive force is liable to damage the walls of the tyre. After inflation make sure that the tyre is fitting evenly all the way round the rim. A line moulded on the wall of the tyre indicates whether or not the tyre is correctly fitted. If the tyre has a white mark indicating a balance point, this should be fitted near the valve.

17. Tyre Pressures

The recommended pressures for the rear tyre are 16 lbs. per square inch for wheel loads not exceeding 200 lb., 18 lb. per square inch for loads up to 230 lb., 20 lb. per square inch for loads up to 260 lb., 24 lb. per square inch for loads up to 320 lb., 28 lb. per square inch for loads up to 380 lb., and 32 lb. per square inch up to 440 lbs.

18. Lubrication

Grease the bearings by packing them with grease after dismantling the hub as described above.

Note that the brake cam is drilled for a grease passage, but the end of this is stopped up with a countersunk screw instead of being fitted with a grease nipple. This is done to prevent excessive greasing by over-enthusiastic owners. If the cam is smeared with grease on assembly it should require no further attention, but in case of necessity it is possible to remove the screw, fit a grease nipple in its place and grease the cam by this means.

SECTION L10

Rear Wheel (Non-Detachable Type)

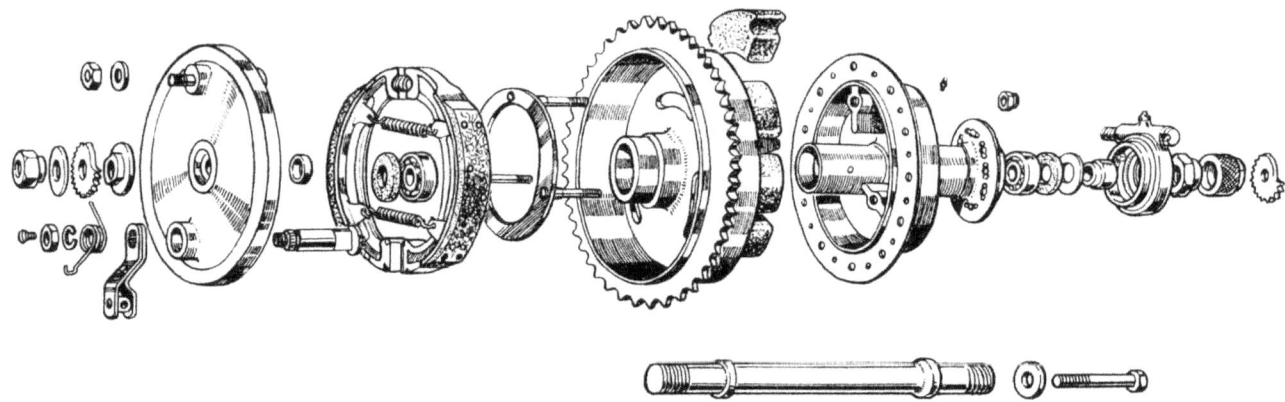

REAR HUB (NON-DETACHABLE TYPE)
Fig. 1

1. Description

The wheel incorporates a rubber cush drive and the chain line is $2\frac{3}{4}$ in. A special feature is the provision of a two-piece spindle with a detachable distance piece, the removal of which enables the inner tube to be changed with the wheel in position in the machine.

2. Removal of Inner Tube with Wheel in Position in Frame

Place the machine on the stand. Deflate the tyre and remove the right-hand side of the tyre from the rim, using tyre levers in the ordinary way. Unscrew the centre bolt and withdraw this completely. Spring the fork ends slightly apart so as to release the slip collar from the spigot which locates it and slide the collar out of the fork end. Disconnect the speedometer driving flex from the speedometer gearbox, remove the inner tube from the tyre and withdraw it through the gap left between the inside of the fork end and the speedometer gearbox.

3. Removal and Replacement of Wheel

Place machine on the stand, if necessary putting packing pieces beneath the legs of the stand to lift the wheel clear of the ground. Remove the rear mudguard unit (see Section H6, subsection 3). Disconnect the rear driving chain at the spring link and remove the chain from the rear wheel sprocket, leaving it in position on the gearbox countershaft sprocket. Unscrew the rear brake rod adjusting nut completely and depress the brake pedal so as to disengage the rod from the trunnion in the brake operating lever. Unscrew the brake cover plate anchor nut and remove this together with the washer behind it. Disconnect the speedometer driving cable, loosen the spindle nut and the centre bolt and mark the chain adjuster cams to ensure replacing in the same position*. Slide the wheel out of the fork ends, tilting it so as to disengage the end of the brake shoe pivot pin from the slot in the fork end.

When replacing the wheel make sure that the dogs on the speedometer drive gearbox are engaged with the slots in the end of the **hub barrel**. Make sure also that the speedometer **drive gearbox** is correctly positioned so that there is no sudden bend in the driving cable. Make sure that the closed end of the spring link points in the direction of travel of the chain. Replace the chain adjuster cams in their original positions or, if necessary, turn each of them the same number of notches to tension the chain and maintain correct wheel alignment. Do not forget to refit the brake rod and adjust the brake so that the wheel turns freely while the brake is off, while at the same time only a small

---

* Note that the wheel is not necessarily correctly lined up when the same notch position is used on both adjuster cams. Once the position of the cams which gives correct alignment has been found this alignment will, however, be maintained if both cams are moved the same number of notches.

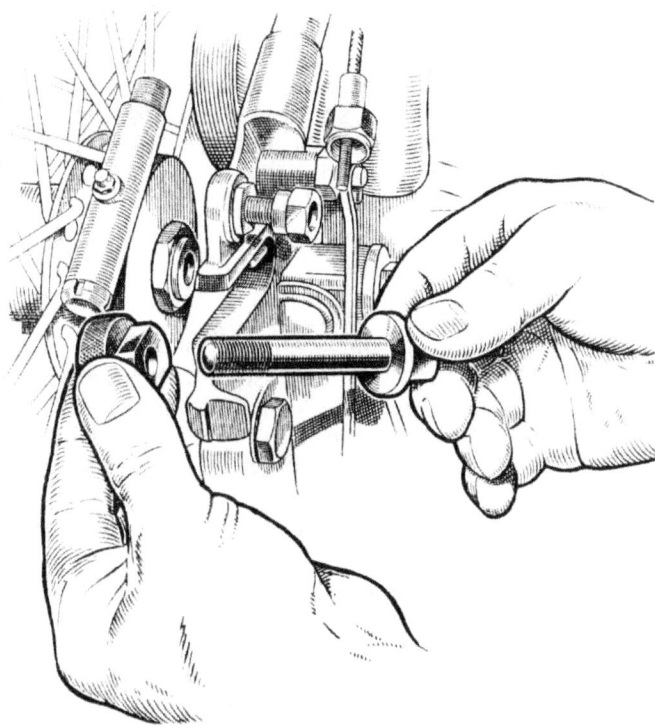

REMOVAL OF CENTRE BOLT AND SLIP COLLAR TO PERMIT REMOVAL OF INNER TUBE

Fig. 2

travel of the brake pedal is necessary to put the brake on.

4. Removal of Brake Shoes for Replacement

Remove the complete wheel as described above, then remove the spindle nut, chain adjuster, and the distance collar, thus permitting the complete brake cover plate with operating cam, pivot pin, shoes and return springs to be lifted off the hub spindle. The brake shoes can then be removed after detaching the return springs.

5. Removal of Brake Operating Cam

To remove the operating cam unscrew the nut which secures the operating lever to the splines on the cam. A sharp tap on the end of the cam spindle will now free the lever, after which the cam can be withdrawn from its housing. **Do not try to remove the brake shoe pivot pin; it is cast into the brake cover plate and cannot be removed.**

6. Replacing Brake Linings

Brake linings are supplied either in pairs ready drilled complete with rivets, or ready fitted to service replacement brake shoes. When riveting linings to shoes secure the two centre rivets first so as to ensure that the lining lies flat against the shoe. Standard linings are Ferodo AM2 which are drilled to receive cheese headed rivets.

A number of early "Crusader 250" models were fitted with brake linings bonded to the shoes. These should be returned for servicing when necessary.

7. Removal of Hub Spindle and Bearings

To remove the hub spindle and bearings, having already removed the brake cover plate assembly and speedometer drive gearbox, lift out the felt washers and distance pieces then hit one end of the spindle with a copper hammer or mallet thus driving it out of the hub, bringing one bearing with it and leaving the other in position in the hub. Drive the bearing off the spindle and insert the latter once more in the hub at the end from which it was removed. Now drive the spindle through the hub in the opposite direction, when it will bring out the remaining bearing.

8. Hub Bearings

These are deep-groove single-row journal ball bearings, $\frac{5}{8}$ in. i./d. by $1\frac{9}{16}$ in. o./d. by $\frac{7}{16}$ in. wide. The Skefko Part No. is RLS5. Equivalent bearings of other makes are Hoffmann LS7, Ransome and Marles LJ$\frac{5}{8}$ in., Fischer LS7.

9. Refitting Ball Bearings

To refit the bearings in the hub a hollow drift is required, as shown in Fig. 3. One bearing is first fitted to one end of the spindle by means of the hollow drift; the spindle and bearing are then entered into one end of the hub barrel which is then supported on one of the hollow drifts. The other bearing is then threaded over the upper end of the spindle and driven home by means of the second hollow drift either under a press or by means of a hammer which will thus drive both bearings into position simultaneously.

In order to make quite sure that there is clearance between the inner faces of the outer bearings and the bottom of the recesses fit the distance washers against the inner races of the bearings and either fit the assembly of brake cover

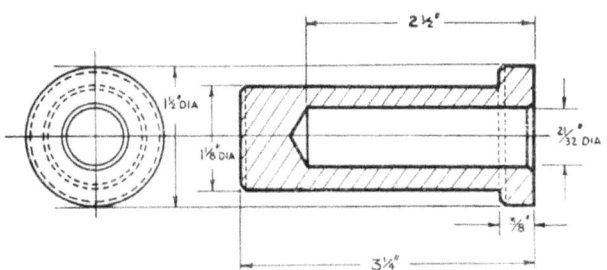

DRIFT FOR REFITTING BEARINGS

Fig. 3

plate, speedometer gearbox, etc., or make up this distance with tubular distance pieces. Fit and tighten the spindle nuts. Tightening the nuts should not have any effect on the ease with which the spindle can be turned. If tightening the nuts makes the spindle hard to turn this may be taken as proof that the bearings are bottoming in the recesses in the hub barrel before they are solid against the shoulders on the spindle. In this case the bearing should be removed and a thin packing shim fitted between the inner race and the shoulder on the spindle.

10. Cush Drive

The sprocket/brake drum is free to rotate on the hub barrel. Three radial vanes are formed on the back of the brake drum and three similar vanes are formed on the cush drive shell. Six rubber blocks are fitted between the vanes on the brake drum and those on the cush drive shell, thus permitting only a small amount of angular movement of the sprocket/brake drum relative to the hub barrel and transmitting both driving and braking torques and smoothing out harshness and irregularity in the former.

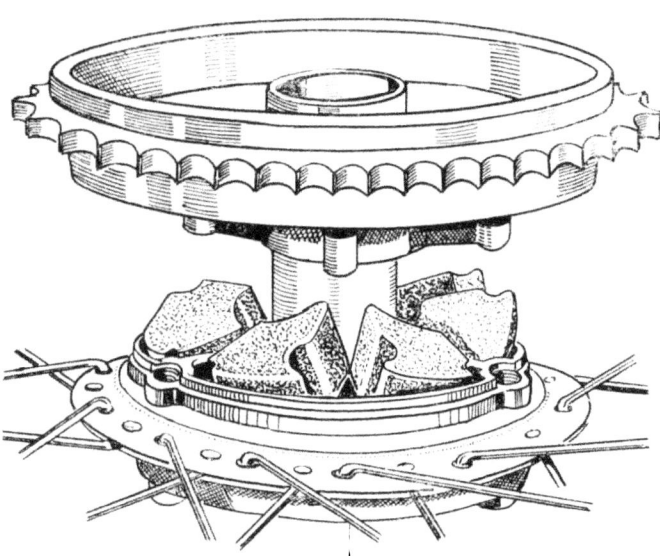

REASSEMBLY OF CUSH DRIVE
Fig. 4

If the cush drive rubbers become worn so that the amount of free movement measured at the tyre exceeds $\frac{1}{2}$ in. to 1 in. the rubbers should be replaced. To obtain access to them remove the complete wheel as described above, remove the brake cover plate complete with the brake shoe assembly, unscrew the three Simmonds nuts at the back of the cush drive shell. Drive out the three studs into the brake drum, tapping each stud evenly and in rotation, as they are each brazed to the lock ring, after which the sprocket/brake drum can be separated from the cush drive shell and the six cush drive rubbers can be lifted out.

When reassembling the cush drive the entry o the vanes between the rubbers will be facilitated if the latter are fitted into the driving shell first and then tilted. The rubbers should be liberally painted with soapsuds to facilitate entry of the vanes.

When reassembling the cush drive coat the inside of the bore of the sprocket/brake drum liberally with grease where it fits over the hub barrel and also put grease on the inner face of the lockring. The three Simmonds nuts should be tightened down solid as there is a shoulder on the stud which prevents tightening of the nuts from locking the operation of the cush drive.

11. Reassembly of Brake Shoes, Pivot Pin and Operating Cam into Cover Plate

No difficulty should be experienced in carrying out these operations. Put a smear of grease on the pivot pin and on the operating face of the cam; also on the cylindrical bearing surface of the operating cam if this has been removed. Fit the operating lever and trunnion on its splines in a position to suit the extent of wear on the linings and secure with the nut. The range of adjustment can be extended by moving the lever on to a different spline.

12. Final Reassembly of Hub before Replacing Wheel

Before replacing the felt washers which form the grease seals, pack both bearings with grease. Recommended greases are Castrolease LM, Mobilgrease M, Esso Multipurpose Grease H, Energrease L2, Shell Retinax A or Marfak Multipurpose 2. These are all medium heavy lime soap or aluminium soap greases. The use of H.M.P. greases which have a soda soap base is not recommended as these tend to be slightly corrosive if any damp finds its way into the hubs.

Make sure that the inside of the brake drum is quite free from oil or grease, damp, etc. Replace the felt washers, distance collars, the brake cover plate assembly, speedometer drive gearbox, distance collars, chain adjuster cams, the loose section of the spindle and the spindle nut. The wheel is then ready for reassembly into the machine.

"250 Trials":

The hub of this model is similar to the above in all respects other than possessing a detachable chain sprocket, secured by eight nuts and bolts.

13. Wheel Rims

The standard wheel rim is WM2-17 in., plunged and pierced with forty holes for spoke nipples.

The spoke holes are arranged in groups of three holes on one side of the centre line, then a single hole on the other side, a further group of three and a single hole and so on. Care must be taken that the rim is built the right way round into the wheel. The rim diameter after building is 17·06 in., the tolerances on the circumference where the tyre fits being 53·642/53·582 in. The standard steel measuring tape for checking rims is ¼ in. wide, ·011 in. thick and its length is 53·702/53·642 in.

The "250 Trials" model is fitted with a WM3-18 rim having a diameter after building of 18·06 in., the tolerances on the circumference being 56·783/56·723 in. and the length of the measuring tape 56·843/56·783 in.

14. Spokes

The spokes are of the single-butted type, 8-10 guage with 90° countersunk heads, thread diameter ·144 in., 40 threads per inch, thread form British Standard Cycle. For the 17 in. rim the spoke length is 6¾ in. on the cush drive side and 7½ in., on the spoke flange side. For the 18 in. rim the spoke lengths are 7¼ in. and 8 in. respectively. All spokes initially have an angle of bend of approximately 100°; those on the outside of the spoke flanges are hit with a hide or wooden mallet after building the wheel but before final truing so as to give a more acute angle of bend of approximately 80°.

15. Wheel Building and Truing

The spokes are laced one over three and the wheel must be built central in relation to the faces of the distance collars which fit between the fork end. The rim should be trued as accurately as possible, the maximum permissible run-out both sideways and radially being plus or minus $\tfrac{1}{32}$ in.

Fig. 5 shows the lacing when using Dunlop rims. The key to correct lacing is the inside spokes to the large flange on the cush drive shell which must slope in the direction shown in Fig. 5. With the Dunlop rim this spoke goes to the middle hole of one of the groups of three (see Subsection 14) and the rim must be built into the wheel so that these groups of three holes are on the right of the centre line when the cush drive is on the left, i.e., the inside spokes to the large flange cross from the left to the right of the centre line.

16. Tyres

The standard tyre is Dunlop 3·25–17 in. Universal tread. When removing the tyre always start close to the valve and see that the edge of the cover at the other side of the wheel is pushed down into the well in the rim. When replacing the tyre, fit the part by the valve last, also with the edge of the cover at the other side of the wheel pushed down into the well.

If the correct method of fitting and removal of the tyre is adopted it will be found that the covers can be manipulated quite easily with the small levers supplied in the tool-kit. The use of long levers and/or excessive force is liable to damage the walls of the tyre. After inflation make sure that the tyre is fitting evenly all the way round the rim. A line moulded on the wall of the tyre indicates whether or not the tyre is correctly fitted. If the tyre has a white mark indicating a balance point this should be fitted near the valve.

A 4·00–18 in. tyre is fitted to the 18 in. wheel of the "250 Trials."

17. Tyre Pressures

The load which the tyre will carry at different inflation pressures is shown below:

Tyre Section Inches	Inflation Pressures—lb. per sq. in.					
	16	18	20	24	28	32
	Load per tyre—lb.					
3·25	200	230	260	320	380	440
3·50	280	310	335	390	450	500
4·00	360	395	430	500	570	640

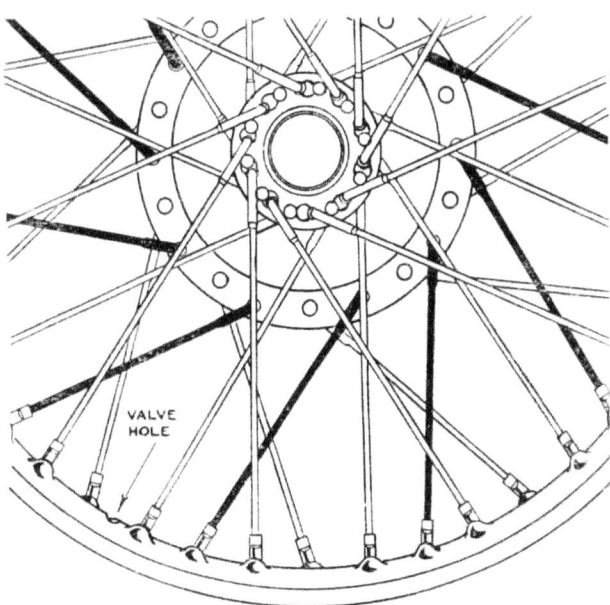

WHEEL LACING—DUNLOP RIM

Fig. 5

18. Lubrication

A greasing point is provided in the centre of the hub barrel. Unless the barrel is packed full with grease on assembly (which is apt to lead to trouble through grease finding its way past the felt seals on to the brake linings) this greasing point is of little value and the best way to grease the bearings is by packing them with grease after dismantling the hub as described above.

Note that the brake cam is drilled for a grease passage but the end of this is stopped up with a countersunk screw instead of being fitted with a grease nipple. This is done to prevent excessive greasing by over-enthusiastic owners. If the cam is smeared with grease on assembly it should require no further attention but in case of necessity it is possible to remove the screw, fit a grease nipple in its place and grease the cam by this means.

SECTION M7

Special Tools

Sub-Section	No.	Use
SECTION C		
1 and 2	DWU05	Screwdriver
16	E7353	Valve Guide Mandrels
18	E.5477 A	Gudgeon Pin Extractor (*Not illustrated*)
20	E.2178	Inlet Valve Seat Cutter. "Crusader 250," "250 Clipper"
	T.1891	Inlet Valve Seat Cutter. "Crusader Sports," Super, Continental, "250 Trials"
20	T.2053	Inlet Valve Seat Arbor
24	E.4870	Camshaft Sprocket Extractor
25	E.6978	Pump Disc Lapping Tool
SECTION D		
2	E.6960	Crankshaft Extractor
5	E.6977	Crankshaft Assembly Tool
SECTION E		
5	E.5414	Clutch Centre Extractor

Special Tools

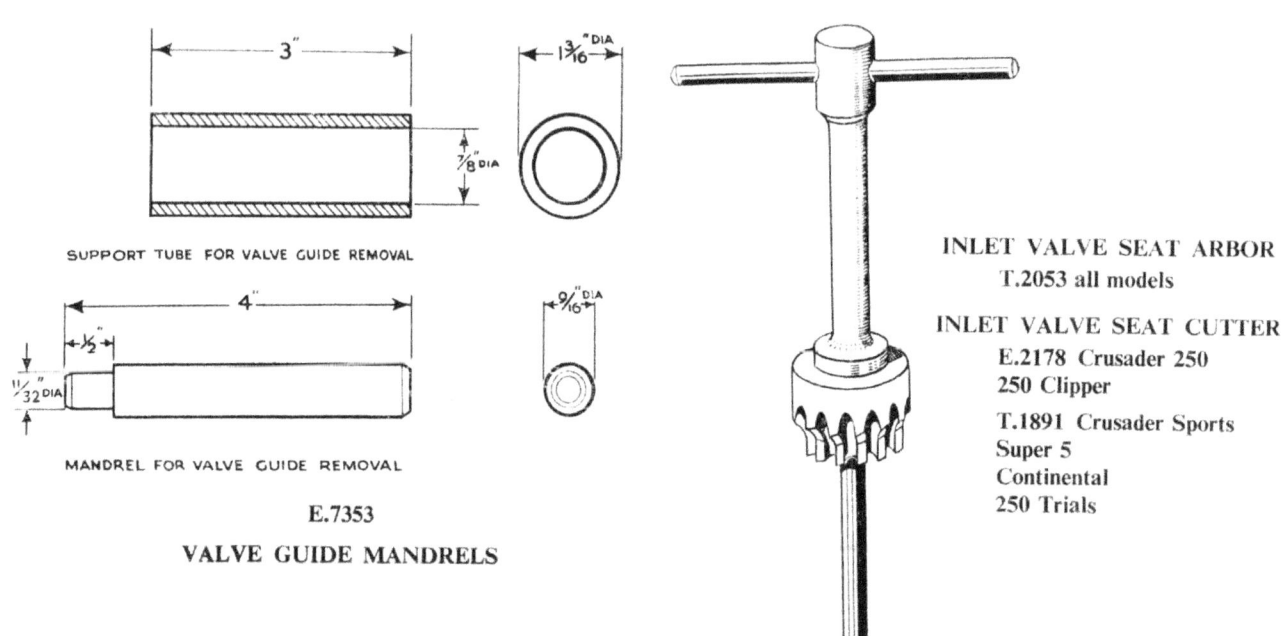

E.7353
VALVE GUIDE MANDRELS

INLET VALVE SEAT ARBOR
T.2053 all models

INLET VALVE SEAT CUTTER
E.2178 Crusader 250
250 Clipper

T.1891 Crusader Sports
Super 5
Continental
250 Trials

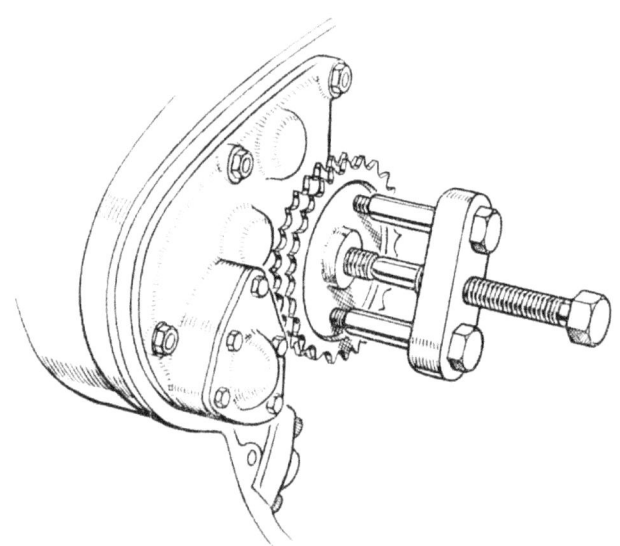

E.4870
CAMSHAFT SPROCKET EXTRACTOR

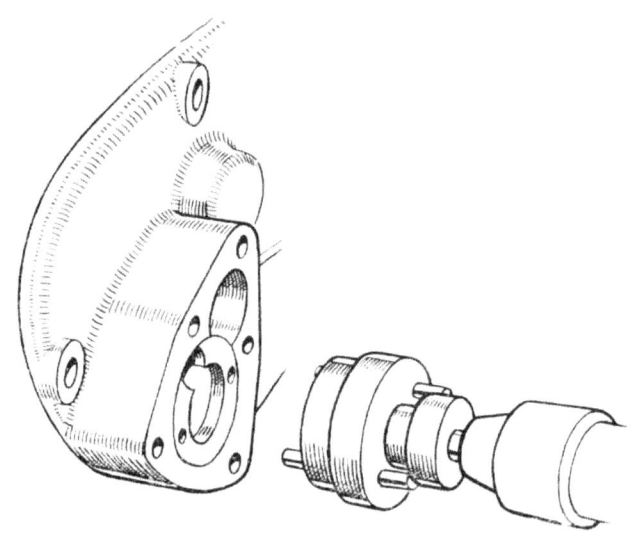

E.6978
OIL PUMP DISC LAPPING TOOL

Special Tools

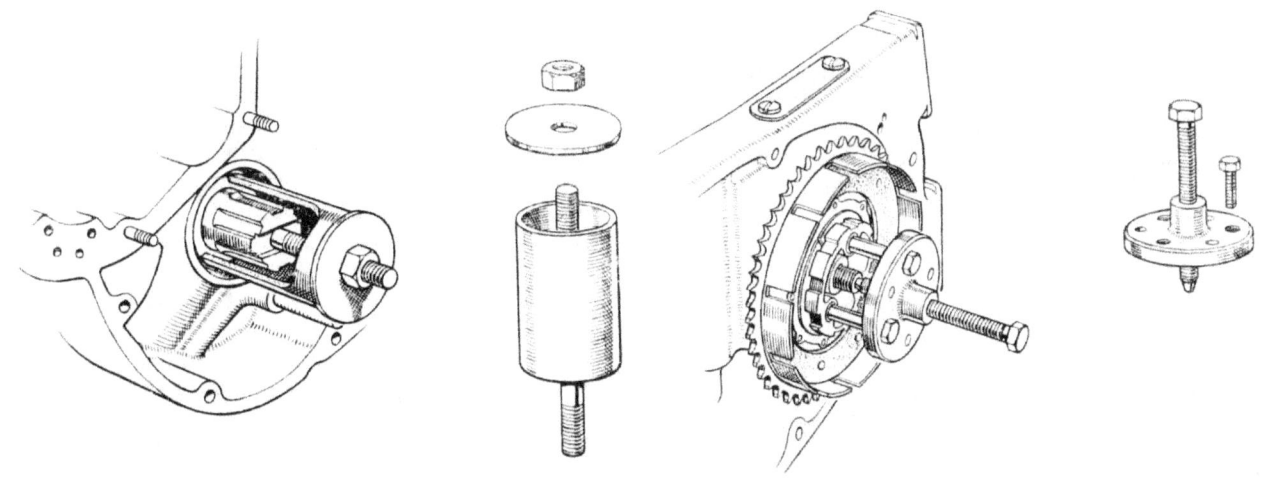

E.6977
CRANKSHAFT ASSEMBLY TOOL

E.5414
CLUTCH CENTRE EXTRACTOR

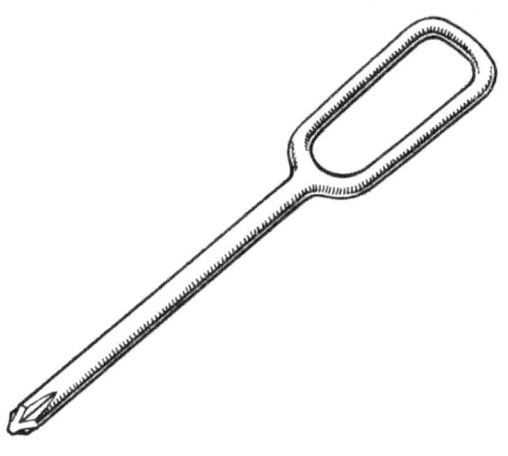

DWU05
SCREWDRIVER

SECTION N2

Accessories

1. Legshields

Legshield (Part Nos. 41399 and 41400) are available for the 1958 to 1963 "250 Clipper" and the 1957 to 1962 "Crusader 250." They are made from steel pressings and, being of double curvature, are particularly robust. Their method of attachment ensures no vibration.

Underneath the tank and welded to the tank tube of the frame is a clip provided for the top attachment of the legshields. The crossbar (41550) is attached to this clip with stud (31160), distance piece (41551), two nuts (27944) and washers (27917). Do not tighten the nuts until the legshields have been fitted, as the crossbar can slide and pivot in the clip for adjustment. The legshields are attached to this bar with screws (14446), and washers (27917). Rubber grommets (40183) are fitted over the bar where it passes through the legshields. For the bottom attachment the middle engine plate stud is replaced by stud (42892). Distance tubes (41552, L.H.) and (42893, R.H.) are fitted between the engine plates and legshield brackets, and the original nuts and washers used to hold the assembly together.

2. Pannier Equipment

Pannier bags (42218), and carriers (42193) and (42194), specially designed for the "250 Clipper," "Crusader" and "Crusader Sports," can be fitted after very little modification. The carriers, made from steel pressings, prevent any dirt from the back wheel soiling the bags.

Each pannier carrier is attached at three points. The forward end is clipped to the mudguard carrier tube with two clips (Part No. 42196), and two screws (42202). The screw heads are on the outside with a large washer (5965) under each head and a collar (23941) between the carrier and each end of the outer clip. Use nuts (27944) and washers (27917). A strut (42199) is attached to the rear mudguard behind the dual seat by the existing screws holding the mudguard to the mudguard bridge. Each carrier is fastened to the strut with a screw (42203) and two washers (5965), one between the strut and the carrier, the other between the carrier and the head of the screw. Drill a $\frac{21}{64}$ in. dia. hole in the valance of the mudguard in line with the bottom fixing hole of each pannier carrier. Position the mudguard bridge (40053) to suit these holes drilled in the valance, and drill two $\frac{9}{32}$ in. dia. holes through the guard to line up with the two in the bridge. Attach the bridge to the guard with screws (18446), nuts (26998) and washers (27916). Place a short distance piece (20199) between the bridge and the inside of the valance and a longer distance piece (42201) and washer (5965) between the valance and back of the carrier, the washer being next to the carrier. A bolt (42204) with washer (5965) under the head is fitted from the outside and tightened up with nut (27944) and washer (8634).

SECTION P1
"Airflow" Fairing

1. Description of the Fairing

The "Airflow" fairing and front mudguard are fibre glass units and therefore very light, rigid and tough. The fairing, with the windscreen, provides full weather protection. It has two cubby holes and incorporates the headlamp, speedometer, ammeter and lighting switch.

On the rare occasions that it may be necessary to remove the mudguard and fairing from the machine, it will be found to present no difficulty if the following sequence is adopted:

2. Removal of the Windscreen

Remove the two screws which attach the number plate to the fairing. Removal of the number plate will expose a screw in the centre of the fairing which may now be taken out, together with the screws at each corner of the screen. The screen and metal back plate may now be lifted clear, taking care not to lose the five slotted sleeve nuts with their plain steel and rubber washers.

3. Removal of the Headlamp

Take out the small screw from the underside of the headlamp rim. Raise the rim to clear its spigot plate from the slot in the lamp body shell and remove. Next take off the rubber ring from the light unit. By slackening the three light unit adjuster screws and rotating the light unit in an anti-clockwise direction, the unit may then be withdrawn sufficiently to disconnect the four leads.

Should it be necessary to remove the lamp body shell this may be done by unscrewing the four screws spaced round its flange. This also releases the rubber washer. Care should be taken not to lose the four screw locking plates inside the fairing.

4. Removal of the Headlamp Switch, Speedometer and Ammeter

Undo the switch knob screw and remove the knob. Unscrew the switch plate nut and remove the switch plate. The switch body may now be pulled out from beneath the fairing. Do not lose the plain washer situated beneath the switch knob.

Disconnect the speedometer drive, and, after removing two nuts, the spring washers and the bridge piece from the bottom of the speedometer, it may be removed.

To remove the ammeter it is only necessary to take off the rubber band from the body of the ammeter, after disconnecting the leads, and press down the small metal tabs which will be found turned outwards. The ammeter will then pull out from the top of the fairing.

5. Removal of the Front Wheel and Fork Legs

To remove the front wheel from the fork, place the machine on the centre stand with sufficient packing (about 2 in.) beneath each side of the stand to lift the wheel clear off the ground when tilted back on to the rear wheel. Slacken the brake cable adjustment and disconnect the cable from the handlebar lever and from the operating cam lever on the hub. Unscrew the four nuts securing the fork leg caps and allow the wheel to drop forward out of the front fork. Make sure that the machine stands securely on the rear wheel and centre stand—if necessary place a weight on the saddle or a strut beneath the fork to ensure this.

Unscrew the plug screws in the fork head, when the sliding fork legs, complete with springs and spring distance tubes, can be withdrawn from the lower ends of the main tubes.

6. Removal of the Front Mudguard

From the top of the fairing the two clamp bolts holding the mudguard to the fork crown can be reached. Unscrew the nuts and push out the bolts.

On Early Models it is necessary to remove the centre pin securing the guard to the bottom of the steering stem. The mudguard may now be withdrawn.

7. Removal of the Fairing

First take off the exhaust pipe. This is held to one of the front engine bearer bolts and to the pillion footrest stud at the rear.

Slacken the hose clips and remove the attachment caps from the ends of the attachment studs to which the lower part of the fairing is anchored.

Unscrew the nuts and push out the stud which secures the upper part of the fairing to the tube extending forward from the steering head.

If desired the two bottom attachment studs may be removed.

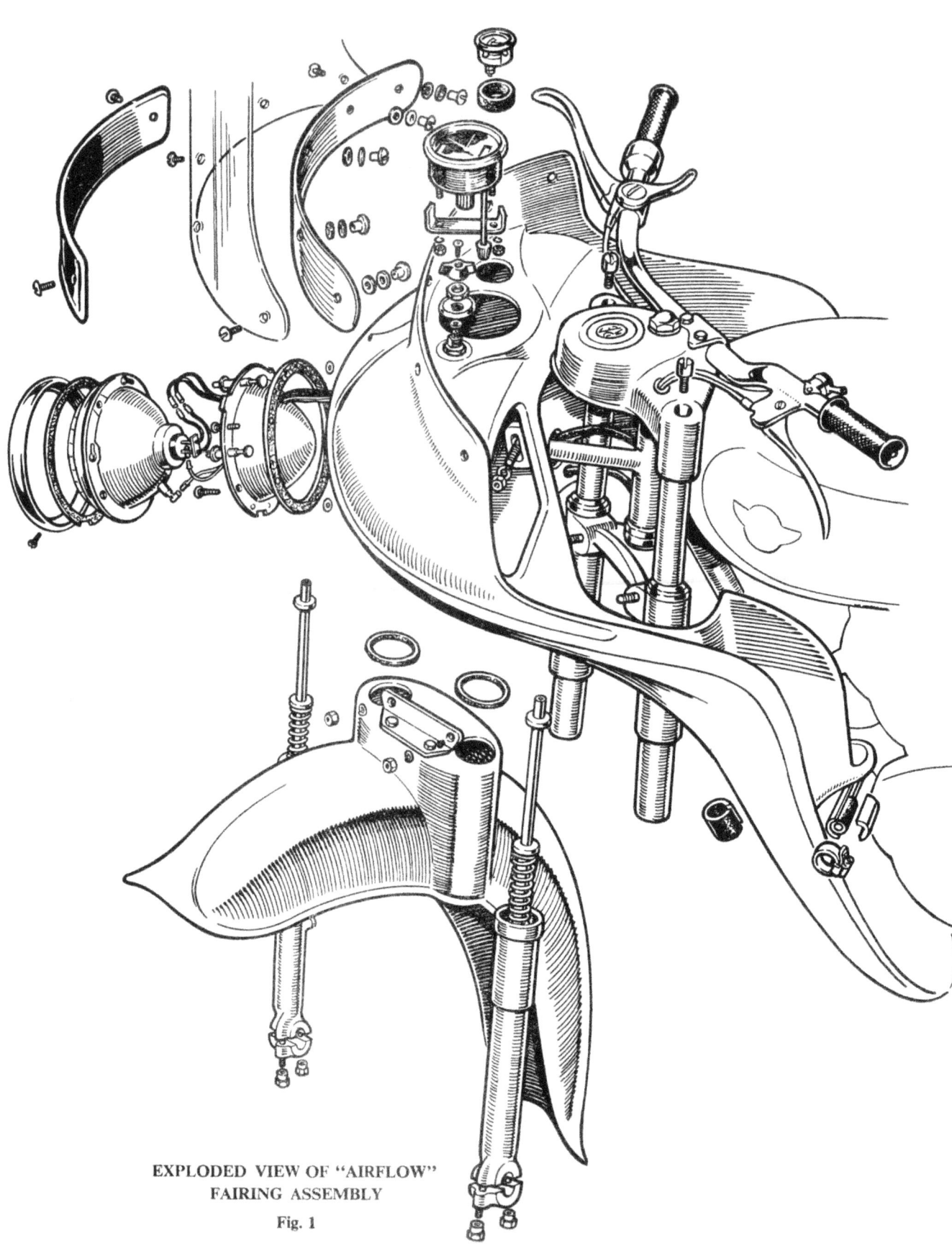

EXPLODED VIEW OF "AIRFLOW" FAIRING ASSEMBLY

Fig. 1

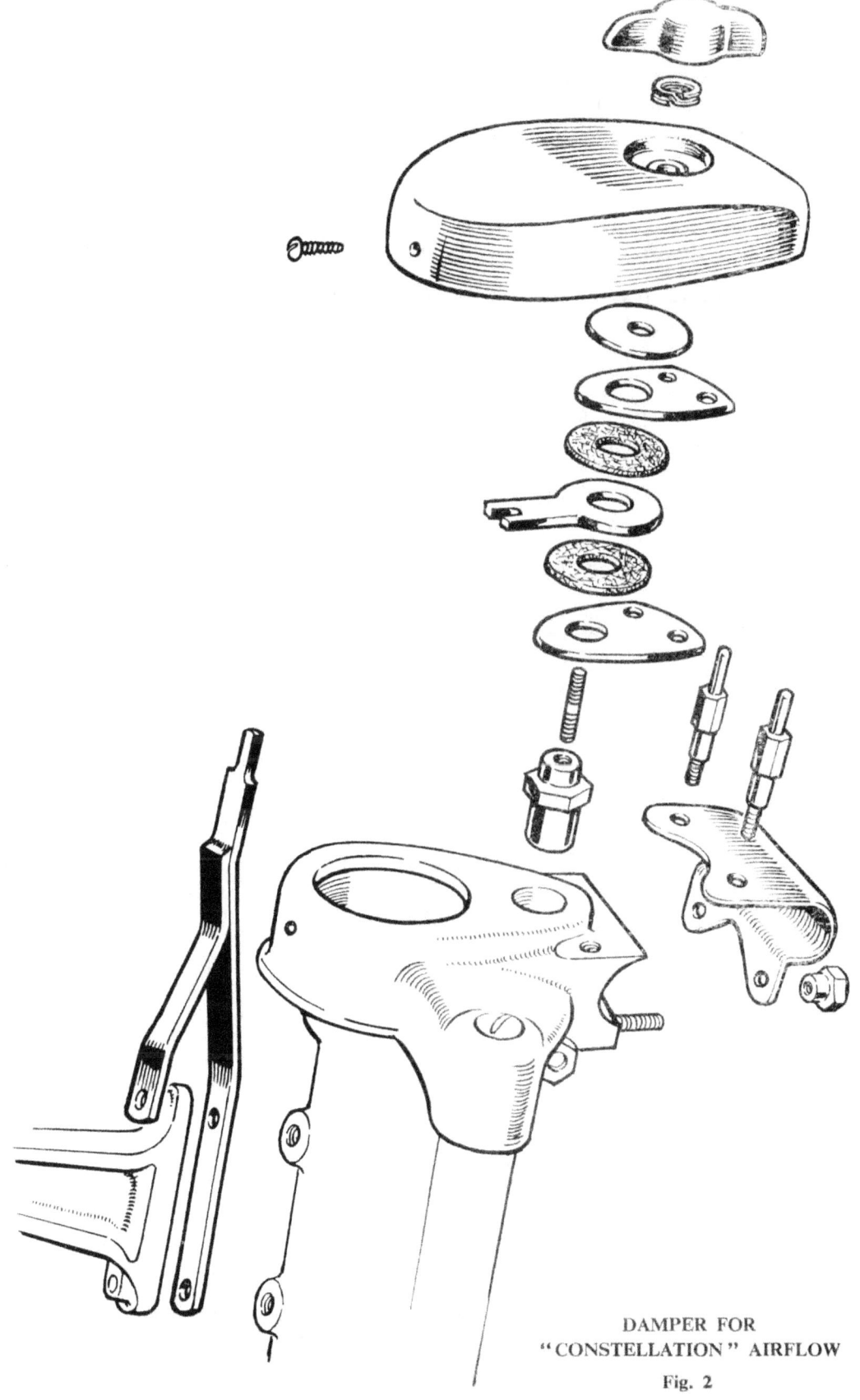

DAMPER FOR
"CONSTELLATION" AIRFLOW

Fig. 2

8. Repairs

In the event of minor damage to the fairing, small repair kits consisting of a quantity of resin, catalyst and glass fibre are available from our Service Department. Instructions for carrying out minor repairs are issued with this kit.

9. Reassembly of the Fairing

If these have been removed replace the two bottom fairing attachment studs, also fit the rubber sleeve to the down tube. Next raise the fairing over the fork cover tubes, locating the bottom attachment plates on each leg shield over the attachment studs.

Incline the fairing outwards and thread the light and switch leads through the strut tube aperture, and the speedometer cable through the smaller hole below it. The fairing can then be pushed towards the forks until the strut tube, complete with buffer assembly, has entered the aperture and is positioned between the strut tube attachment plates. Fit the stud through the buffer assembly and attachment plates and secure washers and nuts to either end.

Complete the fairing assembly to the machine by fixing the attachment cap over the attachment stud rubber. Compress these parts together and secure with the attachment clip. The exhaust system may now be fitted.

10. Reassembly of Mudguard, Fork Legs and Wheel

Fit the two sealing washers to the fork cover tubes—not forgetting the small sealing washer for the fork crown extension tube on Early Models. Raise the mudguard, and thread the cover tubes (and the fork crown extension when fitted) through their respective holes. Line up the mudguard bracket holes with the fork crown clip bolt holes and fit the bolts, washers and nuts finger tight. (On Early Models fit the fork crown extension stud and washer.)

Slide the fork legs up into the fork head. Centralise the fork leg top with the cover tube, and push up to the full extent. Fit and tighten the plug screws in the fork head.

The fork crown clip bolts may now be tightened.

Replace the wheel and connect up the brake cable at both ends. **Do not forget to readjust the brake.**

11. Reassembly of Headlamp

Thread the red earth wire, the blue and red, and the blue and white main bulb wires from the dipper switch, and one green and brown pilot lamp wire, through the hole in the lamp body shell. Fit the body shell rubber washer between the fairing and the lamp body shell rim, and line up the holes in the shell rim, the washer and the fairing aperture rim. Secure with the four screws and locking plates, keeping the threaded plate at the bottom.

Connect the blue and red and the blue and white wires to the main bulb wires in the back of the light unit. Push the green and brown lead into the pilot lamp socket and the single red earth wire from the main harness into the socket on the main bulb fitting.

The light unit may now be pushed over the three adjusters, after first slackening them. Turn the light unit in a clockwise direction to secure. Afterwards tighten all the adjusters as far as possible.

Place the rubber ring over the light unit, with the face marked "BACK" facing the light unit rim. Locate the spigot plate, situated on the top underside of the rim, with the slot in the lamp body shell. Press the rim downwards and screw in the pin at the bottom of the rim.

Finally, adjust the aim of the light beam by turning the adjuster screws in a clockwise direction from the rear as necessary. Do not turn them further than required—not more than two screws will need adjusting.

12. Reassembly of Ammeter, Headlamp Switch and Speedometer

Insert the ammeter into the off-side hole in the fairing, turn up under the fairing the small tabs on the ammeter, and fit the rubber ring, pushing it up as far as possible. Connect up the two wires with the tab washer type connections to the ammeter terminals.

Push the switch up from the underside of the fairing, place in position the switch plate and secure with the nut. Finally, put on the small washer and the switch knob, and secure with the screw.

Push the speedometer into the fairing from above, and secure the bracket with the nuts and washers from below. Fit the speedometer drive and lamp.

13. Reassembly of Windscreen

Put the slotted sleeve nuts, with their plain steel and rubber washers, into the back plate and windscreen, and line up with the holes in the fairing. Be sure to use the shortest screw for the centre countersunk hole, and the two longest for attaching the number plate.

January, 1961.   Price 2/-

A List of
SPARE & REPLACEMENT PARTS
for the
1961
Royal Enfield
'Made like a Gun'

"CRUSADER 250"

"CRUSADER SPORTS"
AND
"CRUSADER AIRFLOW"
MOTOR CYCLES

THE
ENFIELD CYCLE COMPANY LIMITED
Head Office & Works:
REDDITCH, WORCESTERSHIRE
ENGLAND

Telegrams:
"Cycles, Phone, Redditch."

Telephone:
Redditch 4222 (9 lines)

INDEX

	Page
"Airflow" models, special parts	52, 54
Air Filter	38
Battery	48
Brake Control, Rear	32
Carburettor—Amal, Monobloc Type	40, 42
Chains and Covers	32
Clutch	20
Camshaft, Oil Pump, etc.	10
Crankcase	8
Dual Seat	36
Electrical Equipment	44, 46, 48
Engine and Cylinder Head	4
Estimates and Quotations	3
Exhaust System	32
Footrests	32
Frame and Rear Suspension	34
Front Fork, Telescopic	24
Gear Box	16–18
Guarantee	56
Handlebar, Controls and Cables	22
Legshields	50
Mudguard—Front, and number plate	26
" —Rear	36
Oil Cleaner, Non-Return Valve, Oil Feed Pipes	12
Panniers	50
Petrol Tank	26
Pillion Footrests	32
Piston, Connecting Rod & Crankshaft	6
Primary Chaincase, etc.	14
Rocker Assembly	4
Shakeproof Washers. To avoid unnecessary repetition, these are listed separately.	36
Silencer	32
Speedometer	40
Stand, Centre	34
Terms of Business	3
Toolbox and Tools	38
Wheel and Brake, Front	28
" " " Rear (Q.D.)	30
1962 Supplement	57

The letter C or S in the "Description" column, indicates that the part is used only on the "Crusader 250" or "Sports" model, respectively.

TERMS OF BUSINESS

All prices of Spare and Replacement Parts are subject to revision or modification, at our discretion, without notice.

Our terms are STRICTLY NET CASH WITH ORDER, or cash on receipt of PRO-FORMA INVOICE. Repairs and sundries items cannot be booked. Prices do not include cost of carriage or postage which will be covered by a percentage surcharge on the nett invoice value. C.O.D. fees and the cost of packing cases or crates are additional to the fixed surcharge.

Any part or complete motor cycle sent for repair should be consigned CARRIAGE PAID and the sender's name and address should be given in full on the address tally. Parts sent to us carriage forward are liable to be refused, and to lie with the carriers at sender's risk and expense.

Full instructions regarding the necessary repairs to be done, with advice as to the mode of despatch of the machine (or part), should be posted the same day.

When forwarding motor cycles for repair it is advisable to remove all accessories and easily detached fittings, such as badges, mascots, tools, tyre inflator, etc. Besides facilitating the work of repair, it will also prevent any loss during transit.

Order all parts by the name of the article and the No. of Part, also state the number of the engine or machine for which they are intended. The engine number will be found stamped on the driving side of the crankcase below the cylinder barrel and the machine number at the top of the front down tube or head lug.

ESTIMATES AND QUOTATIONS

When customers send complete Motor Cycles or parts thereof to us for repairs, we are always prepared to furnish estimates before proceeding with the necessary work. At the same time, it must be distinctly understood that we can only give approximate quotations. Frequently, when the actual work is in progress, it is found necessary to replace parts other than those specified in the estimate, as we make a practice of including in such estimates only those items and parts which at the time we consider really essential to put the machine (or parts) in a thoroughly satisfactory condition.

If any estimate prepared in this way is not accepted, we reserve the right to make a charge for taking down and re-assembling any parts necessary in preparing it.

We cannot hold ourselves responsible for loss of, or damage to, any parts lying at our Works for repairs, unless instructions to proceed with same are given within twenty-one days of our estimate for the said repairs having been rendered.

All welded repairs to crankcases and other aluminium parts are carried out with extreme care, but we cannot give any guarantee with or accept responsibility for, any parts so treated.

When forwarding a complete Motor Cycle, Engine, or other Assembly with the request that we overhaul the same, we understand by the term "Overhaul" that it is to be entirely dismantled, thoroughly renovated, any worn parts renewed, and put in perfect working order. In case a customer desires only certain parts attended to, full instructions should be given to that effect, otherwise the cost may be in excess of that anticipated.

GUARANTEE

We respectfully refer customers to the terms of guarantee on page 56.

ENGINE AND CYLINDER HEAD

Illus. No.	No. of part.	Description.		No. per set
	‡45271	Engine/Gearbox c/w alternator, contact breaker, carburettor, and gearbox—Alloy head	C	1
	45723	Engine unit, as above—Alloy head	S	1
1	‡45691	Cylinder head Alloy c/w valve guides and studs	C	1
	45693	" " " " " " " "	S	1
2	45701	" " " gasket		1
3	‡35892	Valve, exhaust (for Alloy head)	C	1
4	39156	" inlet	C	1
	44766	" exhaust	S	1
	44765	" Inlet	S	1
5	‡25524	" guide (inlet)—for Alloy head		1
5A	‡44045	" " (exhaust)—for Alloy head		1
6	39659	Valve spring, inner	C	2
7	39660	" " outer	C	2
8	35238	" " collar, top	C	2
9	83508	" " " bottom	C	2
10	11099	" split collar	C	2
11	10672	" stem cap	C	2
	42693	" spring, inner	S	2
	42692	" " outer	S	2
	42651	" " collar, top	S	2
	42652	" " " bottom	S	2
	42492	" split collar	S	2
12	45233	Rocker Housing		1
13	13601	" " stud		4
13A	27305	" " nut		4
14	45351	" spindle		2
15	45349	" arm (push rod end)		2
16	45350	" " (valve end)		2
17	45249	" spindle spring washer		2
18	3570	" " nut		4
19	4501	" " washer		4
	9908	" " washer		4
20	45800	Cylinder head cover		1
21	38872	" " " joint washer		1
22	45648	" " " stud		1
23	45801	" " " " nut		1
24	1846	" " " " washer		1
25	35470	Carburettor flange stud	C	2
	36226	" " "	S	2
26	27001	" " " nut		2
27	44026	Cylinder head alloy screw, $\frac{1}{4}'' \times 2''$ o'all. B.S.F.		2
	44996	Carburettor distance piece	S	1
29	39346	Cylinder head stud (long)		4
30	33036	" " " nut		4
31	5975	" " " washer		4
32	39345	" " stud (short)		1
33	27621	" " " nut		1
34	8634	" " " washer		1
35	45275	Cylinder barrel		1
36	39037	" base gasket		1
37	F192	" head locknut		1

‡ Except "Crusader 250" Airflow.

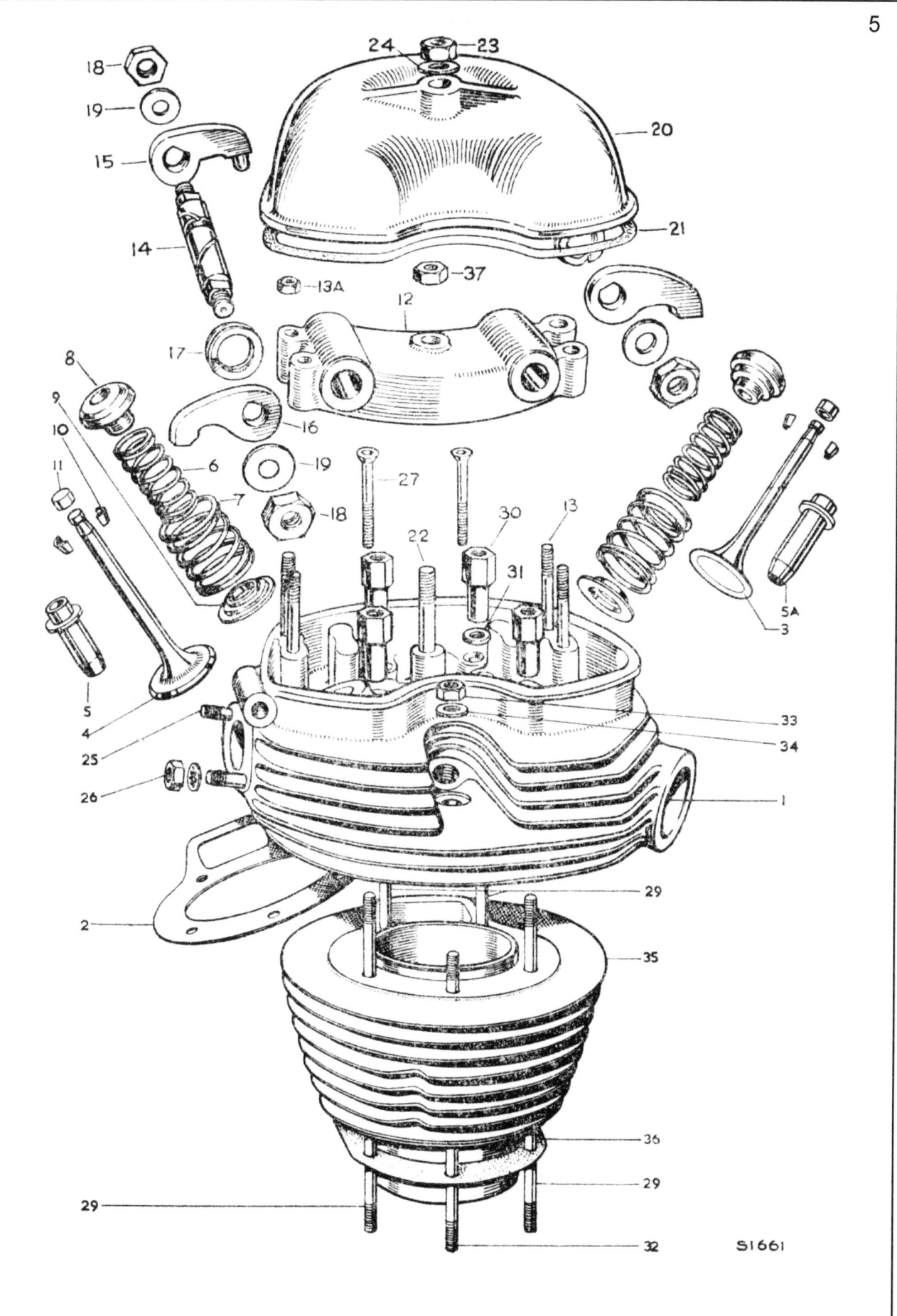

PISTON, CONNECTING ROD & CRANKSHAFT

Illus. No.	No. of part.	Description.	No. per set
1	*43273‡	Piston c/w rings, gudgeon pin, and circlips 8.3:1 C.R.	1
2	*38772	" ring (top compression, chrome plated)	1
3	*38773	" " (lower compression)	1
4	*38774	" " (scraper)	1
5	38770	Gudgeon pin	1
6	38771	" " circlip	2
7	§39358	Connecting rod assy. c/w bolts and B.E. shells	1
8	34056	" " B.E. bolt	2
9	35131	" " " " locating pin	2
10	35130	" " " " nut	2
11	42443	" " " " washer	2
12	30779	" " " " split pin	2
	36017	" " S.E. bush (for Service replacement rods only)	1
13	§39014	" " B.E. bearing shell (one half)	2
14	†44770	Crankshaft c/w oil feed stud & oil plugs	1
16	44649	" oil passage plug	2
17	41831A	" stud (oil feed)	1
	41832	" plug	1
19	42359	" rotor attachment stud	1
20	‡45247	Push rod c/w ends, with alloy head	2
22	45245	" " end (top)	2
23	‡38132	" " " (bottom)	2
24	39160	" " adjusting screw	2
25	34399	" " " " locknut	2
26	39035	Crankshaft distance piece	2
27	41816	" sleeve	1
28	39036	Engine sprocket, 23 teeth	1
29	36852	" " washer	1
30	36853	Timing sprocket, 14 teeth	1
31	5025	" " washer	1
32	DE390	" " nut	1

* Pistons and piston rings are available .020" and .040" oversize. To order, suffix /20 or /40 to the part number. Thus **43273/20**, piston complete .020" oversize.

§ Service replacement Conn. Rod Assys. are available fitted with B.E. bearing shells, .010", .020" undersize to suit crankshafts ground down to these sizes. These rods may also have bronze S.E. bushes. Part numbers of these rods are **39358S/10** and **39358S/20**, respectively. Part numbers of undersize B.E bearing shells only, are **39014/10** and **39014/20**, respectively.

† Service crankshafts are available .010" and .020", undersize on the B.E. journal and are numbered **44770/10** and **44770/20**, respectively.

‡ Except "Crusader 250" Airflow.

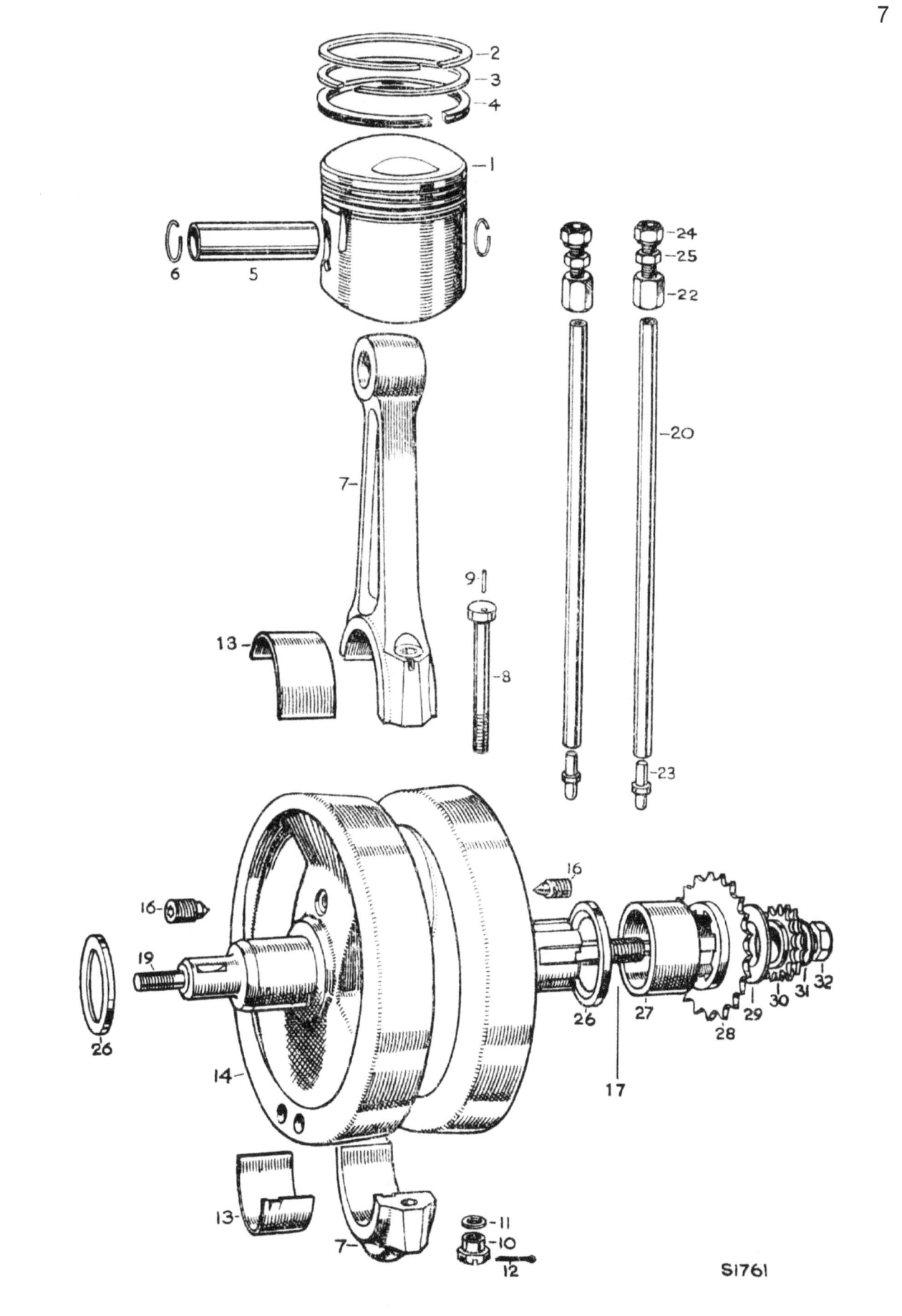

CRANKCASE

Illus. No.	No. of part.	Description.	No. per set
1	44776A	Crankcase assy. with main camshaft and gearbox bearings, oil seals, oil filler collar, fixed studs and dowels.	1
2	SK/6207	Crankshaft bearing, ball, L.H. 35 × 72 × 17mm.	1
3	39353	" " circlip	1
4	SK/N207	" " roller, R.H. 35 × 72 × 17mm.	1
5	41834	" seal, R.H.	1
6	39042	Camshaft bush (short)	1
7	39041	Cam follower spindle	1
8	39144	Idler pinion spindle	1
9	39145	Contact breaker spindle bush	2
10	42010	" " oil seal	1
11	39987	Oil filler collar	1
12	41462	Cored hole cover	1
13	38670	" " " gasket	1
14	28858	" " " screw	4
15	36911	Primary chain tensioner spindle	1
16	41306	Timing chain tensioner stud, $\frac{1}{4}''$ B.S.F. × $1\frac{5}{8}''$	2
17	31166	Cam housing cover stud, $\frac{1}{4}''$ B.S.F. × $\frac{15}{16}''$	5
18	37128	Oil cleaner stud, $\frac{3}{8}''$ B.S.F. × $5\frac{11}{16}''$	1
19	39354	Crankcase stud (front) $\frac{1}{4}''$ B.S.F. × $2\frac{1}{4}''$	1
20	35799	" " (top) $\frac{1}{4}''$ B.S.F. × $3\frac{7}{8}''$	2
21	34714	" " (bottom, rear) $\frac{1}{4}''$ B.S.F. × $4\frac{1}{16}''$	1
22	34370	Gearbox stud $\frac{1}{4}''$ B.S.F. × $4\frac{7}{16}''$	3
23	40064	" " (top) $\frac{1}{4}''$ B.S.F. × $1\frac{7}{16}''$	1
24	37125	" " (bottom) $\frac{1}{4}''$ B.S.F. × $1\frac{7}{16}''$	1
25	34174	Generator stud $\frac{1}{4}''$ B.S.F. × $1\frac{11}{16}''$	3
26	26709	Crankcase dowel	2
27	39355	Gearbox cover dowel	2
28	39370	Crankcase stud (rear—"loose") $\frac{3}{8}''$ B.S.F. × $8\frac{3}{16}''$	1
29	28804	" " (bottom—"loose") $\frac{3}{8}''$ C.E.I. × $5''$	2
30	39371	" " (bottom—"loose") $\frac{1}{4}''$ B.S.F. × $4\frac{3}{8}''$	2
31	39372	" " (inside—"loose") $\frac{1}{4}''$ B.S.F. × $6\frac{7}{16}''$	1
32	44882	" " (Ft. engine plate) $\frac{5}{16}''$ B.S.F. × $3\frac{7}{8}''$	2
	37121	" " (Ft. engine plate) $\frac{5}{16}''$ B.S.F. × $4''$	1
	29854	" " nut $\frac{3}{8}''$ C.E.I. × $\frac{5}{16}''$	4
	27621	" " nut $\frac{5}{16}''$ B.S.F. × $\frac{5}{16}''$	6
	27620	" " nut $\frac{1}{4}''$ B.S.F. × $\frac{1}{4}''$	10
	82	" " washer	10
33	39613	Distance piece (rear c/case stud)	1
34	39291	Engine attachment nut (rear, R.H.)	1
35	45210	" " " (rear, L.H.)	1
36	39290	Rear chain inspection cover	1
37	37104	" " " " screw	2
38	44889	Breather body	1
39	39880	" " backplate	1
40	39892	" " gasket	1
	26648	" " screw, $\frac{3}{16}'' \times \frac{11}{16}''$	2
	26664	" " " $\frac{3}{16}'' \times \frac{3}{8}''$	1
41	39879	" disc valve	2

CRANKCASE — LEFT HAND SIDE INNER FACE

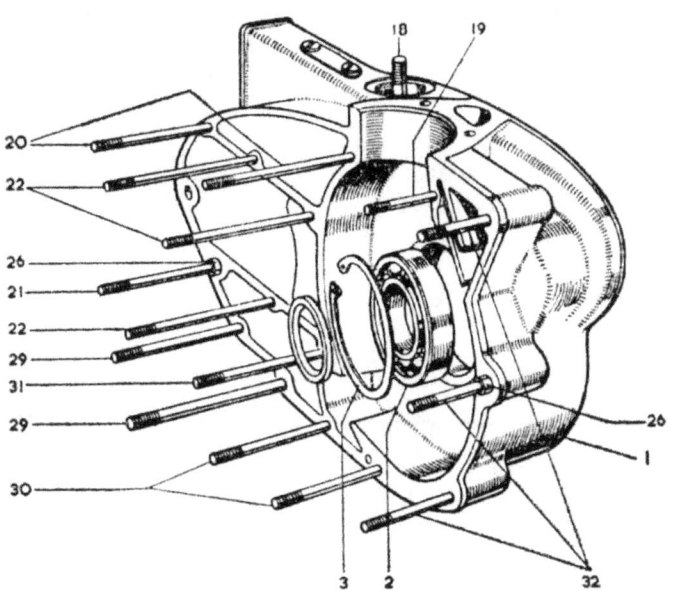

CRANKCASE — LEFT HAND SIDE OUTER FACE

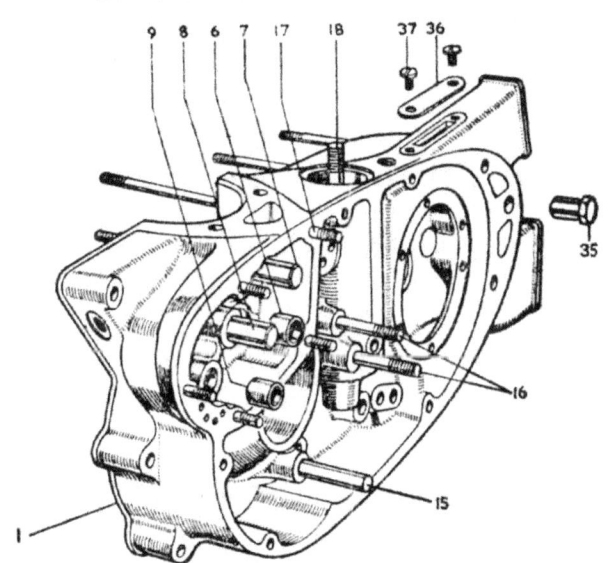

CRANKCASE — RIGHT HAND SIDE

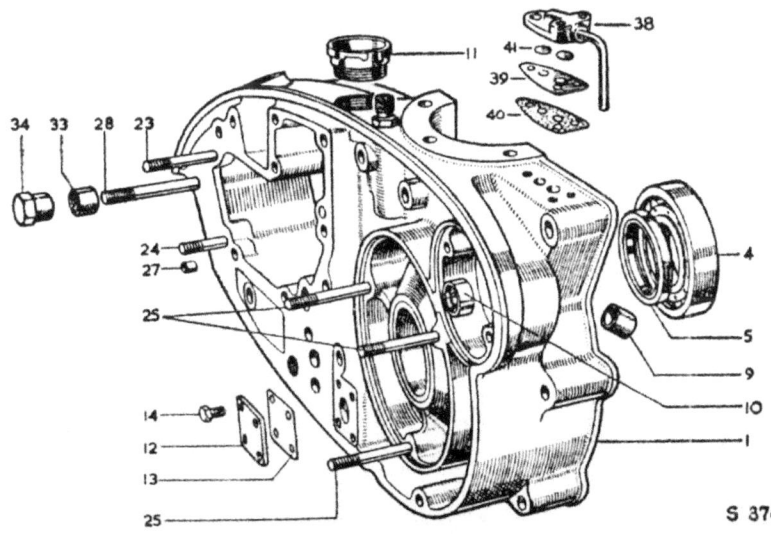

S 3760

CAMSHAFT, OIL PUMP, ETC.

Illus. No.	No. of part.	Description.		No. per set
1	43753	Cam housing cover c/w camshaft bush		1
2	39043	Camshaft bush (long)		1
3	45209	Cam housing cover nut (extended)		2
4	27622	" " " " 1/4" BSF × 3/16"		3
	39360	Camshaft c/w pinion	C	1
6	38695	" only	C	1
	44772	" c/w pinion	S	1
	44773	" only	S	1
7	39141	" pinion		1
8	39142	" " dowel		1
8A	42506	" thrust washer		1
9	39104	" sprocket, 28 teeth		1
10	9410	" " key		1
11	DE627	" " nut		1
12	15641	" " washer		1
13	39143	Idler pinion		1
	39361	Contact breaker and oil pump spindle c/w pinion.		1
14	39151	" " " " " " only		1
15	39141	" " " " " " pinion		1
16	39142	" " " " " " " dowel		1
17	23701	Oil pump plunger (feed—1/8" dia)		1
18	13905	" " " (return—5/16" dia)		1
19	43716	" " disc		1
20	41851	" " " spring		1
21	37669	" " " " end pad		1
22	39101	" " cover		1
23	39102	" " " gasket		1
24	27196	" " " screw		5
25	45247	Cam follower, inlet		1
26	45273	" " exhaust		1
27	36867	" " thrust washer		2
28	35904	" " spring		1

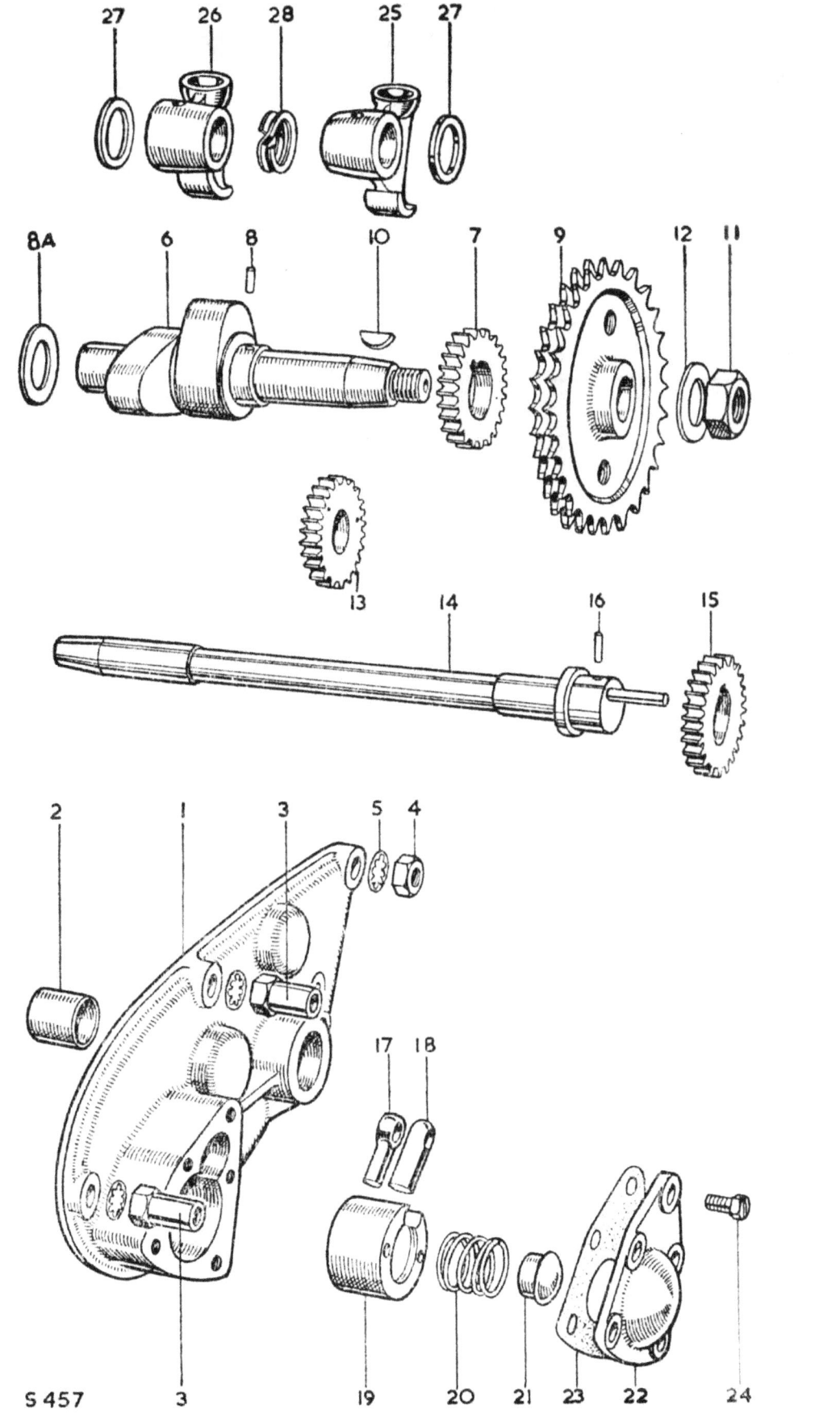

OIL CLEANER, NON-RETURN VALVE, AND OIL FEED PIPES

Illus. No.	No. of part.	Description.	No. per set
1	40792	Oil cleaner element	1
2	43312	" " spring cup	1
3	18793	" " felt washer	1
4	28259	" " spring	1
5	8894	" " " thrust washer	1
6	42281A	" " cap	1
7	39171	" " " washer	1
8	43773	" " " nut	1
9	9732	" " " " washer	1
10	22198	Non-return valve plug	1
11	22199	" " " spring	1
12	32017	" " " ball	1
19	42361A	Oil filler cap	1
20	26472	" drain plug	1
21	9732	" " " washer	1
22	44425	" plug screw	1
23	30394	" " " washer	1
24	39362	Rocker oil feed pipe, complete	1
25	29079	Oil pipe nipple	1
26	29066	" " union nut	1
27	32388	" " banjo	1
28	39152	" " " (double-ended)	1
29	29065	" " union (c/case)	1
30	36032	" " " (cylinder head)	2
31	39469	" " " washer	4
	38621	" " " wire (in Alloy head)	2
32	39365	Oil feed and return pipe, complete (c/case)	1
33	39168	Oil pipe connection (oil pump)	1
34	39169	" " " (double)	1
35	39170	" " " (single)	2
36	39383	" " " screw, $\frac{1}{4}'' \times \frac{3}{4}'' \times 26$ (B.S.F.)	8
37	27916	" " " washer	8
38	43435	" " " gasket (pump)	1
39	43436	" " " " (double)	1
40	43437	" " " " (single)	2

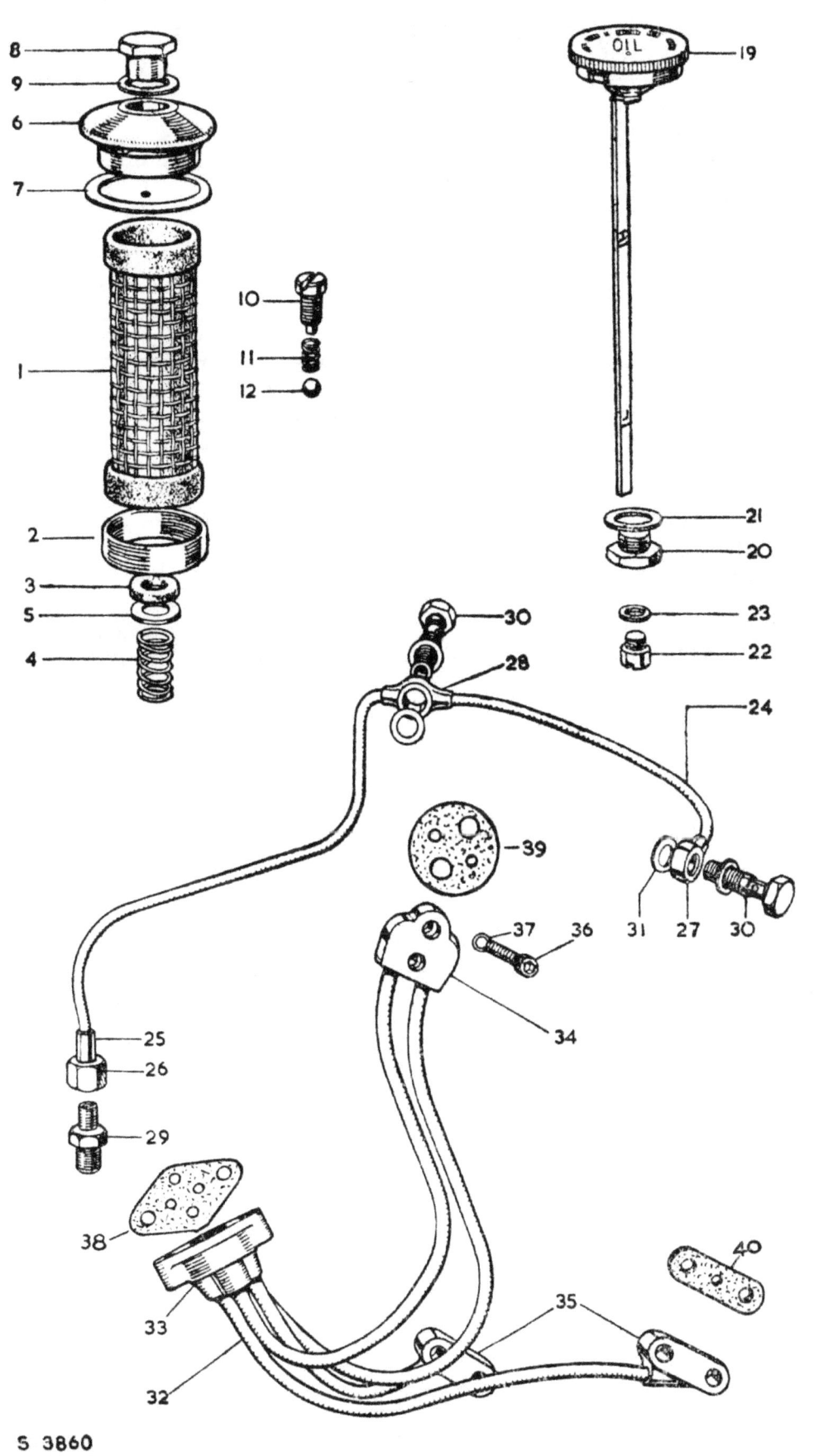

PRIMARY CHAINCASE, CHAINS, TENSIONERS AND GENERATOR COVER.

Illus. No.	No. of part.	Description.	No. per set
1	45074	Primary chaincase.	1
	43469	″ ″ gasket	1
2	39355	″ ″ dowel	1
3	42134	″ ″ screw $\frac{1}{4}'' \times \frac{3}{4}'' \times 26$ (B.S.F.)	2
4	42140	″ ″ ″ $\frac{1}{4}'' \times 1\frac{5}{8}'' \times 26$ (B.S.F.)	6
5	42137	″ ″ ″ $\frac{1}{4}'' \times 1\frac{1}{2}'' \times 26$ (B.S.F.)	2
6	40640	″ ″ inspection plug	1
7	40641	″ ″ ″ ″ washer	1
8	43466	″ ″ back cover	1
9	42503	″ ″ ″ ″ gasket	1
10	43584	″ ″ ″ ″ oil seal	1
11	39375	″ ″ ″ ″ screw	6
	RN/110038/70	Primary chain .375″P × .225″wide × 70 pitches	1
13	36910	″ ″ tensioner pad	1
14	39482	″ ″ ″ spring	1
15	32404	″ ″ ″ adjusting screw	1
16	15771	″ ″ ″ ″ ″ locknut	1
	RN/114500/38	Timing chain 8mm.P × .340″ wide duplex × 38 pitches	1
17	41302	″ ″ tensioner	1
18	40062	″ ″ ″ distance piece	2
19	40063	″ ″ ″ serrated washer	1
20	27620	″ ″ ″ nut	2
21	27916	″ ″ ″ washer	2
22	42192	Crankshaft oil feed seal	1
23	28858	Oil plug screw	1
24	41815	Oil feed tube	1
25	41814	″ ″ ″ washer (rubber)	1
26	38858	Generator cover	1
27	42137	″ ″ screw $\frac{1}{4}'' \times 1\frac{1}{2}'' \times 26$ (B.S.F.)	3
28	42140	″ ″ ″ $\frac{1}{4}'' \times 1\frac{5}{8}'' \times 26$ (B.S.F.)	1
29	45666	Gearbox oil level screw	1
	ST41	Gasket set, decarbonisation only C	1
	ST223	″ ″ complete engine/gearbox unit C	1
	ST228	″ ″ decarbonisation only S	1
	ST229	″ ″ complete engine/gearbox unit S	1

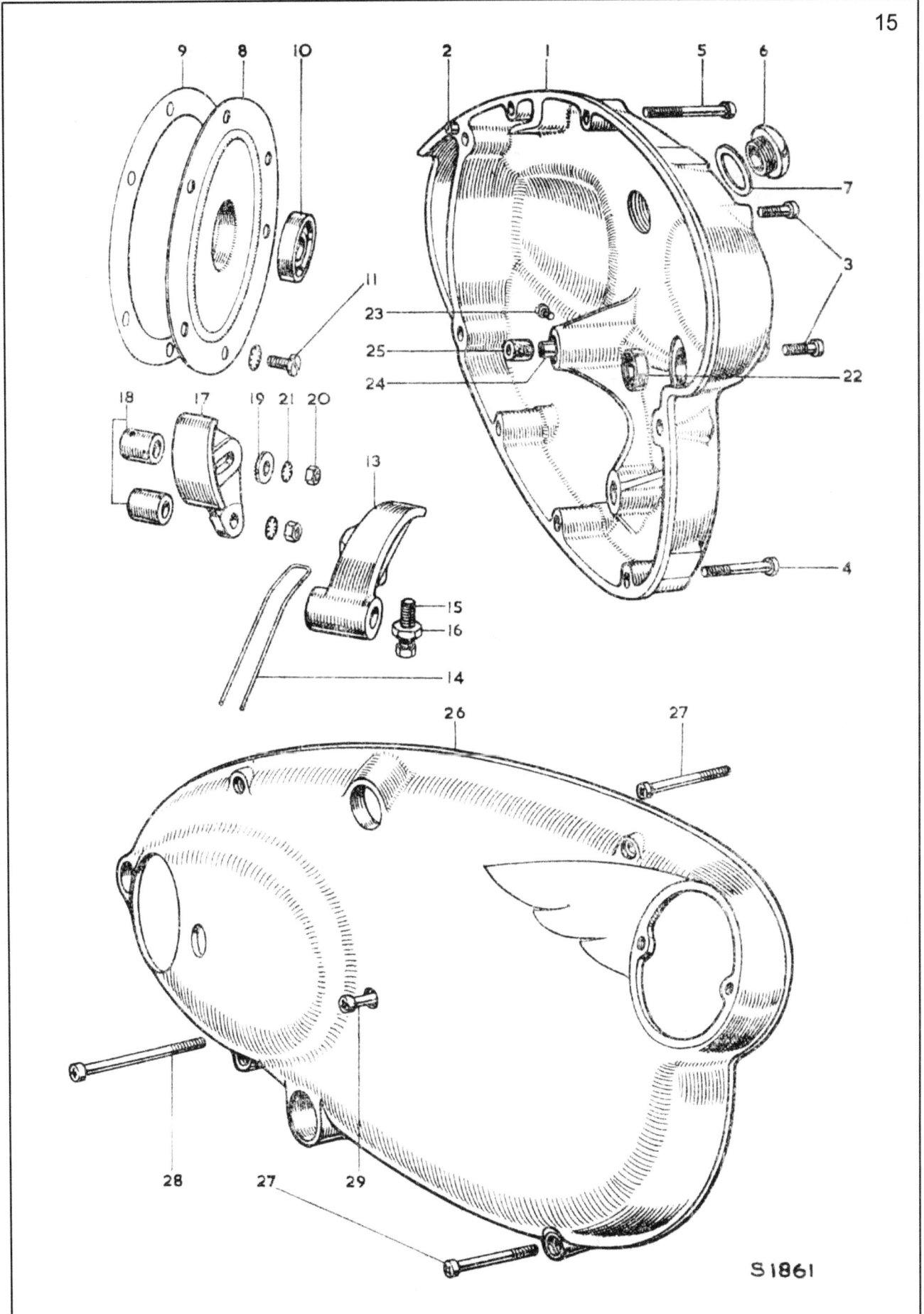

GEAR BOX

Illus. No.	No. of part.	Description.	No. per set
1	39388	Gearbox cover, complete	1
	43949	" " gasket	1
2	27620	" " nut	4
	27622	" " nut	1
3	82	" " " washer	5
4	37707	" " screw	2
5	27916	" " " washer	2
6	35763	" filler plug	1
7	26472	" drain plug	1
8	9732	" filler or drain plug washer	2
9	39214	Mainshaft	1
10	SK/401524	" ball race (large) $2\frac{1}{4}'' \times 1'' \times \frac{5}{8}''$	1
11	HJ3	" oil seal	1
	42508	" " " shim	1
12	HJ4	" dished washer	1
13	SK/6202	" ball race (small) $35 \times 15 \times 11$ mm.	1
14	ST109	" oil thrower	1
15	ST115	" nut (k/starter end, L.H. thread)	1
16	39213	" sleeve	1
17	ST111	" high gear, 15 teeth	1
18	HJ11/21/17	" sliding gear, 21 teeth and 17 teeth	1
19	ST113	" low gear, 26 teeth	1
20	ST117	Layshaft	1
21	ST118	" bush (in case)	1
22	ST120	" washer	1
23	ST121	" low gear, 16 teeth	1
24	ST122	" second gear, 21 teeth	1
25	ST123	" third gear, 24 teeth	1
26	ST124	" high gear and k/starter wheel, 27 teeth	1
27	39215	Kickstarter shaft	1
28	HJ6	" " oil seal ring	1
29	39224	" bush (outer, in cover)	1
30	ST119	" " (inner, layshaft)	1
31	ST126	" pawl	1
32	ST127	" " plunger	1
33	ST128	" " " spring	1
34	ST129	" " stop plate	1
35	ST130	" " " " locating pin	1
36	39937	" return spring	1
37	ST133	" " " cover	1
38	44909	" crank (folding)	1
39	H43/S	" crank pinch bolt and nut	1
40	42691	" " rubber	1
41	HJ21A	" " distance tube	1
42	39185	Gearbox bearing cap	1
43	39382A	" " " screw $\frac{1}{4}'' \times 1\frac{3}{8}'' \times 26$ (B.S.F.)	1
44	39383	" " " " $\frac{1}{4}'' \times \frac{3}{4}'' \times 26$ (B.S.F.)	1
45	HJ33	Gear operator (inside)	1
46	39203	" " fork	1
47	39227	" " anchor pin	1
48	H61A	" " locating plunger box assembly	1

17

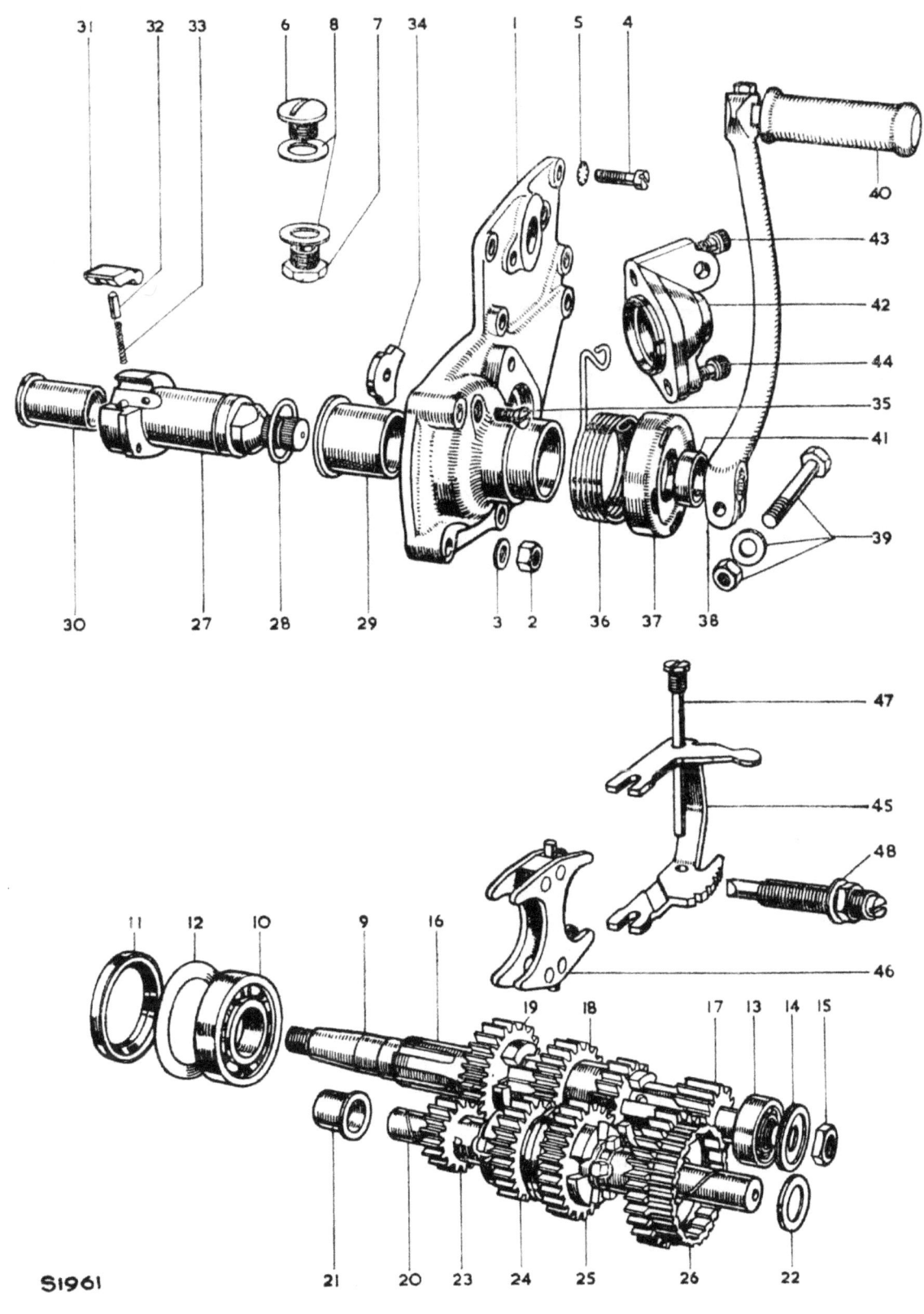

S1961

GEAR BOX—Contd.

Illus. No.	No. of part.	Description.	No. per set
1	39202	Gear change operator bush	1
2	6716	" " " " screw	2
3	39226	" " operator shaft with lever	1
4	39240	" " adjuster plate	1
5	35452	" " " " screw	1
6	30791	" " " " washer	1
7	39242	" " ratchet	1
8	42759	" " operator spring	1
9	39246	" indicator	1
10	42763	" " sleeve	1
11	42774	" " screw	1
12	15641	" " washer	1
	39277	Gear change pawl carrier complete	1
13	39243	" " " " plate, inner	1
13A	42916	" " " " " outer	1
14	39241	" " pawl	2
15	43206	" " " peg	2
16	39244	" " " and link sleeve	3
17	39245	" " " " " rivet	3
18	39252	" " pawl return spring	1
19	39276	" " link	1
20	39266	" " eye bolt	1
21	39275	" " adjusting nut	1
22	7367	" " " locknut, R.H. thread	1
23	40065	" " " " L.H. thread	1
24	39265	" " lever, complete	1
25	39260	" " " spring post	1
26	39261	" " " peg	1
27	41929	" " " " spring clip	1
28	39263	" " stop	2
29	39264	" " centring screw	1
30	39253	" " return spring	1
31	39258	" " lever fulcrum pin	1
32	7914	" " " " " washer	1
33	TC/PZ65	" " " " " grease nipple	1
34	29854	Gear change lever fulcrum pin nut	1
35	15641	" " " " " washer	1
36	39278	" " pedal C	1
	44908	" " pedal S	1
37	43274	" " " clip screw	1
38	G46/FC	" " " rubber	1
39	43234	Final drive sprocket, 17 teeth	1
40	43467	" " " nut	1
41	HJ122	" " " " felt washer	1
42	H51B	" " " locking screw	1

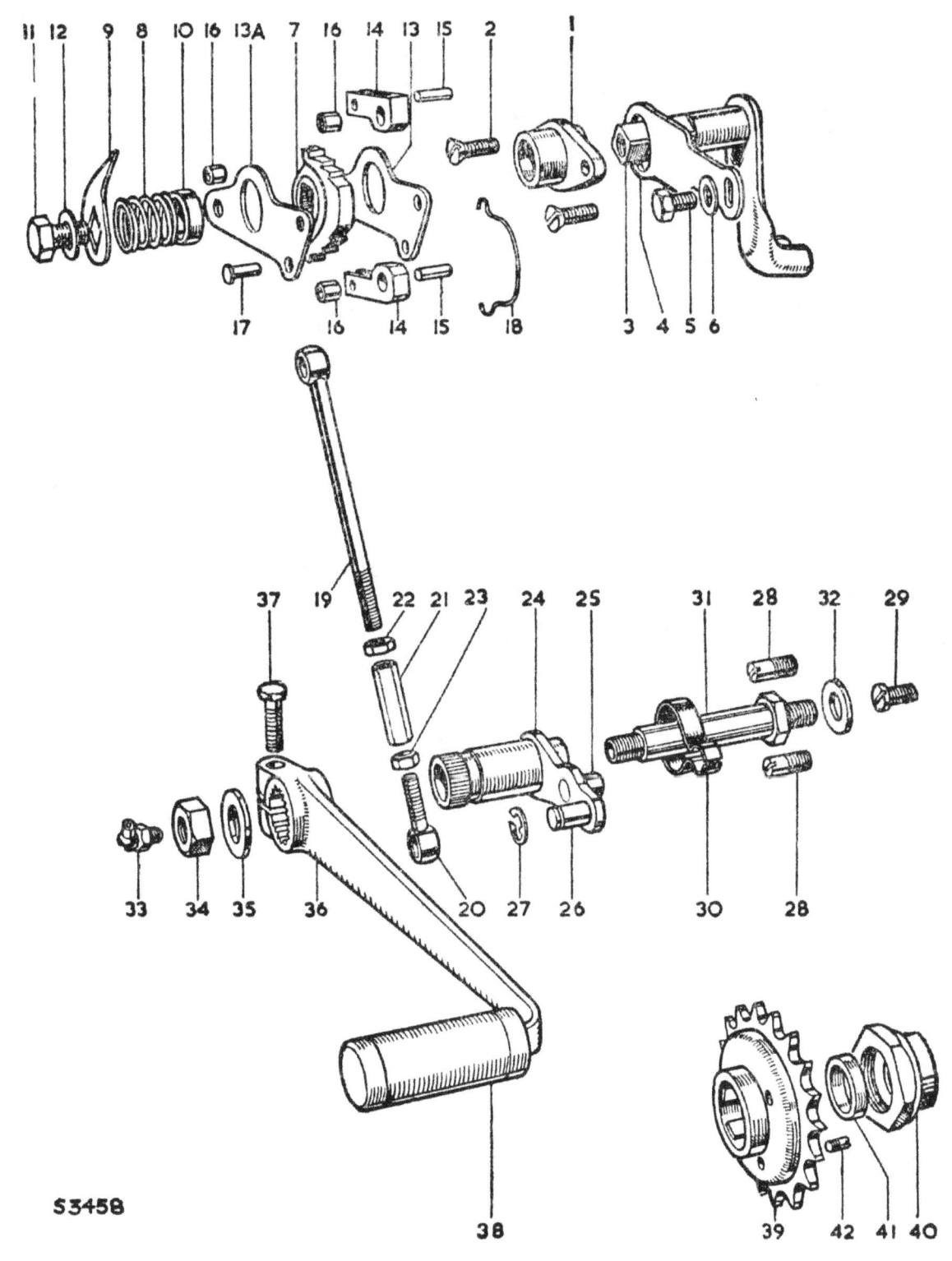

CLUTCH

Illus. No.	No. of part.	Description.	No. per set
	43486	Clutch assembly	1
1	43487	″ centre, complete	1
	43490	″ sprocket 49T. & drum assy.	1
2	43491	″ sprocket	1
3	39308	″ ″ friction plate	2
4	39306	″ ″ ″ ″ rivet	7
5	37057	″ ″ ball cage	2
6	43153	″ ″ ″ ″ rivet	10
7	32017	″ ″ balls	48
8	39305	″ ″ retaining circlip	1
9	39318	″ intermediate plate, dished	2
10	39319	″ ″ ″ plain	1
11	39332	″ plate with inserts	3
12	G67/2	″ ″ insert	60
13	39335	″ ″ retaining washer	1
14	43498	″ front plate	1
15	ST181	″ spring	3
16	39340	″ ″ retaining plate	1
17	48492	″ ″ distance tube	3
18	G80	″ ″ screw	3
19	B.S.30	″ centre key	1
20	31508	″ ″ nut	1
21	39298	″ ″ locking washer	1
22	HJ66B	″ operating pad	1
23	39334	″ ″ rod, $\frac{3}{16}$″ dia. × $7\frac{9}{16}$″ long	1
24	39285	Clutch adjuster body	1
25	32019	″ ″ ball	1
26	37097	″ adjusting screw	1
27	39384	″ ″ ″ washer	1
28	37005	″ ″ ″ locknut	1
29	39284	″ operating lever	1
30	39385	″ ″ ″ pivot pin	1
31	43124	″ ″ ″ ″ ″ locknut	1

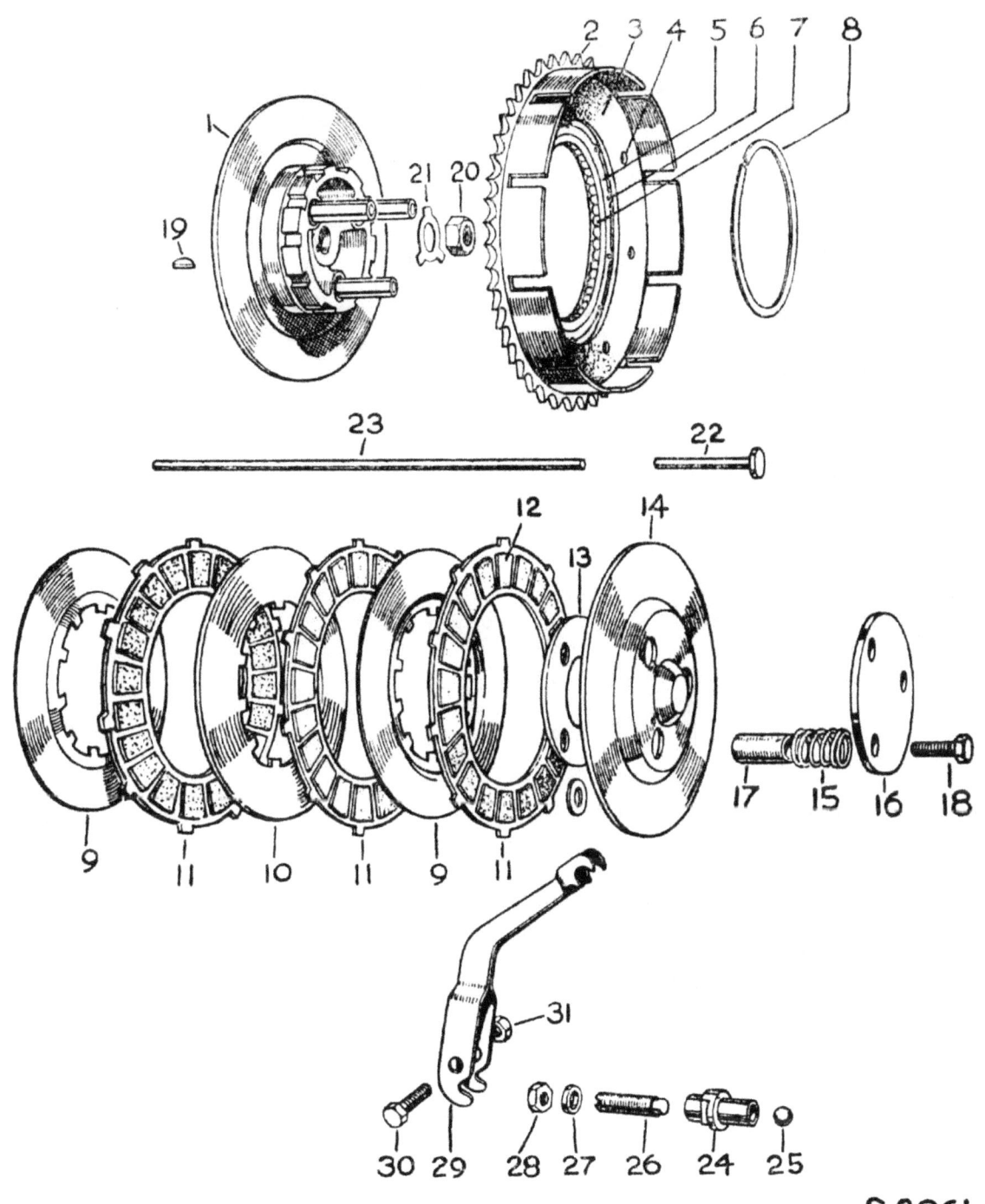

HANDLEBAR, CONTROLS AND CABLES

Illus. No.	No. of part.	Description.		No. per set
	44866	Handlebar c/w controls less cables	C	1
	44867	" " " " cables	S	1
1	40835	" bend only	C	1
	44780	" " "	S	1
	DH/107PA/LH	Clutch control assy.		1
2	DH/1078	" " body		1
3	DH/1008	" " " clip		1
4	DH/1009	" " " " screw		2
5	DH/2071	" " adjuster		1
6	DH/2072	" " " nut		1
7	DH/1070LH	" lever		1
8	DH/5066	" " pivot pin		1
8A	DH/1102	" " " " nut		1
	DH/100/7PA/RH	Brake/Air control assy.		1
9	DH/5000	" " " body screw		2
10	DH/1077RH	Brake control body		1
5	DH/2071	" " adjuster		1
6	DH/2072	" " " nut		1
11	DH/1070RH	" lever		1
12	DH/5066	" " pivot pin		1
12A	DH/1102	" " " " nut		1
13	DH/1001RH	Air control body		1
14	DH/1002RH	" lever		1
15	DH/1005	" " cap		1
16	DH/1006	" " " screw		1
17	DH/1007	" " spring washer		1
	DH/71	Twist grip complete		1
18	DH/711	Rotor		1
19	DH/619	" rubber		1
20	DH/612	Body, top half		1
21	DH/613	" bottom half		1
22	DH/617	" fixing screw		2
23	DH/616	Friction spring		1
24	DH/614	" " screw		1
25	DH/615	" " " locknut		1
26	DH/618	Cable stop		1
27	DH/U4	Dummy grip, rubber		1
30	44891	Clutch cable assembly		1
31	DH/J	" " nipple, handlebar end		1
32	40425	" " " gearbox end		1
33	39286	" " adjusting screw		1
34	39288	" " " " body		1
35	J.195	" " " " locknut		1
36	39289	" " adjuster plastic cover		1
37	39287	" " shouldered ferrule		1
38	40596	" " grommet		1

Control Cables continued on page 28

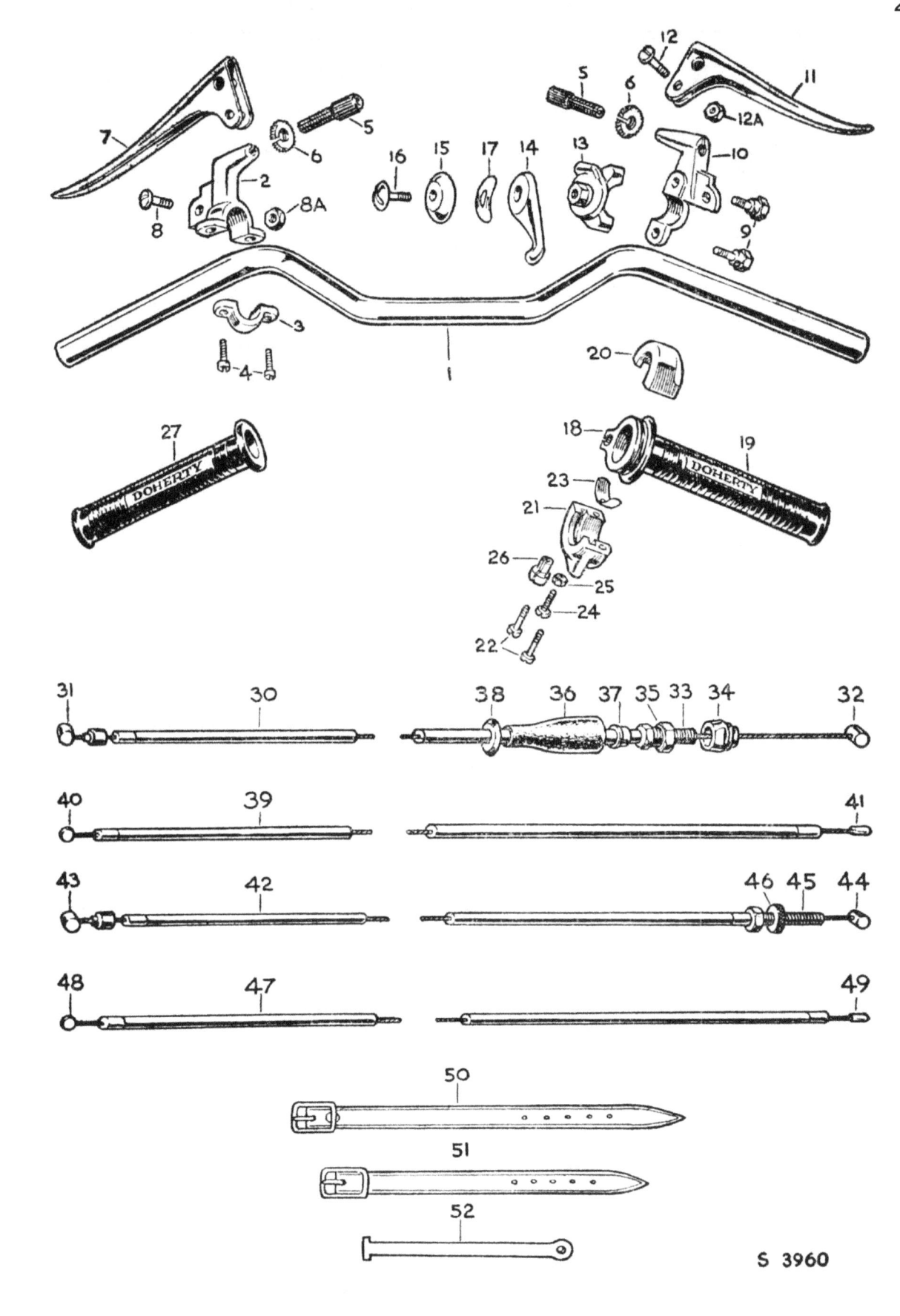

TELESCOPIC FRONT FORK

Illus. No.	No. of part.	Description.	No. per set
	‡45727	Front fork assembly c/w steering stem	1
	‡45728	Steering stem c/w dust covers	1
1	‡39433	" " less dust covers	1
2	39769	" " dust cover only	2
3	‡43600	" " locknut	1
4	36095	" " " washer	1
5	‡45752	Headlamp casing c/w ball race and h'bar clip studs	1
6	‡38888	" " clip bolt	1
7	‡38886	" " " " sleeve (tapped)	1
8	‡38887	" " " " " (plain)	1
	‡45675	" " rubber plug	1
9	‡39038	Fork crown clip bolt	2
11	27944	" " " " nut	2
12	27248	Ball race (fork head)	1
13	27249	" " (crown)	1
14	31302	" " (frame)	2
15	31955	" " cover (bottom head lug race)	1
16	32018	Ball, $\frac{1}{4}$" dia.	38
17	‡42910	Handlebar clip	1
20	‡43004	" " stud $\frac{5}{16}$" × $1\frac{1}{4}$" B.S.F.	4
	DE110	" " " nut	4
23	‡39723	Main tube (fixed)	2
24	39784	Bottom fork leg c/w cap, assy. R.H.	1
25	39783	" " " " " " L.H.	1
26	38063	" " " " cap stud (short) $\frac{5}{16}$" BSF × $1\frac{5}{8}$"	2
27	39762	" " " " " (long)	2
28	34705	" " " " " nut	4
30	32405	" " " oil level screw	2
31	30394	" " " " " " washer	2
32	39770	Fork spring	2
33	39763	" " guide tube (bottom)	2
34	‡41215	" " tube (top)	2
35	45647	" " end screw (top)	2
36	38844	" cover tube bush	2
37	38877	" " " rubber washer	2
38	43604	" crown cover plate	1
40	‡39711	Licence holder bracket	1
41	‡14447	" " " pin	1
42	‡27001	" " " nut	1
	44057	Steering stop block	1
	39002	" " washer (round)	1
	7201	" " pin	1

‡Except "Airflow" models

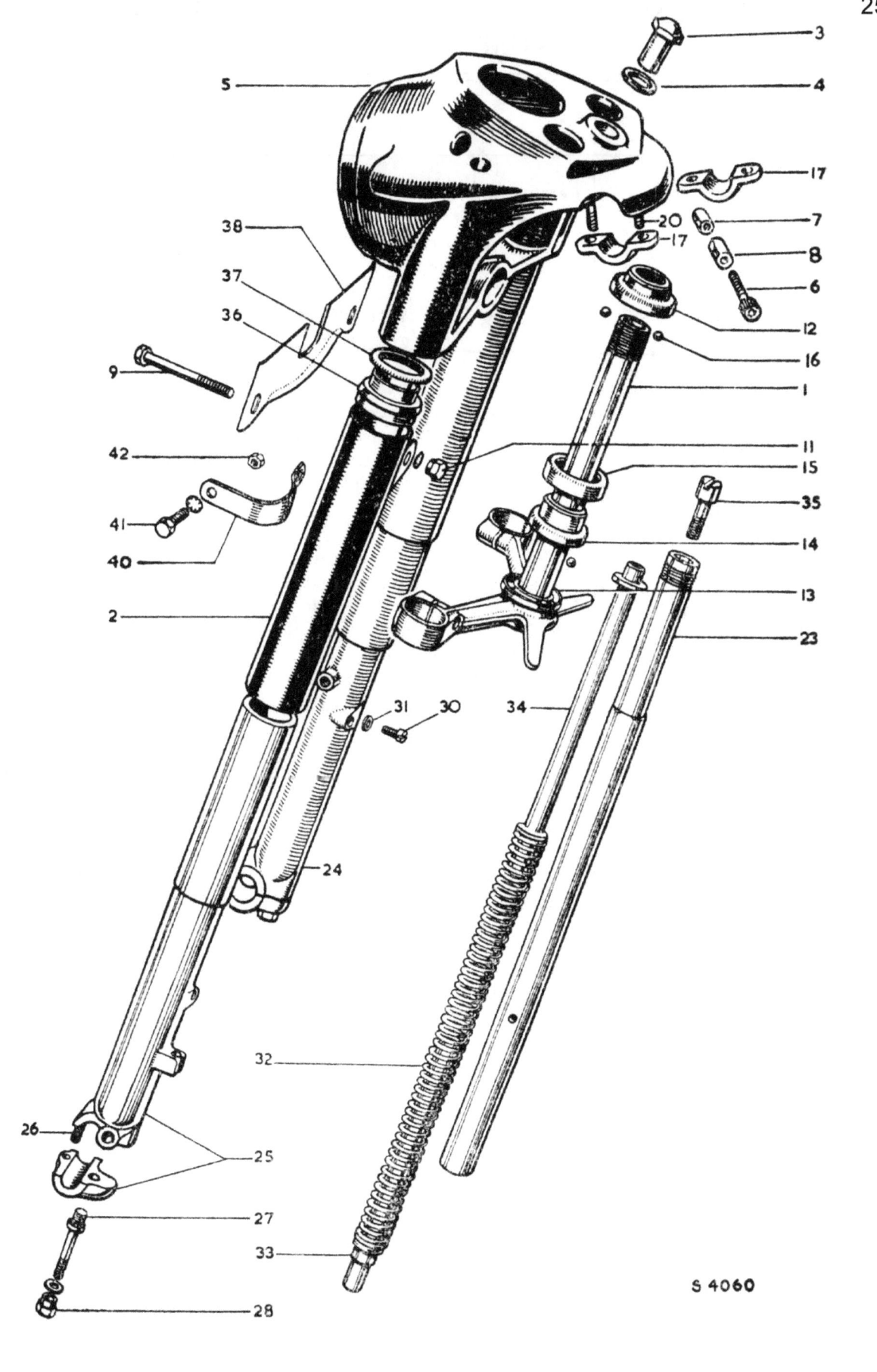

PETROL TANK, FRONT MUDGUARD AND NUMBER PLATE

Illus. No.	No. of part.	Description.		No. per set
	45730	Petrol tank c/w knee grips, badges, tap etc	S	1
	45733	" " " " " " " "	C	1
1	45631	" " only (enamel Crusader, chrome Sports)		1
5	41352	" " badge		2
6	41307	" " " rubber mounting		2
7	42195	" " " screw		4
8	41522	" " knee grip R.H.		1
	41521	" " " " L.H.		1
9	15941	" " filler cap		1
10	25336	" " stud (front) $\frac{3}{8}''$ dia. C.E.1. $\times$ 3"		1
11	41602	" " buffer sleeve assembly		1
14	26995	" " " " nut		2
15	41643	" " steady buffer		2
16	43617	" " clip (rear)		1
	253	" " " pin		2
	29058	" " " " washer		2
16A	45947	" " " rubber sleeve		1
17	36583	Petrol tap		1
18	5662	" " fibre washer		1
19	41361	" pipe complete		1
20	‡43735	Front mudguard c/w bridge and centre brackets	C	1
21	‡39791	" " stay	C	2
22	‡18446	" " " fixing pin	C	2
24	‡26998	" " " " nut	C	2
25	‡39792	" " " stud, $\frac{5}{16}''$ B.S.F. $\times \frac{3}{4}''$		2 or 4
27	‡27944	" " " " nut		4
	‡45484	Front mudguard, chrome	S	1
	‡45487	" " stay (front)	S	1
	‡45489	" " " (rear)	S	1
	‡38767	" " " bolt	S	4
	‡26998	" " " " nut	S	4
	‡38149	" " " stud	S	2
	‡39792	" " " stud		2
	‡45495	Front number plate	S	1
	‡5171	" " " screw	S	3
	‡14904	" " " clip	S	3
	‡25226	" " " washer	S	3
	‡26999	" " " nut	S	3
	‡29058	" " " washer	S	3

‡ Except "Airflow" models.

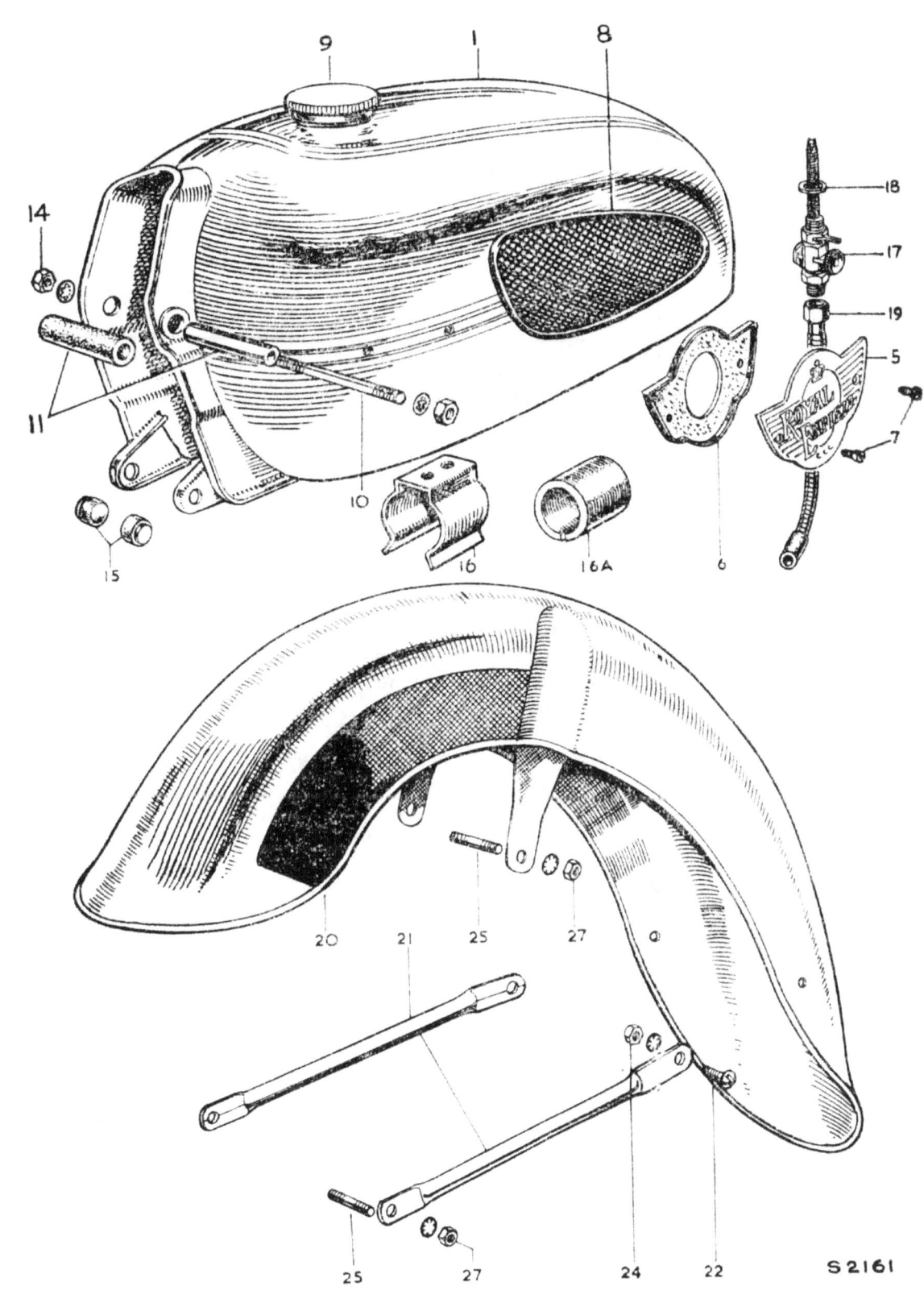

S2161

FRONT WHEEL AND BRAKE

Illus. No.	No. of part.	Description.		No. per set
	40412	Wheel with brake assy. (less tyre)	C	1
	43270	" " " " (less tyre)	S	1
	40414	" rim WM 2-17		1
	41043	* " spoke (outer) $5\frac{3}{4}$" long × 10g butted 8g.	C	20
	40416	* " " (inner) $5\frac{5}{8}$" " " " "	C	20
	43594	* " " $5\frac{5}{16}$" long × 10g butted 8g.	S	40
	29206	* " " nipple		40
1	41025	Hub and barrel, complete	C	1
	43527	" " " complete	S	1
2	36468	" spindle		1
3	SK/RLS5	" journal bearing $\frac{5}{8}$" × $1\frac{9}{16}$" × $\frac{7}{16}$"		2
4	21466	" felt washer		2
5	30538	" distance collar		2
6	40982	" centre		1
7	31347	" spindle nuts		2
8	40981	" cap	C	1
9	40983	" " screw	C	3
10	41251	Brake cover plate	C	1
11	41342A	" shoe c/w lining	C	2
12	41284A/BX	" lining (1 pair c/w rivets)	C	1
	43718	" cover plate	S	1
	43263A	" shoe c/w lining	S	2
	43264A/BX	" lining (1 pr. c/w rivets)	S	1
13	26033	" shoe return spring		2
14	27086	" operating cam	C	1
	43720	" " cam	S	1
15	14472	" " " plug screw		1
	43215	" shoe pivot pin	S	1
	28715	" " " " nut	S	1
	17551	" " " " washer	S	1
16	38905	" lever		1
17	10314	" " nut, $\frac{7}{16}$" dia.		1
18	14613	" " spring washer		1

* Spokes and Nipples screwed .140" dia. × 40 T.P.I.

HANDLEBAR CONTROL CABLES
Continued from page 22

39	43567	Throttle cable assembly	C	1
	45737	" " assembly	S	1
40	AM/12/034	" " nipple, handlebar end		1
41	AM/1482	" " " carburettor end		1
42	44893	Brake cable assembly	S	1
	44916	" " "	C	1
43	DH/J	" " nipple, handlebar end		1
44	38031	" " " brake end		1
45	21872	" " " adjusting screw		1
46	26471	" " " " locknut		1
47	31433	Air cable assembly		1
48	AM/12/034	" " nipple, handlebar end		1
49	AM/1482	" " " carburettor end		1
50	29610	Cable strap with buckle, 7" long		2
51	29609	" " " " 5" long		1

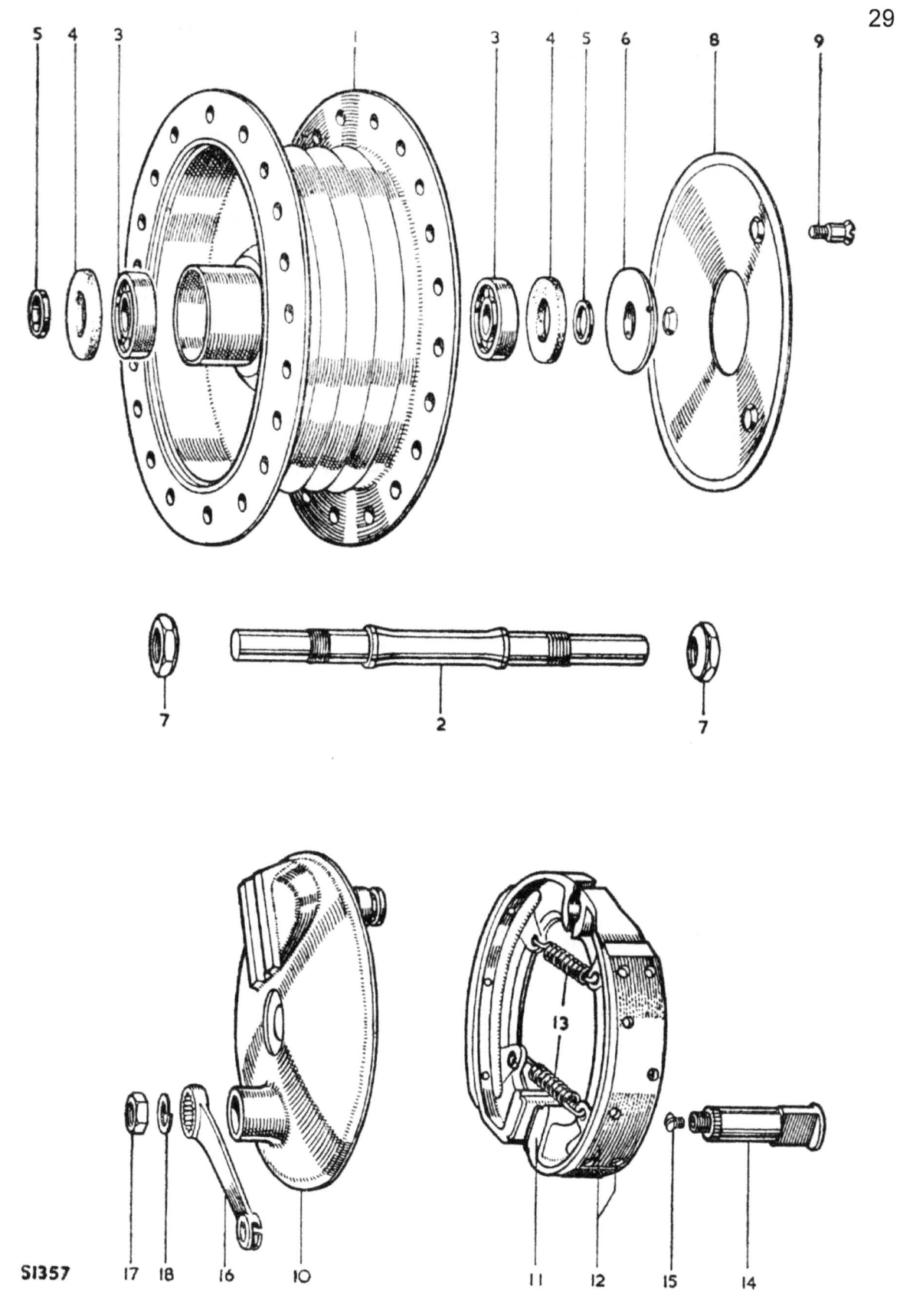

Q.D. REAR WHEEL AND BRAKE

Illus. No.	No. of part.	Description.	No. per set
	40413	Wheel with cush drive and brake assy. (less tyre)	1
	40414	" rim WM 2-17	1
	41043	* " spoke (outer) $5\frac{3}{4}$" long × 10g butted 8g.	20
	40416	* " " (inner) $5\frac{5}{8}$" " " " "	20
	29206	* " " nipple	40
1	40999	Hub & barrel, complete, less sprocket/brake drum and cush drive shell	1
2	40975	Brake drum and sprocket, 49 teeth	1
3	41003	Sprocket lockring c/w studs	1
4	19870	" " stud nut	3
5	41001	" " " " locking washer	3
6	40967	Cush drive shell	1
7	26193	" " rubber block	6
8	41000	Hub driving pin	6
10	DE394	" " " nut	6
11	40981	" cap	1
12	40983	" " screw	3
13	40988	" spindle (fixed section)	1
14	40997	" " (loose section)	1
15	28832	" " nut	1
16	41185	" " washer	2
17	SK/RLS5	" journal bearing $\frac{5}{8}$" × $1\frac{9}{16}$" × $\frac{7}{10}$"	3
18	40995	" " " spacer	1
19	40987	" " " retaining ring	1
20	41032	" " " " circlip	1
21	41006	" felt washer	2
22	39315	" distance collar L.H.	1
23	40990	" " " R.H.	1
24	41256	Brake cover plate	1
	44359	" " " screw (with chainguard only) S	5
25	40984	" " " distance collar	1
26	41342A	" shoe c/w lining	2
27	41284A/BX	" lining (1 pair c/w rivets)	1
28	26033	" shoe return spring	2
29	27086	" operating cam	1
30	14472	" " " plug screw	1
31	27684	" " " lever and trunnion	1
32	10314	" " " " nut	1
33	14613	" " " " spring washer	1
34	41045	" " " " return spring	1
35	1898	" anchor nut	1
36	15111	" " " washer	1
37	40051	Chain adjuster cam	2

* Spokes and Nipples screwed .140" dia. × 40 T.P.I.

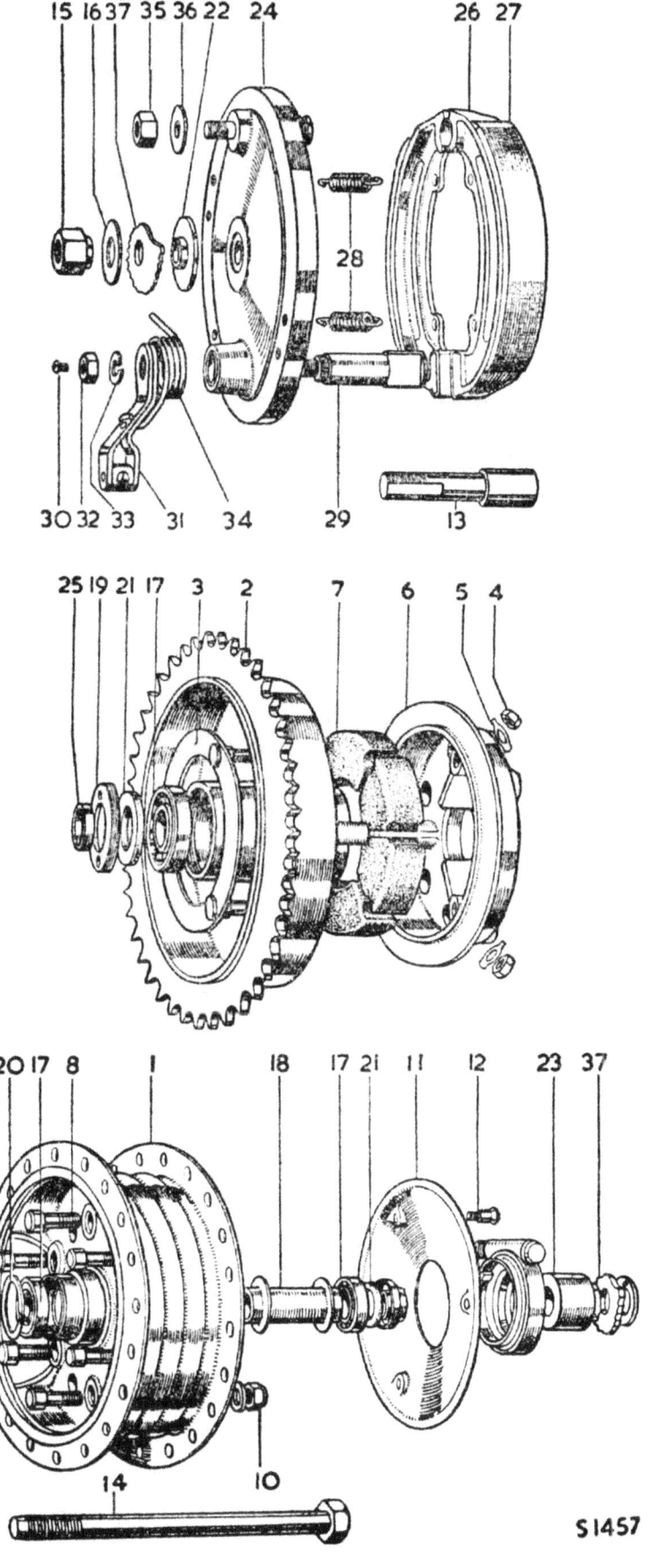

REAR BRAKE CONTROL, EXHAUST SYSTEM, FOOTRESTS, REAR CHAINCASE AND CHAIN

Illus. No.	No. of part.	Description.		No. per set
1	39802B	Brake pedal		1
2	39803	" " fulcrum stud		1
	10314	" " " locknut		1
3	37143	" " " circlip		1
4	4860	" " stop pin $\frac{1}{4}"$ dia. C.E.I. $\times 1\frac{1}{16}"$		1
	27000	" " " " locknut		1
5	TC/PZ6	" " grease nipple		1
6	33860	Brake rod		1
	14691	" " washer, $\frac{5}{16}"$		1
	30779	" " split pin $\frac{1}{16}" \times \frac{3}{4}"$		1
7	17691	" " adjusting nut		1
8	‡46574	Exhaust pipe	C	1
	‡46518	" pipe	S	1
	46589	Silencer complete		1
9	41341	" clip		1
10	4860	" " bolt $\frac{1}{4}"$ dia. C.E.I. $\times 1\frac{1}{16}"$		1
11	12881	" " nut		1
12	46634	" taper section		1
13	46590	" barrel centre		1
14	46635	" stud & baffle assy.		1
15	46336	" barrel seal		1
	18949	" " att. nut		1
	46740	" " " washer		1
16	46776	" " " tab washer		1
17	46203	" outlet end		1
18	18499A	Footrest support bar	C	1
	‡19170A	" " bar	S	1
19	10315	" " " nut, $\frac{3}{8}"$ C.E.I. $\times \frac{3}{8}"$		2
20	6740	" " " " washer		2
21	24238	" distance tube, $\frac{1}{2}"$ long (L.H. on C, R.H. on S.)		1
	‡41017	" " " $\frac{3}{8}"$ " L.H.	S	1
22	19173	" " " centre, $3\frac{13}{16}"$ long		1
23	25839	" arm, L.H.	C	1
24	39968	" " R.H.	C	1
	‡44775	" arm	S	2
25	25838	" rubber		2
26	41526	Pillion footrest		2
27	26324	" " rubber		2
28	41499	" " pivot pin		2
29	3257	" " " " nut		2
30	43253	" " distance tube, L.H.		1
31	41523	" " pivot block		2
32	37207	" " " " stud $\frac{7}{16}"$ dia. C.E.I. $\times 2\frac{9}{16}"$		2
33	30807	" " " " " nut		2

‡ Except "Airflow" models.

(Continued on page 40)

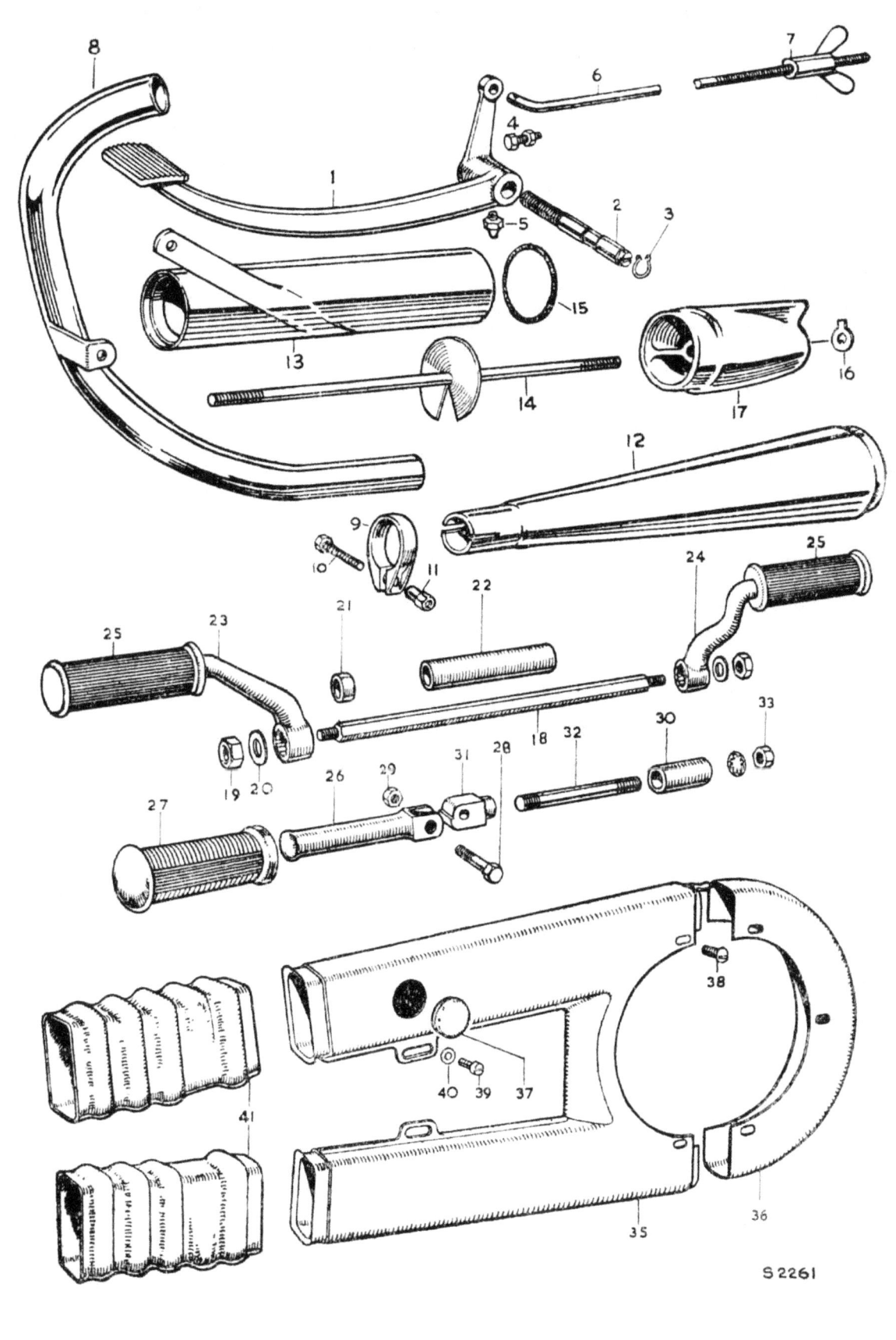

34 FRAME, ENGINE PLATES, CYLINDER HEAD STEADY, REAR SUSPENSION AND CENTRE STAND

Illus. No.	No. of part.	Description.	No. per set
1	‡40503B	Frame with head races, less all other fittings	1
2	43158A	Front engine plate, R.H.	1
3	43159	" " " L.H.	1
4	40418	" " " stud, (frame) $\frac{1}{2}'' \times 4\frac{3}{8}'' \times 26$	2
5	402	" " " " nut	2 or 4
7	39708	Rear engine plate	2
8	39467	Cylinder head steady eye bolt	1
9	35373	" " " sleeve	1
10	35732	" " " locknut	1
11	15267	" " " stud (engine) $\frac{5}{16}'' \times 2\frac{5}{8}'' \times 26$	1
12	19870	" " " " nut	2
14	35033	" " " stud (frame) $\frac{3}{8}'' \times 2\frac{3}{8}'' \times 26$	1
15	26995	" " " " nut	2
17	38853	Chainstay assembly	1
18	38854	" bearing tube	1
19	37762	" " stud	1
20	42124	" " thrust washer	2
21	38894	" " nut	2
	33789A	" " " locking screw	2
23	37770	" " dust excluder	2
24	TC/PZ6	" " grease nipple	2
25	GR/SB3/227	Spring box assy.	2
	GR/9054/152	Dust cover, outer	2
	GR/9054/47	" " inner	2
	GR/9054/316H	Pivot bush (rubber)	4
	GR/9054/277	Suspension spring	2
26	42002	" " pivot pin, top	2
27	26374	" " " " nut	2
28	6740	" " " " washer	2
29	DE394	" " " " nut (bottom)	2
31	33783	" " " " locking washer (bottom)	2
32	38823	Centre stand with spring post	1
	38152	" " only	1
33	33824	" " bearing sleeve	1
34	40461	" " spindle	1
35	TC/PZ65	" " " grease nipple	1
36	10314	" " " nut	2
38	40460	" " spring	1
39	36861	" " " post	1

‡ Except "Airflow" models.

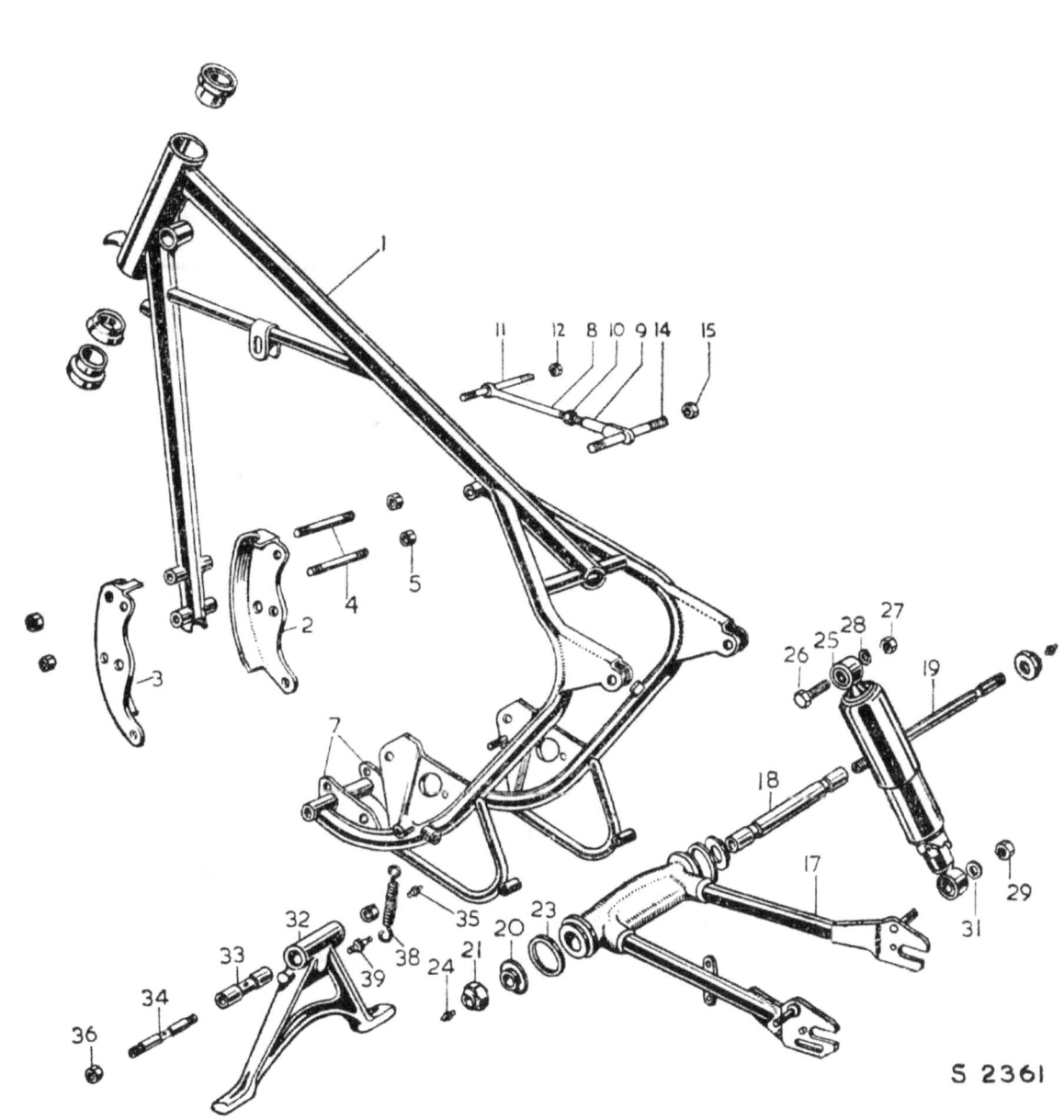

S 2361

DUAL SEAT, REAR MUDGUARD & CARRIER AND NUMBER PLATE

Illus. No.	No. of part.	Description.		No. per set
1	45815	Dual seat		1
2	44620	,, ,, front bracket, R.H.		1
3	44619	,, ,, ,, ,, L.H.		1
4	45822	,, ,, attachment bracket (rear)		1
	12659	,, ,, ,, bolt, $\frac{5}{16}'' \times \frac{1}{2}'' \times 26$ (seat to bracket)		4
	8634	,, ,, ,, ,, washer		2
	10142	,, ,, ,, ,, $\frac{5}{16}'' \times \frac{11}{16}'' \times 26$ (bracket to carrier)		2
	26997	,, ,, ,, ,, nut		2
	251	,, ,, ,, ,, $\frac{1}{4}'' \times \frac{1}{2}'' \times 26$ (rear, to guard)		2
	26998	,, ,, ,, ,, nut		2
	82	,, ,, ,, ,, washer		2
7	46060	Mudguard (enamel)	C	1
	44748	,, (chrome)	S	1
8	18446	,, screw $\frac{1}{4}''$ dia. C.E.1. $\times \frac{9}{16}''$ round head		4
9	26998	,, ,, nut		4
11	40308A	,, carrier		1
12	39767	,, ,, plastic end cover		2
13	41196	,, ,, ,, ,, ,, stiffener		2
14	40053	,, ,, bridge		2
15	10142	,, ,, bolt $\frac{5}{16}''$ dia. C.E.1. $\times \frac{11}{16}''$		4
17	20199	,, ,, bridge distance piece		4
18	41039	Rear number plate		1
19	41087	,, ,, ,, beading, $25\frac{3}{4}''$		1
20	22655	,, ,, ,, attachment pin $\frac{5}{16}''$ dia. C.E.1. $\times \frac{21}{32}''$		1

STANDARD SHAKEPROOF WASHERS

No. of part	Dia.	No. of part	Dia.
29058	$\frac{3}{16}''$	27918	$\frac{3}{8}''$
27916	$\frac{1}{4}''$	27919	$\frac{7}{16}''$
27917	$\frac{5}{16}''$	27920	$\frac{1}{2}''$

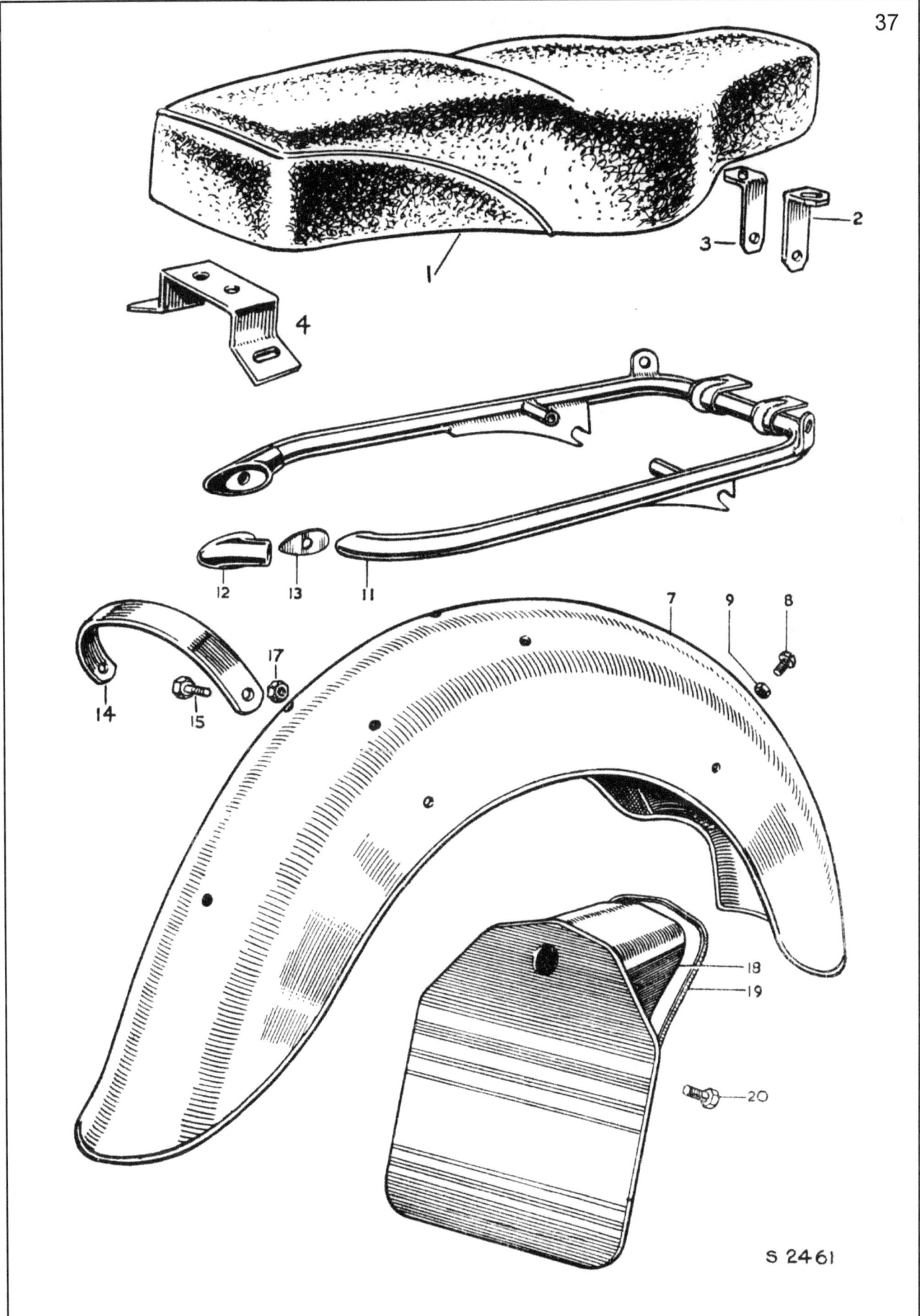

TOOL BOX, TOOLS AND AIR FILTER

Illus. No.	No. of part.	Description.		No. per set
1	43734A	Toolbox (without lids)		1
2	42751	" lid, L.H.		1
3	43292	" " R.H.		1
	43320A	" " post, R.H.	C	1
4	41860	" " screw		2
5	38803	" " " keeper washer		2
6	41932	" clip		1
7	251	" attachment screw $\frac{1}{4}''$ dia. C.E.I. $\times \frac{1}{2}''$		4
8	27000	" " " nut		4
10	18529	" " " washer		8
11	41244	" beading, $15\frac{1}{2}''$		1
12	39826	Air filter element	C	1
13	39825A	" " " cover		1
14	13141	" " " " screw		1
15	18529	" " " " " washer		1
16	39827	" " " connecting tube	C	1
	41516	" " " connecting tube	S	1
17	24094	Tubular spanner, $\frac{11}{16}''$ Whit.		1
18	24095	" " $\frac{1}{2}''$ "		1
19	35635	" " $\frac{3}{8}''$ "		1
20	44710	" " $\frac{7}{16}''$ "		1
21	35634	" " $\frac{1}{4}''$ & $\frac{5}{16}''$ Whit.		1
22	29042	Tommy bar, bent		1
23	24092	D/E spanner, .380'' × .343'' hexagon		1
24	29044	" " $\frac{1}{4}''$ & $\frac{5}{16}''$ Whit.		1
25	27896	" " $\frac{3}{16}''$ & $\frac{1}{4}''$ Whit.		1
26	16008	" " .283'' × .255'' hex. (magneto spanner)		1
27	6406	Combination spanner		1
28	3482	Screwdriver, flat blade		1
	DWU-05	" star blade		1
29	4272A	Tyre lever		2
30	16014	Grease gun		1
31	T3000	Rear suspension "C" spanner		1
	41181	Contact breaker extractor		1
32	16026	Tyre inflator		1
33	16007	Tool roll		1
34	TE/1124	Valve spring compressor		1
35	TE/1167	" grinding tool		1
36	ST71	Leather strap, 42'' × 1''		1

The tools listed above are available but are not necessarily supplied with new machines.

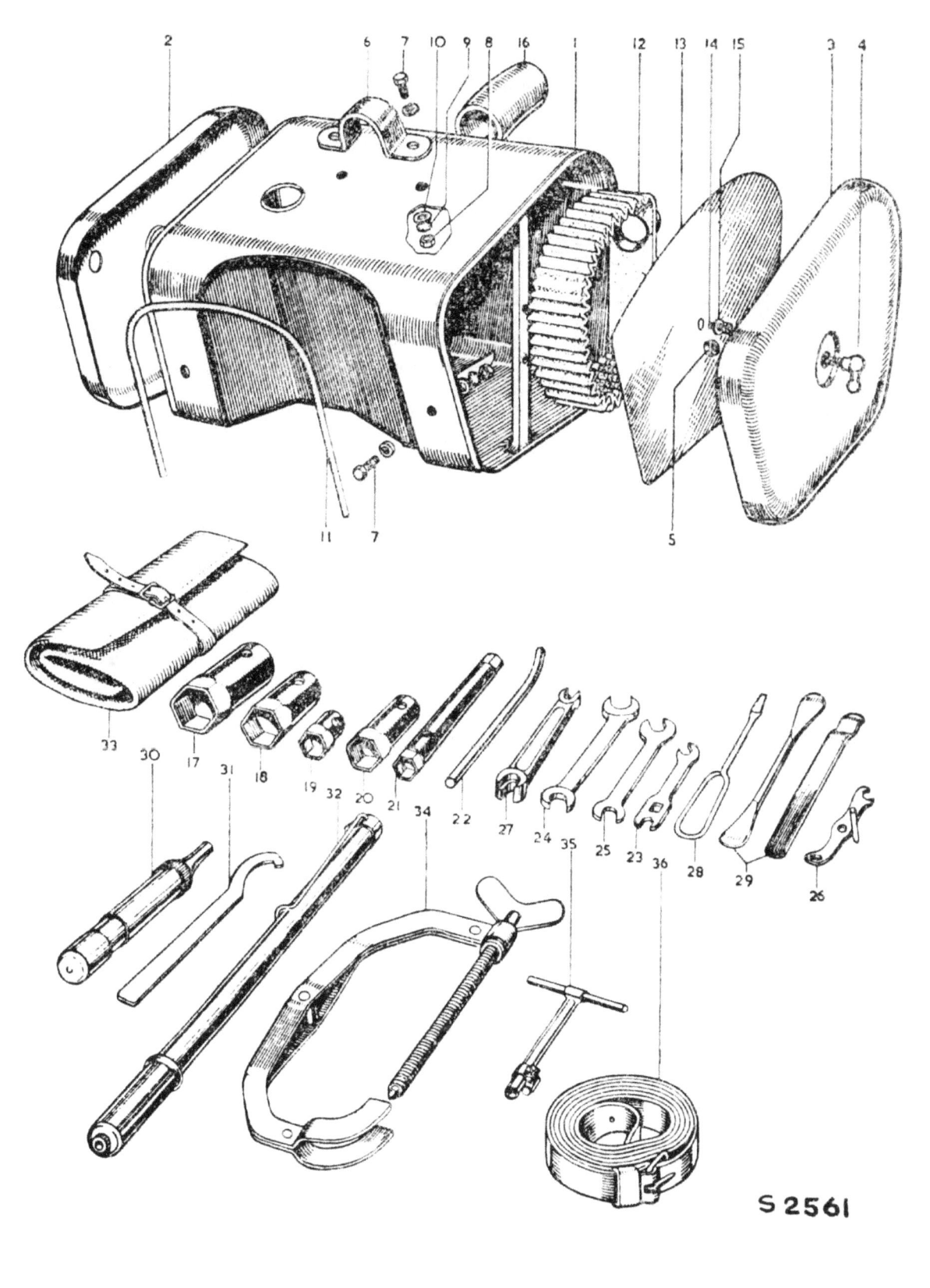

S 2561

SMITH'S SPEEDOMETER

Illus. No.	No. of part.	Description.		No. per set
1	SM/467/241L	Speedometer head 80 m.p.h. illuminated	C	1
	SM/467/245K	″ ″ 140 k.p.h. illuminated	C	1
	SM/467/243	″ ″ 125 m.p.h. ″	S	1
	SM/467/247	″ ″ 180 k.p.h. ″	S	1
2	‡38896	″ ″ clamp		1
	SM/53205	″ light bulb		1
3	SM/N1253	Nut (fixing bracket to head)		2
4	SM/W7216	Spring washer		2
	‡SM/53395/4/52	Flexible drive complete, 52 inches		1
5	‡SM/53398/4/52	″ ″ outer cable assembly		1
6	‡SM/52108/1/52	″ ″ inner cable assembly		1
7	SM/BG5303	Gear box (self-contained) complete		1
8	40989	″ ″ spacing collar (behind box)		1
9	31997	Speedo. drive coupling (on end of hub barrel)		1

‡ Except "Airflow" models.

AMAL "MONOBLOC" CARBURETTOR

Parts special to "Sports" model.

	No. of part.	Description.		No. per set
	AM/376/216	Carburettor complete, less controls and cables	S	1
	AM/376/035	Mixing chamber, $\frac{15}{16}$″ bore	S	1
	AM/376/055	Jet block, $\frac{15}{16}$″ bore	S	1
	AM/376/067	″ ″ washer	S	1
	AM/376/064	″ ″ top	S	1
	AM/376/065	″ ″ ring cap	S	1
	AM/376/060/3½	Throttle valve, No. 3½	S	1
	AM/376/061	″ ″ spring	S	1
	AM/376/063	Taper needle	S	1
	AM/376/062	Air valve	S	1
	AM/376/100/150	Main jet, No 150	S	1
	AM/376/110	Air intake	S	1

REAR CHAINCASE, CHAINGUARD AND CHAIN

(Continued from page 32)

Illus. No.	No. of part.	Description.	No. per set
	39019	Rear chaincase, complete (fixed and loose sections)	1
35	38862	″ ″ fixed section	1
36	38859	″ ″ loose section	1
37	35437	″ ″ inspection plug	1
38	1083	″ ″ attachment pin (brake coverplate)	5
39	6716	″ ″ ″ screw (chainstay)	2
40	82	″ ″ ″ ″ washer	2
41	38804	″ ″ flexible joint	1 or 2
	44109	Chainguard complete	1
	37175	″ fixing pin, rear	1
	27001	″ ″ ″ nut	1
	6716	″ ″ screw, front	2
	82	″ ″ ″ washer	2
	RN/110046/120	Rear chain ½″ P. ×.305″ W. ×120 pitches	1

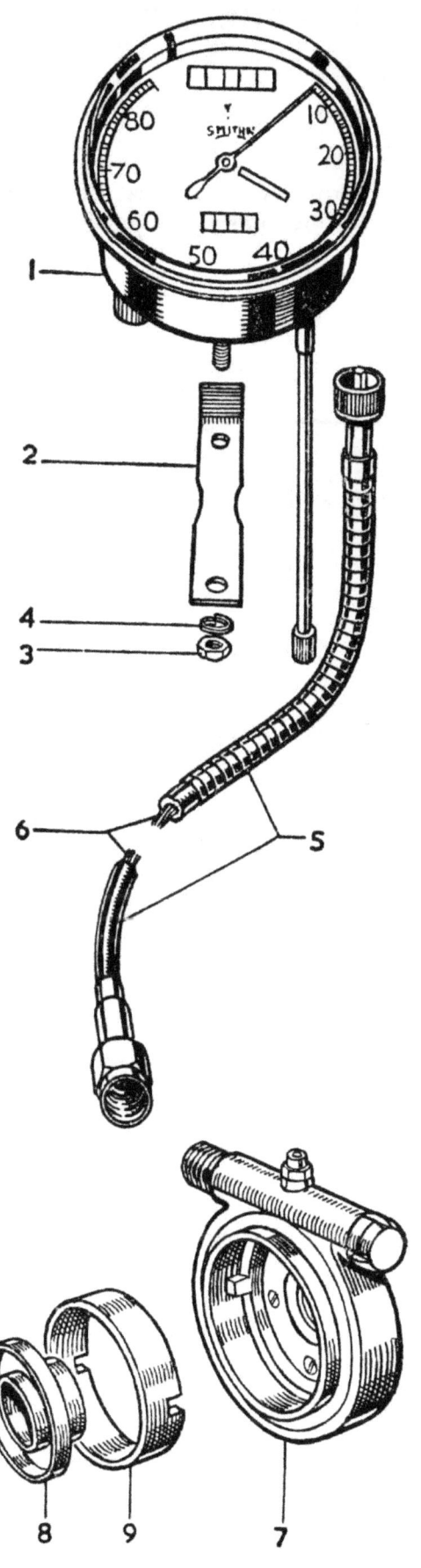

S 1957

AMAL "MONOBLOC" CARBURETTOR

Illus. No.	No. of part.	Description.		No. per set
	AM/375/16	Carburettor complete, less controls and cables	C	1
1	AM/375/005	Mixing chamber body, $\frac{7}{8}$" bore	C	1
	AM/244/765	Flange sealing ring		1
2	AM/375/059	Jet block, $\frac{7}{8}$" bore	C	1
3	AM/376/070	" " locating peg		1
4	AM/375/067	" " washer	C	1
5	AM/375/064	" " top	C	1
6	AM/375/065	" " cap ring	C	1
7	AM/4/235	Cap spring		1
8	AM/4/241	" " screw		1
9	AM/4/035	Cable adjuster		2
10	AM/375/060/3½	Throttle valve, No. 3½	C	1
11	AM/375/061	" " spring	C	1
12	AM/375/063	Taper needle	C	1
13	AM/4/230	Needle clip		1
14	AM/375/062	Air valve	C	1
15	AM/5/047	" " guide		1
16	AM/4/046	" " spring		1
17	AM/376/072/1055	Needle jet		1
18	AM/376/100/120	Main jet, No. 120	C	1
19	AM/376/073	" " holder		1
20	AM/376/074	" " " washer		1
21	AM/376/075	" " cover nut		1
22	AM/376/076/25	Pilot jet, No. 25		1
23	AM/376/095	" " cover nut		1
24	AM/116/162	" " " " washer		1
25	AM/332/017	Air adjusting screw		1
26	AM/4/148	" " " spring		1
27	AM/376/068	Throttle stop screw		1
28	AM/376/069	" " " spring		1
29	39828	Air intake sleeve	C	1
30	AM/376/083	Float, complete		1
31	AM/376/085	" hinge spindle		1
32	AM/376/094	Float spindle bush		1
33	AM/376/089	" needle		1
34	AM/376/088	Needle seating		1
36	AM/376/097	Banjo, single		1
37	AM/14/175	" washer		1
38	AM/376/091	" bolt		1
39	AM/376/092	" " washer		1
40	AM/376/093	Filter gauze		1
41	AM/376/086	Tickler		1
42	AM/343/011	" body		1
43	AM/376/087	" spring		1
44	AM/376/077	Float chamber cover		1
45	AM/376/078	" " " joint		1
46	AM/376/079	" " " screw		3
	AM/244/1037	Monobloc servicing spanner		1

For corresponding parts on the "Sports" model see page 40.

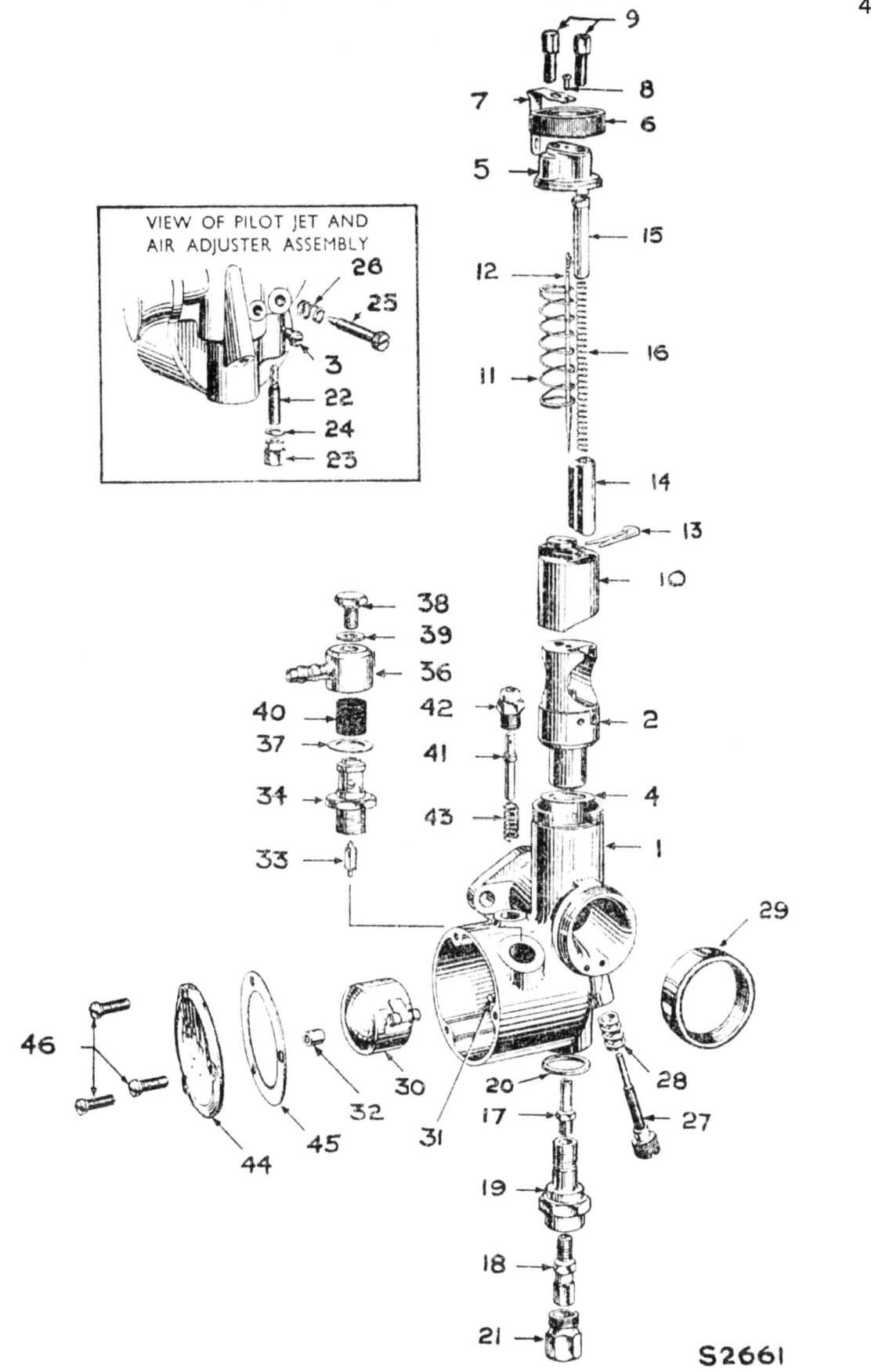

ELECTRICAL EQUIPMENT

Illus. No.	No. of part.	Description.	No. per set
		GENERATOR	
	LU/047519B	Alternator, complete, RM 13	1
1	LU/466125	" rotor assy. only	1
2	DE394	" rotor attachment nut	1
3	41134	" " " " washer	1
4	LU/468678	" stator	1
5	27622	" " attachment nut	3
7	39040	" " locating ring	1
8	41182	" " key	1
9	41133	" " distance washer (behind rotor)	1
10	39281	" " wiring clip	3
		RECTIFIER	
11	LU/47132A	Rectifier unit	1
12	27944	" attachment nut	1
13	35943	" " " washer	1
		CONTACT BREAKER	
	LU/47571D	Contact breaker & Auto Advance Unit CA1A	1
14	LU/420196	Contact set	1
15	LU/420302	Condenser assembly	1
16	LU/465939	Cam assembly	1
17	LU/421457/S	Spring, set, auto-advance	2
18	LU/407131	Toggles	2
19	LU/415730	Weight assembly	2
20	LU/421846	Sleeve and action plate assembly	1
21	41180	Contact breaker centre screw	1
22	7674	" " " " washer	1
23	29781	" " plate attachment screw	2
24	7047	" " " " " washer	2
25	35745	" " cover	1
26	35869	" " " screw	2
		IGNITION COIL	
27	LU/45077B	Ignition coil	1
28	42221	" " bracket	1
29	251	" " attachment screw	2
31	27000	" " " " nut	1

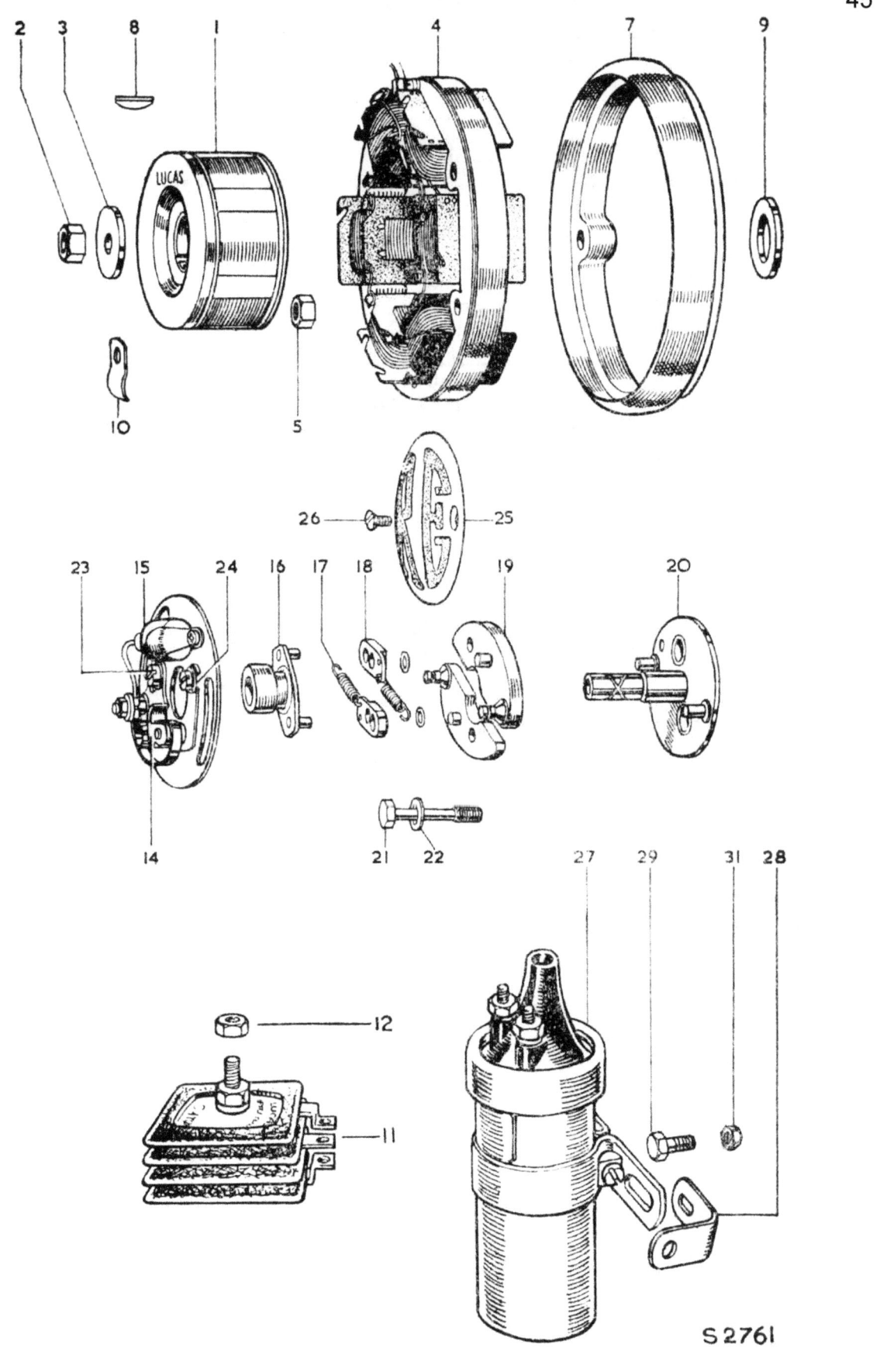

ELECTRICAL EQUIPMENT—Contd. (1)

Illus. No.	No. of part.	Description.	No. per set
	‡LU/50943E	**HEADLAMP** Headlamp MCF 700 comprising unit light with front and fixing rims	1
1	LU/553248	Front rim	1
2	LU/553267	Fixing rim	1
3	39218	Rim fixing screw	2
4	LU/144921	″ adjusting screw	1
5	LU/553925	Unit light	1
6	LU/504665	″ ″ fixing wire	4
7	LU/554602	Bulb holder	1
8	LU/312	Main bulb, 6v., 30 ×24w.	1
	‡LU/52234A	Pilot lamp complete, L550	2
9	LU/526496	Rim	2
10	39218	″ screw	2
11	LU/573615	Lens	2
12	LU/553780	Interior (bulb holder)	2
13	LU/526493	Rubber mounting	2
14	LU/988	Bulb, 6v., 3w.	2
	LU/53394B	**TAIL LAMP** Tail lamp L.564	1
15	LU/573839	″ ″ lens	1
16	LU/575200	″ ″ window	1
17	LU/575219	″ ″ nut for lens	2
18	LU/575208	″ ″ gasket for lens	1
19	LU/575964	″ ″ base	1
20	LU/575209	″ ″ bulb holder	1
21	LU/575207	″ ″ ″ ″ grommet	1
22	LU/573828	″ ″ contact assembly	1
23	LU/166014	″ ″ body securing nut	2
24	LU/188327	″ ″ ″ ″ ″ washer	2
25	LU/573825	″ ″ cable grommet	1
26	LU/352	″ ″ bulb, 6v., 3 ×18w.	1

‡ See special parts list for all components of Headlamp and Pilot lamp for "Airflow" models.

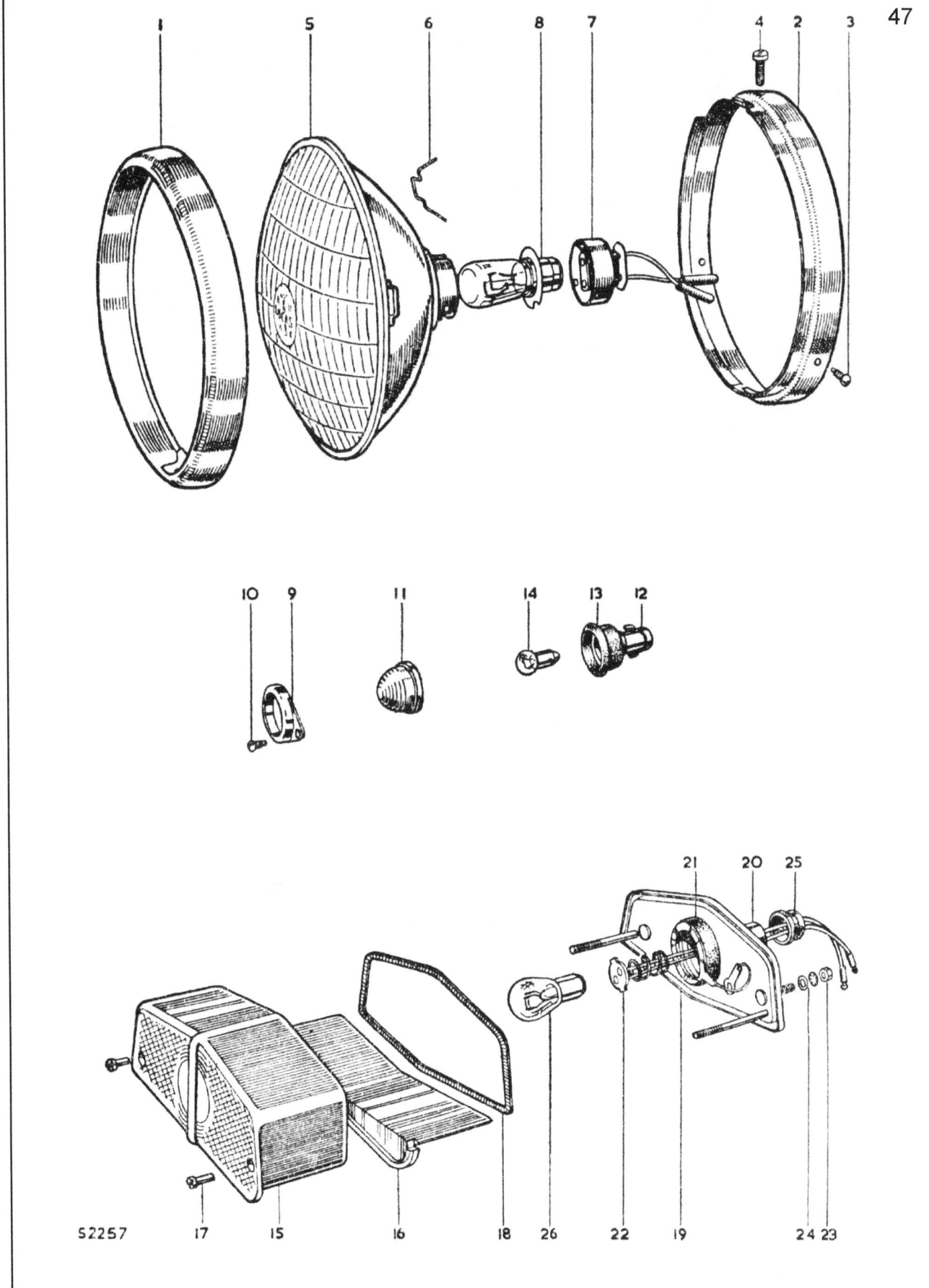

ELECTRICAL EQUIPMENT—Contd. (2)

Illus. No.	No. of part.	Description.		No. per set
		SWITCHES		
1	‡LU/31491A	Lighting switch		1
2	‡LU/351567	Handle and fixing screw		1
3	‡LU/365408	Rubber ring		1
4	LU/34093B	Ignition switch		1
	LU/365408	″ ″ rubber ring		1
	LU/344715	″ ″ key		1
5	37630	″ ″ washer		1
8	LU/31563D	Dipper switch and horn button 25SA	C	1
9	LU/380459	″ ″ ″ ″ rubber base	C	1
10	LU/136291	″ ″ ″ ″ fixing screw	C	2
	LU/31549A	Dipper switch only	S	1
	LU/76204	Horn ″ ″	S	1
		AMMETER		
11	LU/36084F	Ammeter		1
12	LU/365408	″ rubber ring		1
		ELECTRIC HORN AND BATTERY.		
13	LU/70142D	Electric horn, HF1849		1
14	42487	″ ″ clip (R.H.)		1
15	42488	″ ″ ″ (L.H.)		1
16	251	″ ″ ″ screw		2
17	26998	″ ″ ″ ″ nut		2
19	32423	″ ″ attachment screw		2
20	26999	″ ″ ″ ″ nut		2
22	LU/PUZ7E-11	Battery 6v., 12 amp.hr. (dry)		1
23	LU/4183604	″ vent plug		3
24	43222A	″ strap		1
25	13141	″ ″ screw		1
		WIRING		
	‡LU/54940814A	Cable harness complete		1
	‡LU/850641	Pilot lamp 4-way snap connector		1
27	LU/199001	Wiring rubber grommet		3
28	LU/220546	Rear lamp & Ignition coil cable grommet (rear mudguard & toolbox)		3
		STOP LAMP SWITCH		
29	LU/31688	Switch		1
30	45706	″ bracket		1
	36174	″ attachment pin		1
	19870	″ ″ ″ nut		1
31	35603	Stop lamp cable band 3½″ long		3

‡ Except "Airflow" models.

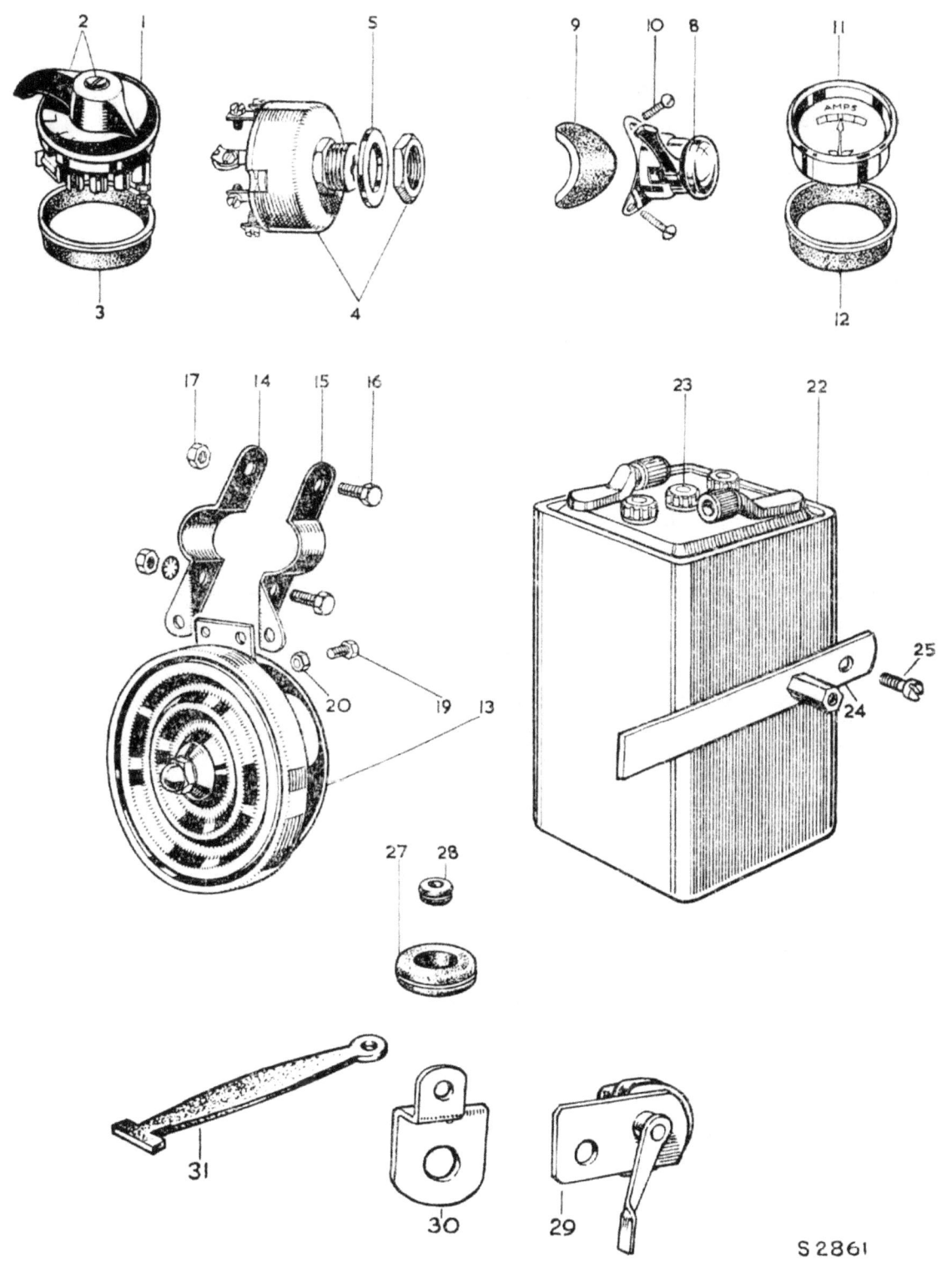

PANNIERS

Illus. No.	No. of part.	Description.		No. per set
1	42218	Pannier bag		2
2	42193	" carrier L.H.		1
3	42194	" " R.H.		1
4	42196	" " clip		4
5	23941	" " " collar, $\frac{7}{8}''$ dia. $\times \frac{1}{4}''$		4
6	42202	" " " screw, $\frac{5}{16}''$ B.S.F. $\times 1''$		4
7	27944	" " " " nut		4
9	42199	" " strut		1
10	42203	" " " screw, $\frac{5}{16}''$ B.S.F. $\times \frac{5}{8}''$		2
11	18446	Strut lug screw, $\frac{1}{4}''$ C.E.I. $\times \frac{9}{16}''$		2
12	26998	" " " nut		2
14	40053	Mudguard bridge		1
15	42201	" " distance piece $\frac{5}{8}'' \times 1\frac{13}{16}''$		2
16	20199	" " " " $\frac{5}{8}'' \times \frac{3}{16}''$		2
17	42204	" " bolt, $\frac{5}{16}''$ B.S.F. $\times 2\frac{11}{16}''$		2
18	27944	" " " nut		2
19	8634	" " " washer, $\frac{5}{8}''$ overall diameter		2
20	5965	Packing washer $\frac{15}{16}''$ overall diameter		12

LEGSHIELDS

EXCEPT "AIRFLOW" MODELS

Illus. No.	No. of part.	Description.		No. per set
21	41399	Legshield, L.H.	C	1
22	41400	" R.H.	C	1
	41885	" L.H.	S	1
	41886	" R.H.	S	1
23	41550	" cross-bar		1
24	31160	" clip stud, $\frac{5}{16}''$ B.S.F. $\times 1\frac{7}{8}''$		1
25	27944	" " " nut		2
27	41551	" " distance piece, $\frac{3}{4}''$ dia. $\times \frac{3}{4}''$		1
28	14446	" attachment screw (top)		2
30	40183	" rubber grommet		2
31	42892	" attachment stud, $\frac{5}{16}''$ B.S.F. $\times 12\frac{3}{16}''$	C	1
32	41552	" support tube, L.H. $\frac{5}{8}''$ dia. $\times 3\frac{1}{4}''$	C	1
	42893	" " " R.H. $\frac{5}{8}''$ dia. $\times 4\frac{3}{4}''$	C	1
	37121	" attachment stud	S	1
	42409	" bracket, bottom	S	1
	44408	" " pin	S	2
	26545	" " " collar	S	2
	27621	" " " nut	S	2

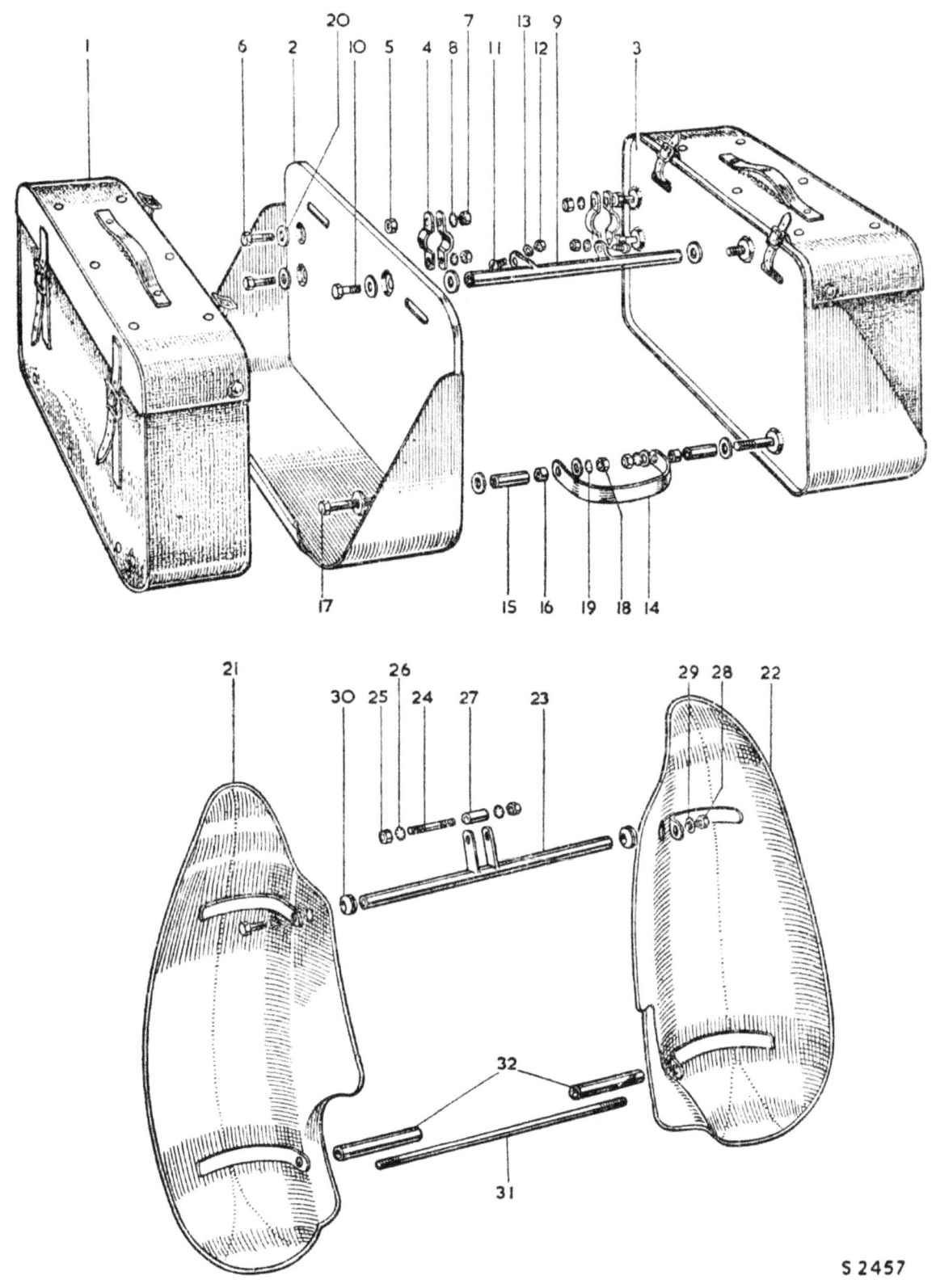

SPECIAL PARTS FOR "AIRFLOW" MODELS

Illus. No.	No. of part.	Description.		No. per set
	39630A	Engine/gearbox unit c/w alternator, contact breaker and carburettor, Iron head, $7\frac{3}{4}:1$ piston	C	1
	39629	Cylinder head (iron) c/w valve guides and studs	C	1
	44947	Valve, exhaust	C	1
	22641	" guide, inlet	C	1
	21322	" " exhaust	C	1
	45357	Piston c/w rings, gudgeon pin and circlips, C.R. $7\frac{3}{4}:1$	C	1
	39164	Push rod c/w ends, inlet	C	1
	39165	" " " " exhaust	C	1
	39161	" " end, bottom	C	2
	43496	Frame with head races, less all other fittings		1
	44508	Front fork assy., c/w steering stem		1
	44509	Steering stem c/w dust covers		1
1	44379	" " less dust covers		1
1A	36094	" " locknut		1
2	43989	Fork crown clip bolt		2
3	43993	" head c/w ballrace and H'bar clip studs		1
4	35694	" " clip bolt		1
5	35695	" " " " sleeve		1
6	32093	" " " " nut		1
7	38895	Handlebar clip		1
8	36304	" " stud		2
9	43982	Main tube		2
10	43984	Fork spring tube		2
	33587	Licence holder pin		1
11	26962	Badge (on fork head)		1
12	44003	" plate		1
13	44004	" clamp		1
	44002	" screw		2
	30206	" " nut		2
14	46737	Exhaust pipe		1
	SM/53395/4/57	Speedo flex drive complete		1
	SM/53398/4/57	" " " outer cable		1
	SM/52108/1/57	" " " inner cable		1
	44009	" head clamp		1
	LU/58258A	Headlamp F700		1
15	LU/555415	" body rubber gasket		1
16	44262	Fixing screw		4
17	44263	" " nut		4
18	44007	Adjusting screw		3
19	25226	" " washer		3
20	44008	" " knurled nut		3
21	30204	" " locknut		3
22	LU/552813	" " spring		3

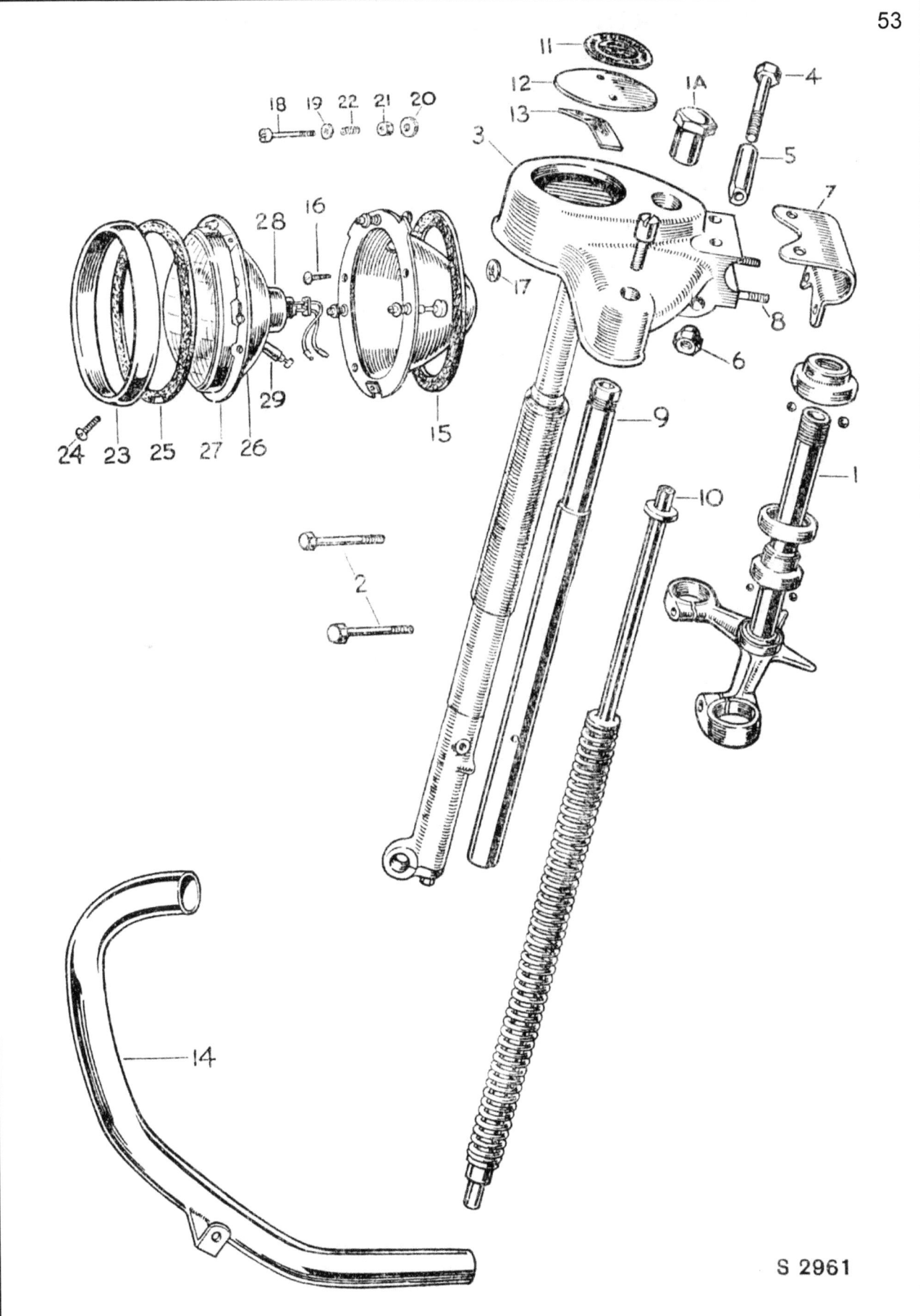

SPECIAL PARTS FOR "AIRFLOW" MODELS—Contd.

Illus. No.	No. of part.	Description.	No. per set
23	LU/554440	Rim assembly	1
24	LU/198898	" fixing screw	1
25	LU/552906	Dust excluder rubber ring	1
26	LU/516798	Light unit	1
27	LU/554872	" " retaining plate	1
28	LU/554602	Bulb holder, main	1
29	LU/554710	" " pilot	1
	LU/312	" main	1
	LU/988	" pilot	1
1	LU/31784A	Lighting switch, 41SA	1
2	LU/351815	" " knob	1
3	LU/127301	" " " screw	1
4	LU/351803	" " plate, chrome	1
5	LU/839870	Cable harness	1
6	43962	Front fairing complete (less windscreen)	1
7	43956	Engine plate stud nut	2
8	43957	Legshield stud	2
9	43961	" " rubber sleeve	2
10	43960	" " sleeve cap	2
11	43965	" " cap clip	2
12	43997	Fairing rubber buffer (head fixing)	1
13	19043	" " " washer	2
14	41603	" " " tube	1
15	39891	" attachment stud	1
	26995	" " " nut	2
	6740	" " " washer	2
16	44179 A	" rubber edging, 24"	1
17	44141	Fairing badge	1
	44140	" " stud	1
	5916	" " " washer	1
	26998	" " " nut	1
18	43737	Windscreen	1
19	1083	" screw	5
20	43996	" " rubber washer	5
21	15641	" " steel washer	5
22	44014	" " nut	5
23	44699	" backing strip	1
24	44010	Number plate	1
25	44463	Front mudguard	1
26	44462	" attachment bracket	1
27	43995	Mudguard rubber sealing washer (fork tubes)	2
	38913	" fixing bolt	3
	27621	" " " nut	3
28	44883	Brake cable grommet	1

Illustrations to top 7 items on page 53.

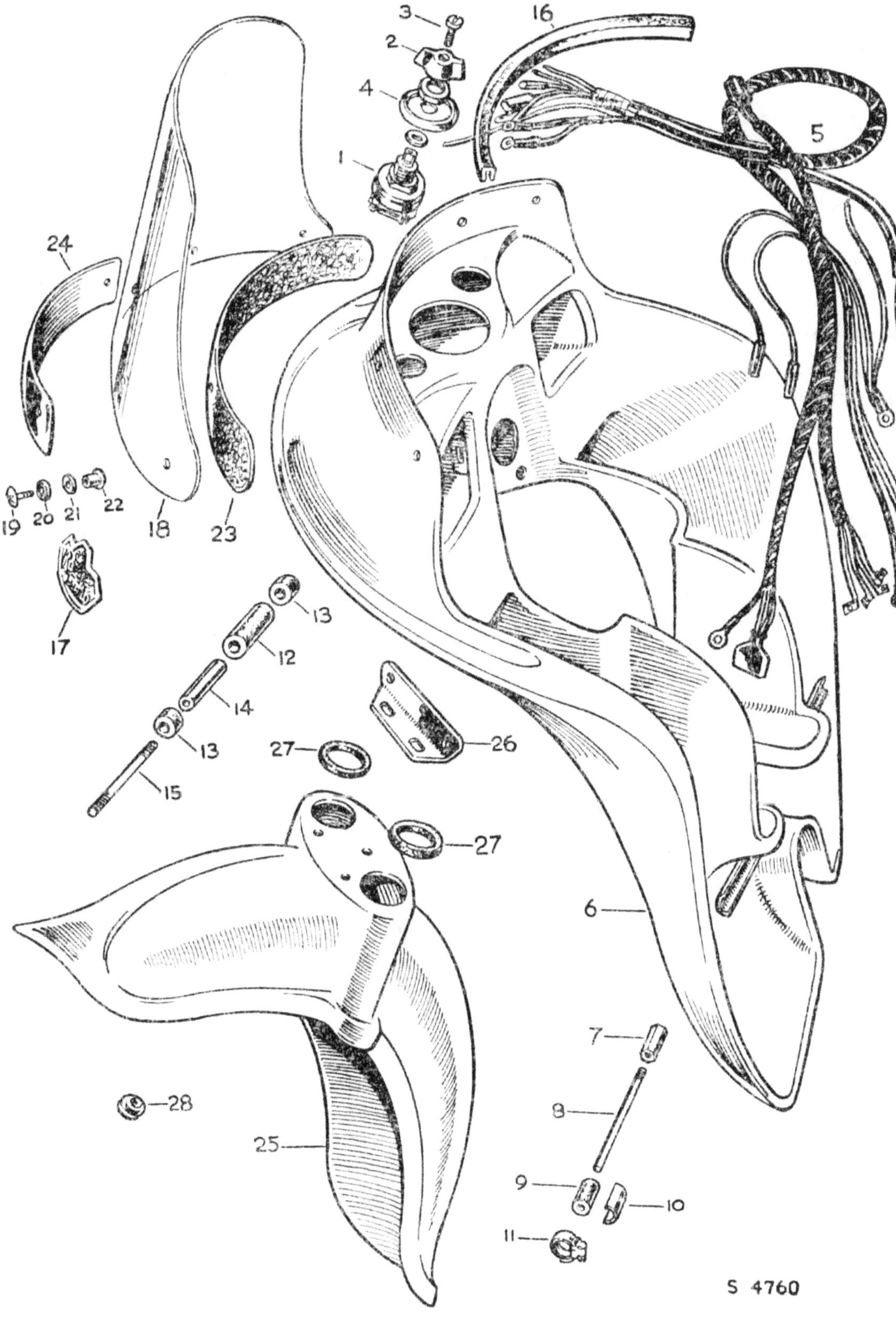

3
16
2
4
5
1
24
19
20
21
22
18
23
17
13
12
14
13
27
26
15
27
6
7
28
8
25
9
10
11
S 4760

Guarantee

TERMS AND CONDITIONS OF SALE AND GUARANTEE

1. In this Guarantee the word "machine" refers to the new motor cycle, scooter, motor cycle combination or sidecar, as the case may be, purchased by the Purchaser.
2. In order to obtain the benefit of this Guarantee, the Purchaser must correctly complete the registration form and return it to us within fourteen days of the purchase.
3. We will supply, free of charge, a new part in exchange for, or, if we consider repair sufficient, will repair free of charge any part proved within six months of the date of purchase of any new machine, or within three months of its renewal or repair in the case of a part already renewed or repaired, to be defective by reason of our faulty workmanship or materials. We do not undertake to bear the cost of fitting such new or repaired part or accessory.
4. Any part considered to be defective must be sent to our Works, carriage paid, accompanied by the following information:—
    (a) Name of Purchaser and his address.
    (b) Date of purchase of machine.
    (c) Name of dealer from whom the purchase was made.
    (d) Engine and frame numbers of machine.
5. This Guarantee shall not extend to defects or damage appearing after misuse, neglect, abnormal stress or strain, or the incorporation or affixing of unsuitable attachments or parts and in particular:—
    (a) Hiring out.
    (b) Racing and competitions.
    (c) Adaptation or alteration of any part or parts after leaving our Works.
    (d) The attaching of a sidecar in a manner not approved by us or to an unsuitable motor cycle.
    This Guarantee shall not extend to machines whose trade mark, name, or manufacturing number has been altered or removed, or in which has been used any part not supplied or approved by us, or to tyres, saddles, chains, speedometers, revolution counters, and electrical equipment or to parts supplied to the order of the Purchaser and different from our standard specification.
6. Our liability and that of our dealer who sells the machine shall be limited to that set out in paragraph 3 and no other claims including claims for consequential damage or injury to person or property, shall be admissible.
    All other conditions and warranties statutory or otherwise and whether express or implied are hereby excluded and no guarantee other than that expressly herein contained applies to the machine to which this Guarantee relates or any accessory or part thereof.

REPAIRS GUARANTEE

1. While the highest standard of workmanship and materials is aimed at, we cannot accept liability for any defects appearing more than three months after the machine, assembly or component, has left our Works after being repaired.
2. We will repair or replace at our option free of charge any defective work, materials or parts relating to the repairs carried out by us appearing within that time but shall not be under any further or other liability for any other loss or damage whether direct or consequential and our liability shall be limited to the cost of so making good.
3. We do not accept liability in respect of parts of proprietary manufacture, e.g. tyres, saddles, chains, speedometers, revolution counters and electrical equipment which may be used by us in effecting a repair. All other conditions and warranties statutory or otherwise express or implied are hereby excluded.

NOTICE

We do not appoint Agents for the sale on our behalf of our Motor Cycles or other goods but we assign to Motor Cycle Dealers areas in which we supply to such Dealers exclusively for re-sale in such areas. No such Dealer is authorised to transact any business, give any warranty, make any representations or incur any liability on our behalf.

February, 1962

SUPPLEMENTARY SPARE PARTS LIST
FOR
1962 "CRUSADER 250" & "CRUSADER SPORTS" MOTOR CYCLES

This list must be used in conjunction with the 1961 Spares Book for these models dated January, 1961.

Page 4
  Part No. 9908. Rocker spindle washer should read Rocker housing stud washer.

Page 6
  Part Nos. 39358 to 30779, inclusive, apply to Early Model.
  The Later Model, with wire inserts, is fitted with the following:

39358B	Connecting rod assy. c/w screws and B.E. shells ..	1
37311A	" " B.E. screw	2
47026	" " " " washer..	2
45444	" " " wire insert	2

  Part No. 39014 should read 46709.
  In the footnote on Service Replacement Connecting Rod Assemblies, the Part Nos. 39358S/10 and 39358S/20 should read 39358B/S/10 and 39358B/S/20 respectively. Part Nos. of undersize B.E. bearing shells only, 39014/10 and 39014/20 should read 46709/10 and 46709/20 respectively.

Page 8
  Part No. 44776A should read 46743.
  After Part No. 82 add item:

45666	Crankcase screw	1

Page 10
  Part No. 45247 should read 45274.

Page 12
  Part No. 38621 description should read:
        Oil pipe union wire insert (in alloy head).
  Illus. Nos. 32 and 33 should be bracketed Early Type.
  After Illus. 33 add 4 items:

46672	Oil feed and return pipe (complete)	⎡ Later Type	1
46668	" pipe filter body	⎢ fitted	1
47045	Pump oil filter cap	⎢ with oil	1
47044	" " " element ..	⎣ filter	1

Page 14
  Illus. 8 should read:

43466ASSY.	Primary chaincase back cover & oil seal assy. ..	1

  Part No. ST41 should read ST236 and the code letter C should be deleted.
  Part No. ST223 should read ST237 and the code letter C should be deleted.
  Delete Part Nos. ST228 and ST229.

58 Page 16
    After Illus. 42 add item:
        46775   Gearbox bearing cap gasket   1
    Part No. 39227 should read 46729 and the description should read:
        Gear operator anchor pin (top)
    After Illus. 47 add two items:
        46730   Gear operator anchor pin (bottom)   1
        46731   "   "   "   " spacer (top)   1

Page 22
    Part No. DH/107PA/LH should read DH/407PA/LH.
    Part No. DH/1070LH should read DH/407LH
    Part No. DH/1077RH should read DH/1077A/RH.
    Part No. DH/619 should read DH/719.
    Part No. DH/612 should read DH/712.
    Part No. DH/613 should read DH/713.
    Part No. DH/617 should read DH/717.
    Part No. DH/616 should read DH/716.
    Part No. DH/614 should read DH/714.
    Part No. DH/615 should read DH/715.
    Part No. DH/618 should read DH/718.

Page 24
    Add code letter C (Crusader) to Part Nos. 39002 and 7201 to complete the descriptions.

Page 26
    Part No. 36583 should read 46895.

Page 28
    Part No. 31433, add code letter S to complete the description.
    After Illus. 47 add item:
        47015   Air cable assembly   C   1
    Part Nos. AM/12/034 should read DH85303.

Page 30
    Illus. 23 description should read:
        Hub distance collar, R.H. (with speedo gearbox
        B.G.5303)   1
    After Illus. 23 add item:
        46875   Hub distance collar, R.H. (later fitting with speedo
        gearbox B.G.5331/247)   1

Page 32
    Part No. 46336 should read 46950.
    Part No. 18949 should read 27001.
    In the description of Part No. 43253, "L.H." should be deleted and the quantity should read 2 per set not 1.

Page 34
    Part No. 4050B should read 46271.
    Part No. 38853 should read 47043 and add "with bearings" to description.
    Part No. 38854 should read:
        46262   Chainstay bearing   2

Page 34 continued
  Part No. 37762 should read 46270.
  Part No. 42124 should read:
     46265   Chainstay bearing collar   2
  Part No. 38894 should read 46264.
  To Part No. 33789A add Illus. No. 22.
  After Illus. 22 add two items:
    23   47033   Front fork stop   ..   ..   ..   S   1
    24   251   ″ ″ ″ pin   ..   ..   ..   S   1
  Delete Part Nos. 37770 and TC/PZ6.
  Delete Part No. 6740.

Page 35
  Frame, etc. For illustration ref. S 2361 substitute S 1062 (see page 4 of this leaflet).

Page 36
  Delete all text matter under heading Dual Seat, Rear Mudguard & Carrier & Number Plate, and substitute:

1	46810	Dual seat		1
	12659	″ ″ bolt (front), $\frac{5}{16}" \times \frac{1}{2}" \times 26$ B.S.F.		4
	8634	″ ″ ″ washer		2
	10142	″ ″ ″ (rear), $\frac{5}{16}" \times \frac{11}{16}" \times 26$ B.S.F.		2
	5965	″ ″ ″ washer		2
2	46806	Mudguard (tail section)		1
3	46826	″ (front section)		1
	251	″ bolt, $\frac{1}{4}"$ C.E.I. $\times \frac{1}{2}"$		1
	26998	″ ″ nut		1
	5916	″ ″ washer		1
	45250	″ pin (carrier end to guard)		2
	4693	″ ″ packing collar		2
	27621	″ ″ nut		2
4	46759	″ carrier		1
5	46779	Rear number plate		1
6	45967	″ ″ ″ beading, 30″		1
	16284	″ ″ ″ attachment pin, $\frac{5}{16}"$ C.E.I. $\times \frac{13}{16}"$		1
	7915	″ ″ ″ ″ ″ washer		1
	45960	Tail lamp platform		1
	45974	″ ″ ″ distance piece		2

Page 37
  Dual Seat, etc. For illustration ref. S 2361 substitute S 1162 (see page 6 of this leaflet).

Page 38
  Illus. 1 & 2 should be bracketed reading: All "Crusader 250"s & early fitting on "Sports".
  After Illus. 2 add two items:
      46340   Toolbox (without lids) ⎰ Later fitting on "Sports"   S   1
      46451   ″ lid, L.H.   ⎱ with plug type ignition switch   ..   ..   S   1
  Illus. 10 should read 2 per set not 8.
  After Illus. 10 add item:
      18229   Toolbox packing washer (rear)   2

1962 FRAME ASSEMBLY

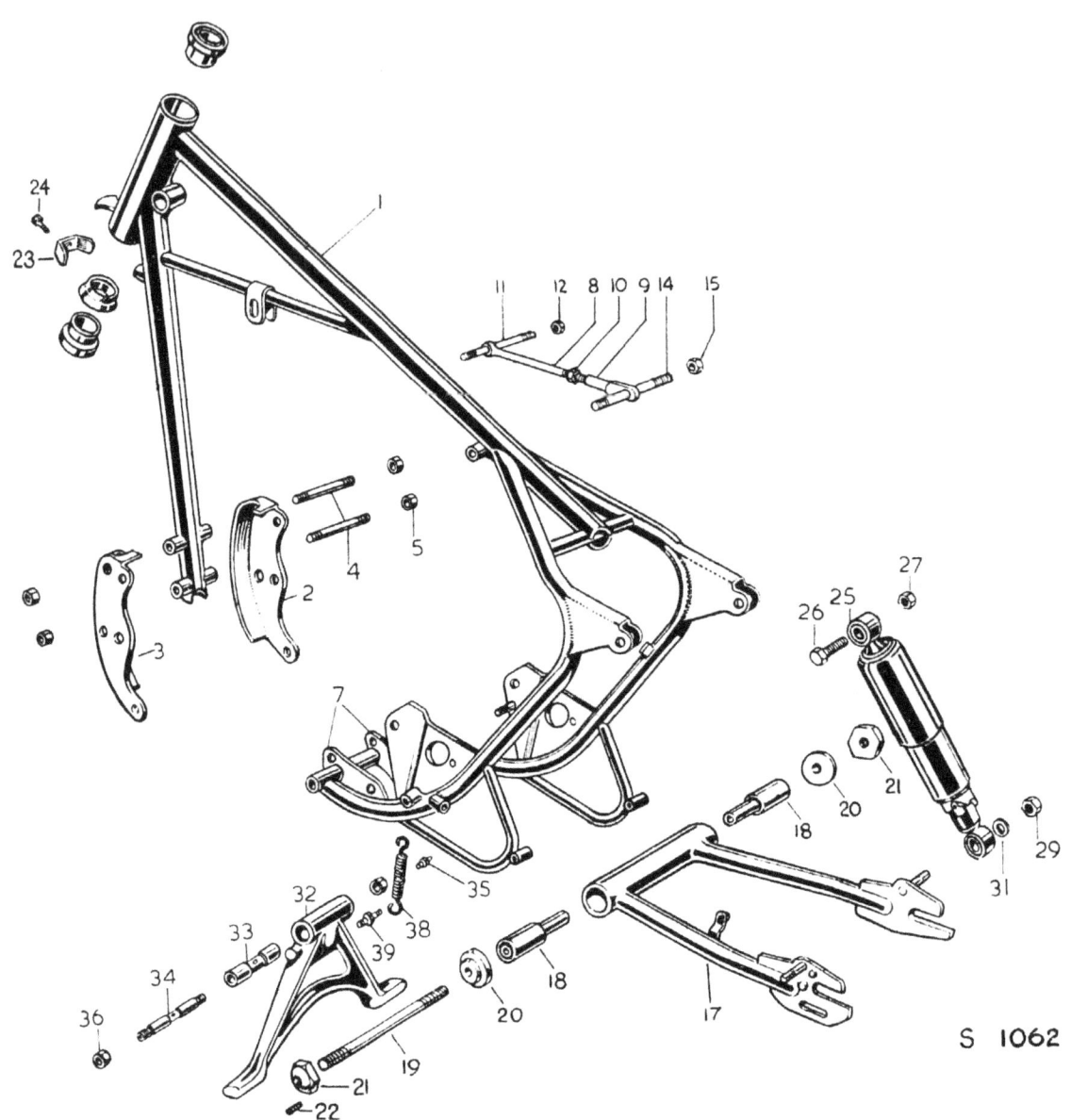

S 1062

Page 38 continued

After Illus. 12 add item:
    41805   Air filter element (not fitted as standard) .. .. S 1

After Illus. 36 add item:
    29912   Pliers, 5″ long 1

Page 40

Part No. SM/467/241L should read:
    Speedometer head 85 m.p.h., illuminated .. .. C 1

After Part No. SM/467/245K add two items:
    SM/SC3303/03   Speedometer head 85 m.p.h. { Alternative .. C 1
    SM/SC3303/04   ″ ″ 140 k.p.h. { Code Nos. .. C 1

After Part No. SM/467/247 add two items:
    SM/SC3303/20   Speedometer head 125 m.p.h. { Alternative .. S 1
    SM/SC3303/39   ″ ″ 180 k.p.h. { Code Nos. .. S 1

Illus. 7, 8 & 9 should read Early fitting.

After Illus. 9 add three items:
    SM/BG5331/247   Gearbox (self-contained), complete   1
    46868   ″ spacing collar. Behind box   } Later   1
    46869   Speedo drive coupling (on end of hub } fitting 1
        barrel) .. ..

Part Nos. 44109, 37175, 27001, 6716 and 82 add code letter S.

Page 44

Part Nos. LU/047519B and LU/466125 should read Early fitting.

After Illus. 1 add two items:
    LU/54021025   Alternator (complete), R.M.18 { Later .. 1
    LU/54213903   ″ rotor assy. only .. { fitting .. 1

Illus. 4 should read:
    LU/468678   Alternator stator RM 13, Early fitting 1

After Illus. 4 add item:
    LU/47161   Alternator stator RM 18, Later fitting 1

Illus. 9 should read:
    41133   Alternator distance washer (behind rotor) with
        RM 13 alternator.

After Illus. 9 add item:
    46958   Alternator distance washer (behind rotor) with
        RM 18 alternator 1

Part No. 251 should read 7201.

After Illus. 31 add item:
    20199   Ignition coil attachment distance piece 2

Page 48

Illus. 1 to 5 should read: All "Crusaders" & Early fitting on "Sports".
Later fittings on "Sports" are:
    LU/34289A   Lighting switch type 88SA 1
    LU/180316   ″ ″ fixing nut 1
    LU/185128   ″ ″ ″ ″ washer 1
    LU/54330934   ″ ″ knob 1
    46949   ″ ″ adaptor (in headlamp casing) .. 1
    16510   ″ ″ ″ washer 1
    LU/34427A   Ignition switch type 88SA 1
    LU54336176   ″ ″ key 1

62 1962 DUAL SEAT, REAR MUDGUARD AND CARRIER AND NUMBER PLATE

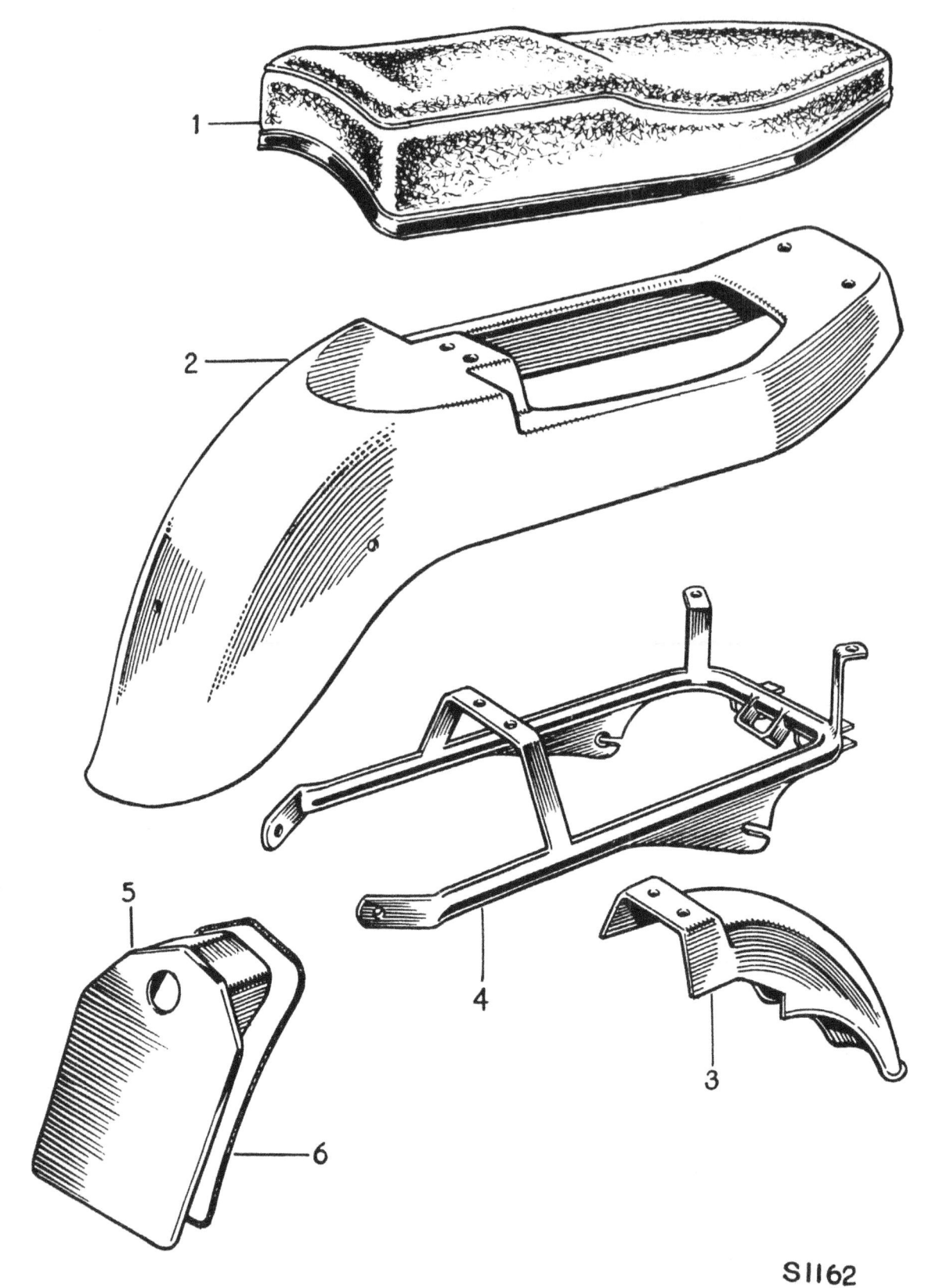

S1162

Page 48 continued

LU/54336177	,, ,, fixing nut		1
LU/54336178	,, ,, ,, ,, cover		1

Illus. 13 should read (Early fitting).
After Illus. 13 add two items:

LU/70163A	Electric horn type 8H { Later fitting		1
LU/54680850	,, ,, bracket {		1

Part No. LU/PUZ7E-11 should read:

LU/54028423	Battery, 6 v., 12 amp.-hr. (dry), type MLZ9E ..		1

After Illus. 22 add item:

46319	Battery cushion		1

Delete Illus. 23.
Part No. 43222A should read 46342.
After Illus. 24 add item:

46345	Battery buffer strip		1

After Illus. 25 add item:

18529	Battery strap screw washer		1

Part. No. LU/54940814A should read: All "Crusaders" & Early fitting on "Sports".
After Part No. LU/54940814A add item:

LU/54930058	Cable harness (Later fitting on "Sports" with 88SA plug & socket lighting & ignition switches) ..		1

Page 49

Electrical Equipment. For illustration ref. S 2861 substitute S 1662
(see page 8 of this leaflet).

Page 50

Delete all text matter under heading Panniers and substitute:

42218	Pannier bag		2
42193	,, carrier, L.H.		1
42194	,, ,, R.H.		1
47096	,, support clip (front)		2
12659	,, ,, ,, bolt $\frac{5}{16}$" C.E.I. $\times \frac{1}{2}$" ..		4
26998	,, ,, ,, ,, nut		4
47095	,, ,, bracket (front)		2
47097	,, ,, ,, (rear)		2
47186	,, ,, ,, bolt $\frac{5}{16}$" C.E.I. $\times \frac{1}{2}$" (thin head)		4
26997	,, ,, ,, ,, nut		4
38767	,, ,, ,, (rear) bolt $\frac{1}{4}$" C.E.I. $\times \frac{1}{2}$"		2
26998	,, ,, ,, ,, ,, nut		2
47098	,, ,, post		2
10142	,, ,, ,, bolt		2
47186	,, ,, bolt $\frac{5}{16}$" C.E.I. $\times \frac{1}{2}$" (thin head) ..		2
5965	,, ,, ,, washer		6

Page 52

Part No. 43496 should read 47185.

ENFIELD CYCLE Co Ltd.   REDDITCH   WORCS.

799/1½m. 262   Printed in England

1962 ELECTRICAL EQUIPMENT

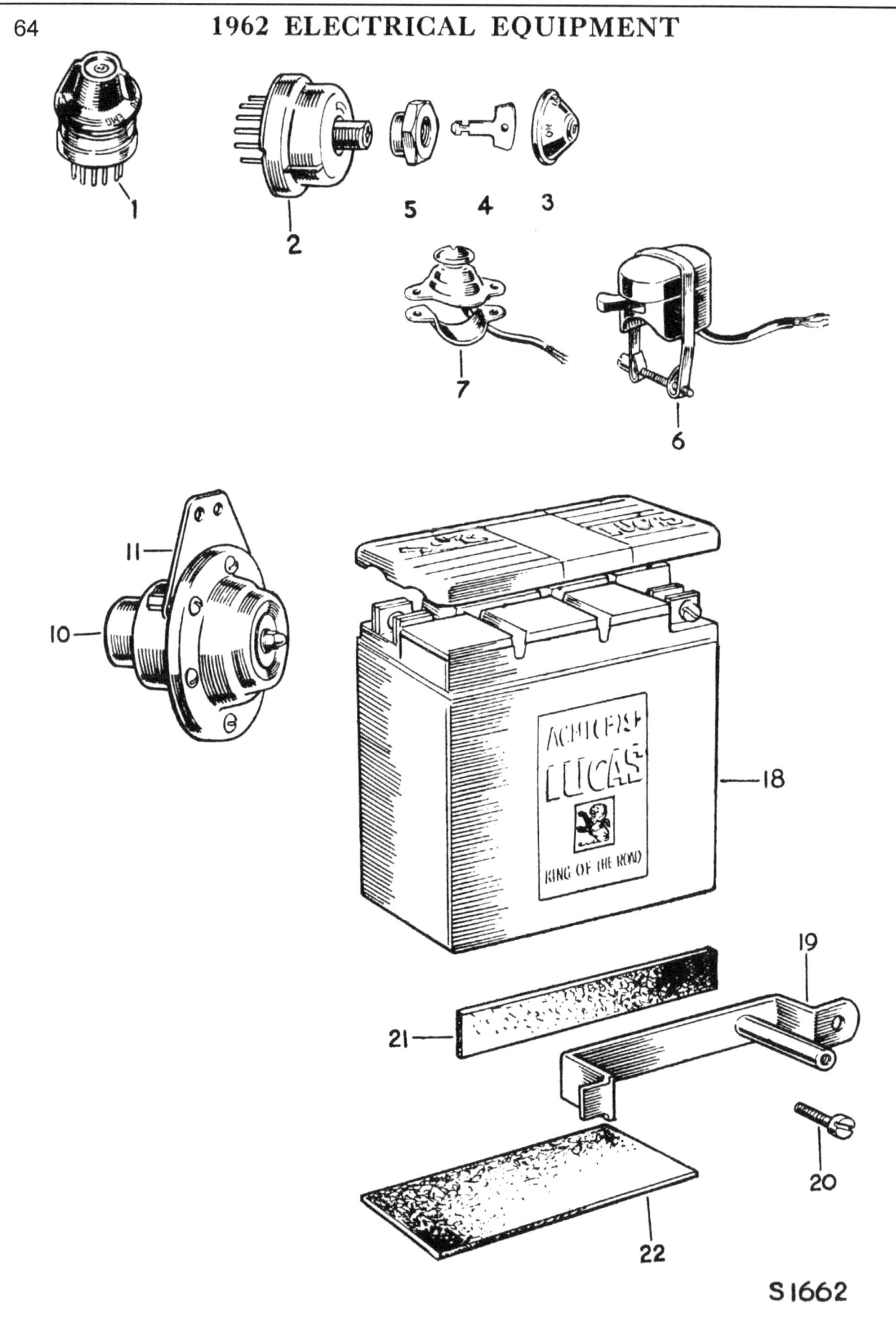

S1662

VELOCEPRESS MANUALS – MOTORCYCLE BY MAKE

AJS 1932-1948 SINGLES & TWINS 250cc THRU 1000cc (BOOK OF)
AJS 1945-1960 SINGLES 350cc & 500cc MODELS 16 & 18 (BOOK OF)
AJS 1955-1965 SINGLES 350cc & 500cc (BOOK OF)
AJS 1957-1966 FACTORY WSM - ALL SINGLES & TWINS
ARIEL UP TO 1932 (BOOK OF)
ARIEL 1932-1939 PREWAR MODELS (BOOK OF)
ARIEL 1933-1951 (WORKSHOP MANUAL)
ARIEL 1939-1960 4 STROKE SINGLES (BOOK OF)
ARIEL 1958-1964 LEADER & ARROW FACTORY WSM & PARTS LIST
ARIEL 1958-1964 LEADER & ARROW (BOOK OF)
BMW R26 R27 (1956-1967) FACTORY WORKSHOP MANUAL
BMW R50 R50S R60 R69S (1955-1969) FACTORY WORKSHOP MANUAL
BRIDGESTONE 90 SERIES FACTORY WSM & PARTS CATALOGUE
BRIDGESTONE 175 SERIES FACTORY WSM & PARTS CATALOGUE
BRIDGESTONE 350 SERIES FACTORY WSM & PARTS CATALOGUES
BSA SERVICE SHEETS MASTER CATALOGUE ALL MODELS 1945-1967
BSA BANTAM D1 TO D7 1948-1966 FACTORY SERVICE SHEETS MANUAL
BSA BANTAM ALL MODELS FROM 1948 ONWARDS (BOOK OF)
BSA DANDY FACTORY WORKSHOP MANUAL (COMPILATION)
BSA SINGLES & V-TWINS UP TO 1927 (BOOK OF)
BSA SINGLES & V-TWINS UP TO 1930 (BOOK OF)
BSA SINGLES & V-TWINS 1936-1939 (BOOK OF)
BSA C10, C11 & C12 1945-1958 FACTORY SERVICE SHEETS MANUAL
BSA OHV & SV SINGLES 250-600cc 1945-1959 (BOOK OF)
BSA C15 & B40 1958-1967 FACTORY SERVICE SHEETS MANUAL
BSA OHV & SV SINGLES 250cc (ONLY) 1954-1970 (BOOK OF)
BSA B31, B32, B33 & B34 1945-60 FACTORY SERVICE SHEETS MANUAL
BSA OHV SINGLES 350 & 500cc 1955-1967 (BOOK OF)
BSA M20, M21 & M33 1945-1963 FACTORY SERVICE SHEETS MANUAL
BSA TWINS A7 & A10 1948-1962 FACTORY SERVICE SHEETS MANUAL
BSA TWINS A7 & A10 1948-1962 (BOOK OF)
BSA TWINS A50 & A65 1962-1965 FACTORY WORKSHOP MANUAL
BSA TWINS A50 & A65 1962-1969 (SECOND BOOK OF)
DOUGLAS 1929-1939 PREWAR ALL MODELS (BOOK OF)
DOUGLAS 1948-1957 POSTWAR ALL MODELS FACTORY SHOP MANUAL
DUCATI 160cc, 250cc & 350cc OHC MODELS FACTORY SHOP MANUAL
HONDA 50cc ALL MODELS UP TO 1970 INC MONKEY & TRAIL (BOOK OF)
HONDA 90cc ALL MODELS UP TO 1966 (BOOK OF)
HONDA TWINS & SINGLES 50cc THRU 305cc 1960-1966 (BOOK OF)
HONDA TWINS ALL MODELS 125cc THRU 450cc UP TO 1968 (BOOK OF)
HONDA C100 50cc SUPER CUB O.H.C. 1959-1962 FACTORY WSM
HONDA C110 50cc SPORT CUB O.H.C. 1960-1962 FACTORY WSM
HONDA 50-65-70-90cc O.H.C. SINGLES 1959-1983 FACTORY WSM
HONDA 100-125cc SINGLES CB/CD/CL/SL/TL 1970-1984 FACTORY WSM
HONDA 125-150cc TWINS C/CS/CB/CA 1959-1966 FACTORY WSM
HONDA 125-160-175-200cc TWINS 1965-1978 WORKSHOP MANUAL
HONDA 250-305cc TWINS C/CS/CB 1961-1968 FACTORY WSM
HOHDA 250-350cc TWINS CB/CL/SL 1968-1973 FACTORY WSM
HONDA 250-360cc TWINS CB/CL/CJ 1974-1977 FACTORY WSM
HONDA 350F & 400F 4-CYLINDER 1972-1977 FACTORY WSM
HONDA 450cc TWINS CB/CL 1965-1974 K0 to K7 WORKSHOP MANUAL
HONDA 500cc & 550cc 4-CYL 1971-1978 FACTORY WORKSHOP MANUAL
HONDA 750cc SHOC 4-CYL 1969-1978 K0~K8 WORKSHOP MANUAL
INDIAN PONYBIKE, BOY RACER & PAPOOSE ILL PARTS LIST & SALES LIT
J.A.P. ENGINES 1927-1952 & MOTORCYCLES 1934-1952 (BOOK OF)
MATCHLESS 1931-1939 ALL MODELS 250cc THRU 990cc (BOOK OF)
MATCHLESS 1945-1956 350 & 500cc SINGLES (BOOK OF)
MATCHLESS 1955-1966 350 & 500cc SINGLES (BOOK OF)
MATCHLESS 1957-1966 FACTORY WSM - ALL SINGLES & TWINS
NEW IMPERIAL ALL SV & OHV FROM 1935 ONWARDS (BOOK OF)
NORTON 1932-1939 PREWAR MODELS (BOOK OF)
NORTON 1932-1947 (BOOK OF)
NORTON 1938-1956 (BOOK OF)
NORTON 1945-1963 MODELS 16H, Big4, ES2, 19 & 50 WSM'S & PARTS
NORTON 1955-1963 MODELS 19, 50 & ES2 (BOOK OF)
NORTON 1948-1970 DOMINATOR TWINS FACTORY WSM'S & PARTS
NORTON 1955-1965 DOMINATOR TWINS (BOOK OF)
NORTON 1960-1970 TWIN CYLINDER FACTORY WORKSHOP MANUAL
NORTON 1970-1975 COMMANDO 850 & 750cc FACTORY WSM
NORTON 1975-1978 MK 3 COMMANDO 850 cc FACTORY WSM
PANTHER 1932-1958 LIGHTWEIGHT MODELS 250 & 350cc (BOOK OF)
PANTHER 1938-1966 HEAVYWEIGHT MODELS 600 & 650cc (BOOK OF)
RALEIGH MOTORCYCLES 1919-1933 (BOOK OF)
ROYAL ENFIELD 1934-1946 SINGLES & V TWINS (BOOK OF)
ROYAL ENFIELD 1937-1953 SINGLES & V TWINS (BOOK OF)
ROYAL ENFIELD 1946-1962 SINGLES (BOOK OF)
ROYAL ENFIELD 1948-1963 500cc TWIN & METEOR MINOR WSM's
ROYAL ENFIELD 1952-1963 700cc TWINS FACTORY WORKSHOP MANUAL
ROYAL ENFIELD 1956-1966 250cc CRUSADER SERIES & 350cc BULLET
ROYAL ENFIELD 1958-1966 250cc & 350cc SINGLES (SECOND BOOK OF)
ROYAL ENFIELD 1962-1970 INTERCEPTOR WSM'S & PARTS (Compilation)
RUDGE 1933-1939 (BOOK OF)
SACHS 1968-1975 100cc & 125cc ENGINES WSM & M/CYCLE PARTS LIST
SUNBEAM 1928-1939 (BOOK OF)
SUNBEAM 1946-1957 S7 & S8 (BOOK OF)
SUZUKI 50cc & 80cc UP TO 1966 (BOOK OF)
SUZUKI T10 1963-1967 FACTORY WORKSHOP MANUAL
SUZUKI T20 & T200 1965-1969 FACTORY WORKSHOP MANUAL
SUZUKI TWINS 1962 ONWARDS 125-500cc WORKSHOP MANUAL
TRIUMPH 1935-1949 SINGLES & TWINS (BOOK OF)
TRIUMPH 1937-1951 (WORKSHOP MANUAL)
TRIUMPH 1945-1955 FACTORY WORKSHOP MANUAL
TRIUMPH 1945-1959 TWINS (BOOK OF)
TRIUMPH 1956-1969 TWINS (BOOK OF)
TRIUMPH 1963-1970 UNIT CONSTRUCTION 650cc FACTORY WSM
TRIUMPH 1963-1974 UNIT CONSTRUCTION 350-500cc FACTORY WSM
TRIUMPH 1968-1974 TRIDENT T150 & T150V FACTORY WSM
VELOCETTE 1925-1970 ALL SINGLES & TWINS (BOOK OF)
VELOCETTE 1933-1952 MOV-MAC-MSS RIGID FRAME FACTORY WSM
VELOCETTE 1954-1971 MSS-VENOM-THRUXTON-VIPER FACTORY WSM
VILLIERS ENGINE UP TO 1959 INC. 3 WHEELERS (BOOK OF)
VILLIERS ENGINE UP TO 1969 (BOOK OF)
VINCENT 1935-1955 (WORKSHOP MANUAL)
YAMAHA 1961-1967 YA5 & YA6 (WORKSHOP MANUAL & ILL PARTS LIST)
YAMAHA 1971-1972 JT1& JT2 (WORKSHOP MANUAL & ILL PARTS LIST)

VELOCEPRESS TECHNICAL BOOKS – MOTORCYCLE

1930'S BRITISH MOTORCYCLE CARBS & ELEC COMPONENTS (BOOK OF)
1930'S BRITISH MOTORCYCLE ENGINES (OVERHAUL & MAINTENANCE)
1930'S BRITISH MOTORCYCLE GEARBOXES & CLUTCHES (BOOK OF)
CATALOG OF BRITISH MOTORCYCLES (1951 MODELS)
LUCAS ELECTRONICS BRITISH M/CYCLES REPAIR & PARTS (1950-1977)
MOTORCYCLE ENGINEERING (P.E. Irving)
MOTORCYCLE ROAD TESTS 1949-1953 (Motor Cycle Magazine UK)
SPEED AND HOW TO OBTAIN IT (Motor Cycle Magazine UK)
TUNING FOR SPEED (P.E. Irving)
WIPAC (COMBO) MANUAL NUMBER 3 + M/CYCLE & SCOOTER MANUAL

VELOCEPRESS MANUALS – SCOOTERS BY MAKE

BSA SUNBEAM SCOOTER WORKSHOP MANUAL 1959-1965
BSA SUNBEAM SCOOTER 1959-1965 (BOOK OF)
LAMBRETTA 1947-1957 ALL 125 & 150cc MODELS (BOOK OF)
LAMBRETTA 1957-1970 LI & TV MODELS (SECOND BOOK OF)
NSU PRIMA 1956-1964 ALL MODELS (BOOK OF)
TRIUMPH TIGRESS SCOOTER WORKSHOP MANUAL 1959-1965
TRIUMPH TIGRESS SCOOTER (BOOK OF)
VESPA 1951-1961 (BOOK OF)
VESPA 1955-1963 125 & 150cc & GS MODELS (SECOND BOOK OF)
VESPA 1955-1968 GS & SS (BOOK OF)
VESPA 1963-1972 90, 125 & 150cc (THIRD BOOK OF)

VELOCEPRESS MANUALS – MOPEDS & MOTORIZED BICYCLES

CYCLEMOTOR (BOOK OF)
NSU QUICKLY 1953-1963 ALL MODELS (BOOK OF)
PUCH MAXI N & S MAINTENANCE & REPAIR (3 MANUAL COMPILATION)
RALEIGH MOPEDS 1960-1969 (BOOK OF)

VELOCEPRESS MANUALS - THREE WHEELER'S

BOND MINICAR THREE WHEELER 1948-1967 (BOOK OF)
BMW ISETTA FACTORY WORKSHOP MANUAL
BSA THREE WHEELER (BOOK OF)
RELIANT REGAL THREE WHEELER 1952-1973 (BOOK OF)
VINTAGE MORGAN THREE WHEELER (BOOK OF)

VELOCEPRESS MANUALS – AUTOMOBILE BY MAKE

ALFA ROMEO GIULIA WORKSHOP MANUAL 1300 TO 2000cc 1962-1975
ALFA ROMEO GIULIA TECH MANUAL CARBURETED CARS FROM 1962
ALFA ROMEO GIULIA TECH MANUAL FUEL INJECTED CARS FROM 1969
ALFA ROMEO GIULIETTA & GIULIA 750 & 101 SERIES 1955-1965 WSM
AUSTIN-HEALEY SPRITE & MG MIDGET WORKSHOP MANUAL 1958-1971
BMW 600 LIMOUSINE FACTORY WORKSHOP MANUAL
BMW 600 LIMOUSINE OWNERS HAND BOOK & SERVICE MANUAL
BMW 2000 & 2002 1966-1976 WORKSHOP MANUAL
CORVAIR 1960-1969 WORKSHOP MANUAL
CORVETTE V8 1955-1962 WORKSHOP MANUAL
FERRARI HANDBOOK ROAD & RACE CARS (SERVICE/SPECS) 1948-1958
FERRARI 250/GT SERVICE & MAINTENANCE MANUAL 1956-1965
FIAT 500 FACTORY WORKSHOP MANUAL 1957-1973
FIAT 600, 600D & MULTIPLA FACTORY WORKSHOP MANUAL 1955-1969
JAGUAR E-TYPE 3.8 & 4.2 SERIES 1 & 2 WORKSHOP MANUAL
JAGUAR MK 7, 8, 9 & XK120, 140, 150 WORKSHOP MANUAL 1940-1961
METROPOLITAN FACTORY WORKSHOP MANUAL
MGA & MGB OWNERS HANDBOOK & WORKSHOP MANUAL
MG MIDGET TC, TD, TF & TF1500 WORKSHOP MANUAL
PORSCHE 356 1948-1965 WORKSHOP MANUAL
PORSCHE 911 2.0, 2.2, 2.4 LITRE 1964-1973 WORKSHOP MANUAL
PORSCHE 911 2.7, 3.0, 3.2 LITRE 1973-1989 WORKSHOP MANUAL
PORSCHE 912 WORKSHOP MANUAL
PORSCHE 914/4 & 914/6 1.7, 1.8, 2.0 LITRE 1970-1976 WSM
TRIUMPH TR2, TR3, TR4 1953-1965 WORKSHOP MANUAL
VOLKSWAGEN TRANSPORTER, TRUCKS & WAGONS 1950-1979 WSM
VOLVO 1944-1968 ALL MODELS WORKSHOP MANUAL

VELOCEPRESS TECHNICAL BOOKS - AUTOMOBILE

HOW TO BUILD A FIBERGLASS CAR
HOW TO BUILD A RACING CAR
HOW TO RESTORE THE MODEL 'A' FORD
MASERATI OWNER'S HANDBOOK
PERFORMANCE TUNING THE SUNBEAM TIGER
SOUPING THE VOLKSWAGEN
SOLEX CARBURETORS (EMPHASIS ON UK & EU AUTOMOBILES)
SU CARBURETORS (EMPHASIS ON UK AUTOMOBILES)
WEBER CARBURETORS (EMPHASIS ON ALFA & FIAT)

VELOCEPRESS BOOKS & GUIDES - AUTOMOBILE

COMPLETE CATALOG OF JAPANESE MOTOR VEHICLES
FERRARI 308 SERIES BUYER'S AND OWNER'S GUIDE
FERRARI BROCHURES AND SALES LITERATURE 1968-1989
FERRARI SERIAL NUMBERS PART I - ODD NUMBERS TO 21399
FERRARI SERIAL NUMBERS PART II - EVEN NUMBERS TO 1050
HENRY'S FABULOUS MODEL "A" FORD
MASERATI BROCHURES AND SALES LITERATURE

VELOCEPRESS BOOKS – RACING

CARRERA PANAMERICANA - MEXICAN ROAD RACE (BOOK OF)
DIALED IN - THE JAN OPPERMAN STORY
VEDA ORR'S NEW REVISED HOT ROD PICTORIAL

www.VelocePress.com

Please check our website:

www.VelocePress.com

for a complete
up-to-date list of
available titles